AMERICAN LEGAL AND CONSTITUTIONAL HISTORY ★ A Garland Series of Outstanding Dissertations

Edited by
HAROLD HYMAN
William P. Hobby Professor of History,
Rice University

STUART BRUCHEY
Allan Nevins Professor of American
Economic History, Columbia University

WHAT SAYETH THE LAW ★ The Treatment of Slaves and Free Blacks in the State and Local Courts of Tennessee

Arthur F. Howington

Garland Publishing, Inc.
New York & London ★ 1986

Library of Congress Cataloging-in-Publication Data

Howington, Arthur F., 1945–
What sayeth the law.

(American legal and constitutional history)
Bibliography: p.
Includes index.
1. Slavery—Law and legislation—Tennessee—History.
2. Afro-Americans—Legal status, laws, etc.—Tennessee—History. 3. Slavery—Tennessee—Emancipation. I. Title.
II. Series.
KFT411.5.A34H68 1986 342.768′0872 86-4652
ISBN 0-8240-8273-7 347.6802872

All volumes in this series are printed on acid-free, 250-year-life paper.

Printed in the United States of America

What Sayeth the Law:
The Treatment of Slaves and Free Blacks in the State and Local Courts of Tennessee

Arthur F. Howington

ACKNOWLEDGMENTS

This study would never have been completed had it not been for the aid of my parents, Jean and Flether Howington, and those of my wife, Nancy and Harold Wilkerson. Equally essential was my Nashville "family," Margaret and Bill Gray, also without whom the task simply could not have been accomplished. I can never fully repay my debt to Samuel McSeveney and James Ely, my counselors as I struggled to produce a Vanderbilt dissertation. There were everything advisers should be and more. Whatever merit this work has is directly attributable to their always gentlemanly insistance that I try to achieve the standard of excellence that for them is the norm. I must also extend my appreciation to Phillp Schwarz of Virginia Commonwealth University and to an anonymous reader from the University of Georgia Press. Both will find that, in the process of revising the dissertation, I have incorporated many of their suggestions and recommendations, always to the substantial improvement of the product. Kermit Hall introduced me to Loyd Ford and his slaves, a meeting which marked the beginning of the journey for which this book probably marks the end. He has been "in my corner" at many important points along the way. I will always be grateful. The staff of the Tennessee State Library and Archives always provided me cheerful and capable assistance. They became partners in my research, and, happily, we became friends in the process. Finally, I want to dedicate this book to my wife, Nancy, and my daughter, Channing. My project, in one form or another, has been spread across the kitchen and dining room tables, the spare bedroom, and their lives for many years. They alone can count its full cost.

Chapter I, "The Tennessee Supreme Court and the Law of Manumission," is a revised version of an article which appeared in the Fall 1985 issue of the _Tennessee Historical Quarterly_. The author wishes to thank the editor of that journal for permission to publish the material in this work.

PREFACE

This is a study of the Tennessee courts' treatment of slaves whose liberation required judicial sanction and of slaves and free blacks put on trial as criminal defendants. It also examines judicial efforts to protect slaves against unlawful violence in the hands of whites. Like many books, I suspect, this one originated as a seminar paper, a detailed examination of Ford v. Ford, a notable Tennessee manumission case.[1] Researching that paper, I became acquainted with the pathbreaking studies of A.E. Keir Nash and Daniel Flanigan, scholars whose work demonstrated that antebellum southern supreme courts treated blacks and whites with strikingly similar formality and, perhaps, fairness.[2] In my work on the Ford case, I found evidence of the same pattern of treatment in the county court and circuit court. It seemed appropriate, then, to expand

---

[1]Arthur F. Howington, "Not in the Condition of a Horse or an Ox: Ford v. Ford, the Law of Testamentary Manumission and the Tennessee Courts' Recognition of Slave Humanity," Tennessee Historical Quarterly 34 (Fall 1975): 249-63.

[2]A.E.Keir Nash, "Negro Rights and Judicial Behavior" (Ph.D. dissertation, Harvard University, 1967); "A More Equitable Past? Southern Supreme Courts and the Protection of the Antebellum Negro," North Carolina Law Review 48 (February 1970): 197-242; "Fairness and

that research beyond a single case, to examine a broader range of issues encompassing the entire judicial process, in effect, to test whether the type of treatment Nash and Flanigan found at the appellate level penetrated the court structure and prevailed throughout the judicial system.

I soon discovered that I was raising new questions. Except for Michael Hindus' work on South Carolina, there was, at that time, no similar study for any other southern state. Moreover, Hindus' study concerned only slave criminal cases in two upcountry districts of a state that was atypical in its method of dealing with slave defendants[3].

Formalism in the Trials of Blacks in the State Supreme Courts of the Old South," Virginia Law Review 56 (February 1970): 64-100; "Negro Rights, Unionism, and Greatness on the South Carolina Court of Appeals: The Extraordinary Chief Justice John Belton O'Neal," South Carolina Law Review 21 (Spring 1969): 141-90; "The Texas Supreme Court and Trial Rights of Blacks, 1845-1860," The Journal of American History 58 (December 1971): 622-42; "Reason of Slavery: Understanding the Judicial Role in the Peculiar Institution," Vanderbilt Law Review 32 (January 1979): 7-223; Daniel J. Flanigan, "The Criminal Law of Slavery and Freedom, 1800-1868" (Ph.D. dissertation, Rice University, 1973); "Criminal Procedure in Slave Trials in the Antebellum South," The Journal of Southern History 40 (November 1974): 537-64.

[3]Flanigan has observed that "no other slaveholding states adopted procedural systems that consistently weighed so heavily on accused slaves as those of Virginia and South Carolina." Flanigan, "The Criminal Law of Slavery," p. 100.

Michael S. Hindus, "Black Justice Under White Law: Criminal Prosecutions of Blacks in Antebellum South Carolina," The Journal of American History 63 (December 1976): 575-99; Prison and Plantation: Crime, Justice., and Authority in Massachusetts and South Carolina, 1767-1878 (Chapel Hill: University of North Carolina Press, 1980), pp. 129-61. Note certainly should be made of the work

As far as possible, my approach was ethnographic. Seeking neither to praise nor to condemn the antebellum Tennessee whites who controlled or participated in the judicial system, I sought to learn, to describe, and, perhaps, to understand--to illuminate, in U.B. Phillips' phrase, the "true nature of the living order."[4] The study is the kind called for over a decade ago by Eugene Geovese and Elinor Miller when they wrote of the need for the "introduction of new data" into the discussion of antebellum slavery and observed that, in this field, "the job itself remains that of research, of empirical investigation--of getting at the story."[5]

My strategy for "getting at the story" of the treatment of slaves and free blacks by the Tennessee courts was traditional. First, I read the statutes. One should never lose sight that, in most cases, the courts acted within parameters set by the legislature. One cannot describe, much less understand, the actions of the

---

of Phillip J. Schwarz and Judith K. Schafer. There have been a few isolated case studies of a very narrow range of lower court trials of slaves; see below, pp. 125, 170.

[4]Ulrich B. Phillips, American Negro Slavery: A Survey of the Supply, Employment, and Control of Negro Labor as Determined by the Plantation Regime (New York: D. Appleton and Company, 1918; reprint ed., Baton Rouge: Louisiana State University Press, 1966): p. 514.

[5]Elinor Miller and Eugene D. Genovese, eds., Plantation, Town, and County: Essays on the Local History of American Slave Society (Urbana: University of Illinois Press, 1974): pp. 1-2.

courts without reference to the written law. Next, I read the published opinions of the Tennessee Supreme Court, assuming that, as in the modern era, appellate court judgments about the proper application of the law in particular cases influenced the implementation of the law in all cases. This assumption proved correct; after the statutes, Supreme Court decisions are the most important point of reference in examining how slaves and free blacks were treated in the lower courts. Finally, I turned to the records of the county, circuit, criminal, and chancery courts themselves, a rich depository of material on slavery that even now remains largely untapped.[6] I have not read all the extant court records for antebellum Tennessee. I have, however, read records of courts across Tennessee and, I think, in sufficient number so that my description of their activities is valid for the state as a whole.[7]

---

[6]Most counties tried criminal offenses in the circuit courts, but, in a few, Davidson for example, circuit court business became so heavy that separate tribunals were established to handle criminal offenders.

Most of the records cited in this study are on microfilm in the Tennessee State Archives (TSA). The exceptions are the minutes of the criminal court and chancery court of Davidson county, which are located in the Davidson county courthouse in Nashville; the minutes of the Shelby county county court, circuit court, and the Memphis Criminal Court, which are located in the Shelby County Microfilm and Public Records Office in Memphis; and the minutes of the Memphis Recorder's Court, located in the Memphis/Shelby County Archives, also in Memphis.

[7]Originally, I planned to use the court records of the counties selected by Chase C. Mooney in Slavery in Tennessee. Because of the unavailability of records in

Some geographic and demographic background is in order. Antebellum Tennessee was an Upper South state and one in which a minority of whites held slaves. In his study of slavery in Tennessee, Chase C. Mooney found that, in 1860, about forty-five percent of the landowners and thirteen percent of non-landowners owned slaves.[8] Slaves constituted a minority of the population. In 1820, there were 80,107 slaves in the state, about nineteen percent of the population. By 1860, this number had grown to 275,716, slightly less than twenty-five percent of the population. In 1860, Tennessee ranked eighth among the fifteen slaveholding states in the number of slaves and eleventh in the proportion of slaves to the total

---

some of those counties, that proved impossible. For example, no circuit court records are available for Fentress, Dekalb, Montgomery, Dyer, and Fayette counties. Circuit records are available for the other counties chosen by Mooney, and those counties are included in this study. For the chancery courts, records were unavailable for Johnson, Fentress, Dekalb, Lincoln, Robertson, Montgomery, Dyer, and Fayette counties. All others chosen by Mooney are cited. For county courts, adequate records are unavailable for Fentress, DeKalb, Dyer, and Hardin counties. Again, all the others selected by Mooney are cited. I chose some counties not selected by Mooney, either because I simply wanted more raw data or because, in the case of Knox and Shelby counties, they contained important urban centers. See Chase C. Mooney, *Slavery in Tennessee* (Bloomington: Indiana University Press, 1957), pp. 1-6; "Slavery in Tennessee" (Ph.D. dissertation, Vanderbilt University, 1939), pp. 5-9.

[8]All together, Mooney found that in 1860 thirty-seven percent of the heads of agricultural families owned slaves. Mooney, *Slavery in Tennessee*, pp. 105, 109; Frank L. Owsley and Harriet C. Owsley, "The Economic Structure of Rural Tennessee, 1850-1860," *The Journal of Southern History* 8 (May 1942): 165.

population.[9]

Free blacks were a smaller element of the Tennessee population. In 1820, there were 2,727 free blacks in the state, less than one percent of the population. In 1860, the number of free blacks had increased to 7,300, but their percentage of the population remained unchanged. Tennessee ranked eighth among the slaveholding states both in the size of its free black population and in the proportion of free blacks to the total population.[10]

In some ways, Tennessee is three states rather than one. Throughout most of its history, the state has been divided into three distinct "grand divisions," East, Middle, and West Tennessee.[11] There are noteworthy differences among these divisions. For example, slaves were not distributed equally across the state. The largest

---

[9] Mooney, Slavery in Tennessee, p. 102; Mary Emily Robertson Campbell, The Attitude of Tennesseans Toward the Union, 1847-1861 (New York: Vantage Press, 1961), p. 14; Population of the United States in 1860; . . . the Eighth Census.

[10] J. Merton England, "The Free Negro in Antebellum Tennessee" (Ph.D. dissertation, Vanderbilt University, 1941), pp. 3-4; Roger Raymond Van Dyke, "The Free Negro in Tennessee, 1790-1980" (Ph.D. dissertation, Florida State University, 1972), pp. 2-3; Population of the United States in 1860, . . . the Eighth Census, pp. 456-69.

[11] There are other geographical subdivision, a total of eight, for the state as a whole. Physiography is the basis for all these subdivisions. However, the Grand Divisions became political, as well as geographic subdivisions. Mooney, Slavery in Tennessee, pp. 4-6; Stanley J. Folmsbee, Robert E. Corlew, and Enoch L. Mitchell, Tennessee: A Short History (Knoxville: University of Tennessee Press, 1969): pp. 5-11, 534-35.

number of slaves lived in Middle Tennessee; indeed that division contained more slaves than the other two divisions combined.[12] In 1860, for example, fifty-three percent of the slaves resided in Middle Tennessee. Thirty-seven percent lived in West Tennessee, and only ten percent in East Tennessee. The counties under study in this book reflect the overall distribution of slaves. In the counties used to investigate the circuit and criminal courts, for example, the Middle Tennessee counties contained fifty percent of the slaves, the West Tennessee counties forty-seven percent, and the East Tennessee counties only three percent.[13]

Although slaves were most numerous in Middle Tennessee, slavery was most important in West Tennessee and

---

[12]Middle Tennessee also contained the majority of slaveowners. Folmsbee, et. al., Tennessee, p. 217; Bell Irvin Wiley, "Cotton and Slavery in the History of West Tennessee," (M.A. thesis, University of Kentucky, 1929), pp. 30-34; Chase C. Mooney, "Some Institutional and Statistical Aspects of Slavery in Tennessee," Tennessee Historical Quarterly 1 (September 1942): 217.

[13]Population of the united States in 1860, . . . the Eighth Census, pp. 456-69. Mooney found that, in 1860, in East Tennessee twelve percent of the heads of agricultural families held slaves. In both Middle and West Tennessee, that same year, about forty percent of the heads of agricultural families were slaveowners. Mooney's computations were based on manuscript census schedules, and I have not duplicated his efforts for the counties used in this study. However, of the counties used by Mooney, both East Tennessee counties, five of seven in Middle Tennessee, and five of six in West Tennessee, were also used in this study. The common counties are Greene and Johnson in East Tennessee; Lincoln, Maury, Davidson, Montgomery, and Robertson in Middle Tennessee; and Fayette, Haywood, Gibson, Henry, and Hardin in West Tennessee.

least important in East Tennessee. In 1860, in West Tennessee, the slave population was fifty-three percent as large as the white population. In Middle Tennessee, the slave population was forty-one percent of the white population, while in East Tennessee it was only ten percent as large as that of the whites. In the counties investigated for this study, in West Tennessee, the slave population was sixty-seven percent as large as that of whites; in Middle Tennessee, it was sixty-two percent; and in East Tennessee, nine percent.[14]

Not only did West Tennessee contain the highest ratio of slaves to whites, but large slaveowners, those with at least fifty slaves, were most numerous in that division. They were more numerous by far in both Middle and West Tennessee than they were in East Tennessee. Of two hundred and nineteen Tennessee slaveowners who held at least fifty slaves in 1860, only seven resided in East Tennessee, compared with ninety-five in Middle Tennessee and one hundred and seventeen in West Tennessee. Three West Tennessee counties, Fayette, Shelby, and Haywood, each had over twenty such owners. No other Tennessee county has so many as twenty.[15]

Free blacks were concentrated in the eastern and

---

[14] _Population of the United States in 1860, . . . the Eighth Census_, pp. 456-69.

[15] _Agriculture of the United States in 1860, . . . the Eighth Census_, pp. 238-39.

central regions of Tennessee. In 1860, Shelby was the only Western Division county with at least one hundred free blacks. The division as a whole contained only eleven percent of the free blacks in the state. East Tennessee contained thirteen counties with at least one hundred free blacks and forty-five percent of the total free black population. The remaining forty-four percent of free blacks lived in Middle Tennessee, where nine counties had at least one hundred free blacks in their population[16] (see Table 1). Because only three East Tennessee counties are included in this study, the distribution of free blacks in the sample counties differs from the distribution for the state as a whole. Seventy-two percent of the free blacks in these counties resided in East and Middle Tennessee, but a majority, fifty-seven percent, of them lived in the central region of the state.

For this study, nineteen counties were examined, representing the three Grand Divisions. In addition to the three East Tennessee counties, seven were chosen from Middle Tennessee and nine from West Tennessee (see Table 1). The size of the slave population in these counties varied. For example, in 1860, Johnson county in East Tennessee contained only 233 slaves, less than five percent of the population.

---

[16] _Population of the United States in 1860; . . . the Eighth Census_, pp. 456-69; England, "The Free Negro in Tennessee," pp. 4, 44; Van Dyke, "The Free Negro in Tennessee," p. 5; Campbell, _The Attitude of Tennesseans_, pp. 15-16.

That same year, Fayette county in West Tennessee had 15,473 slaves, more than sixty percent of that county's total population.[17] The size of the free black population in the counties under study also varied considerably. Tipton county in West Tennessee in 1860 contained only nine free blacks, while Davidson county that year had 1,209, the largest number of any Tennessee county.[18]

Most of the counties included in the study were rural. However, Tennessee slavery had its urban dimension. In 1860, for example, 3,266 slaves lived in Nashville, and 3,684 lived in Memphis. These slaves represented about twenty-two percent of the total slave population in Davidson and Shelby counties respectively, both of which are included in this study. In East Tennessee, Knox county contained the largest number of slaves, 2,370, in 1860. The population of the city of Knoxville was not included in the census of that year, but ten years earlier, Knoxville had a slave population of 462, twenty-two percent of the total slave

---

[17] Also included in this study are the other two counties, Williamson in Middle Tennessee and Haywood in West Tennessee, that in 1860 had populations containing over fifty percent slaves.

[18] Knox county had the largest slave population and the largest free black population of all the East Tennessee counties. In 1860, the size of its free black population was second only to Davidson. Shelby county had the largest free black population in West Tennessee; both Knox and Shelby counties are included in this study.

population of the county.[19] Like Davidson and Shelby, Knox county is included in those under study.

A significant proportion of Tennessee free blacks resided in cities. In 1850, Nashville, Knoxville, and Memphis contained 789 free blacks, slightly over twelve percent of the total number of free blacks in the state. By contrast, only 2.2 percent of the Tennessee slave population lived in the three cities. Ten years later, Nashville and Memphis contained 917 free blacks, again over twelve per cent of the statewide total free black population. Only 2.5 percent of the state's slave population lived in Memphis and Nashville. In 1860, one hundred and ninety-eight Shelby county free blacks lived in Memphis, seventy-two percent of all free blacks in that county. That same year, 719 Nashville free blacks represented fifty-nine percent of those in Davidson county.

In the following study, counties were chosen to represent the geographic and demographic dimension of Tennessee slavery, but it has not always been possible to take such variations fully into account in studying the court system. For instance, city-dwellers who violated state laws were likely to be tried in the circuit or criminal court that had jurisdiction over the entire

---

[19] In contrast to Davidson and Shelby counties in 1860, in 1850 Knox county slaves were more concentrated in the city than the total population, only eleven percent of which lived in Knoxville. The Seventh Centus of the United States: 1850, pp. 573-74; Population of the United States; . . . the Eighth Census, pp. 459-67.

county. Thus it proved impossible to distinguish between the trials of those who lived in the city and those who lived in the countryside. However, cities established special courts to try offenders who violated municipal ordinances, and such tribunals have been investigated. Also, in analyzing the courts and manumission and the treatment of slaves accused of capital offenses, it has been possible to investigate whether differences existed among the three Grand Divisions. Thus the study is representative of a diversity of settings in which the interactions of Tennessee's judicial system and its Peculiar Institution took place.

TABLE OF CONTENTS

LIST OF TABLES

Table		Page

Table Page

LIST OF ILLUSTRATIONS

LIST OF ABBREVIATIONS

TSA	Tennessee State Archives, Nashville, Tennessee
TSLmd	Tennessee State Library, Manuscript Division, Nashville, Tennessee

CHAPTER I

THE TENNESSEE SUPREME COURT AND THE LAW OF MANUMISSION

The Tennessee Supreme Court unquestionably treated slaves as property. Like those of other southern states, Tennessee court reports "are full of wrangles about sales, gifts, mortgages, and bequests of slaves."[1] However, the Court singled out humanity as the feature which gave slave property its unique character. Recognition of a bondsman's humanity did not lessen his standing as property. Rather, the Court focused on humanity as the factor which gave slave property its "special and peculiar value."[2]

---

[1]Lawrence M. Friedman, _A History of American Law_ (New York: Simon and Schuster, 1973), p. 73. Also see Helen Tunnicliff Catterall, ed., _Judicial Cases Concerning American Slavery and the Negro_, vol. 2: _Cases from the Courts of North Carolina, South Carolina, and Tennessee_ (Washington, D.C.: Carnegie Institution of Washington, 1929), pp. 479-601.

[2]_Henderson v. Vaulx and Wife_, 18 Tenn. 28 (1836). Also see, _Loftin v. Espy and others_, 12 Tenn. 74-75 (1833).

The legal issues concerning slaves as property have not been examined fully either for the Tennessee Supreme Court or for southern appellate courts in general. However, important contributions have been made by Thomas Morris, John Stealey, and Mark Tushnet. Thomas D. Morris, "'As If the Injury Was Effected by the Natural Elements of Air or Fire': Slave Wrongs and the Liability of Masters," _Law and Society Review_, 16 (1981-82): 569-99; "'Society

For example, the Tennessee Supreme Court allowed courts of equity to have jurisdiction in cases of disputed title to slave property. This provided an owner with means to compel the actual return of a specific individual bondsman. Such a remedy was unavailable in a court of law where an owner's just claim could be satisfied fully by payment for the slave in question. Slaves, however, were "property in intellectual and moral and social qualities, in skill, in fidelity, and in gratitude," property for which the market value was an insufficient measure. The "mutual feelings of dependence, affection, and humanity" that existed between master and slave "[had] no cash price and [could] not be compensated in money."[3]

Humanity not only made slave property uniquely valuable, but, as Tennessee Supreme Court Justice John Catron put it, in slaves "the rights of humanity combined themselves with the rights of property."[4] In 1846,

---

is Not Marked by Punctuality in the Payment of Debts': The Chattel Mortgages of Slaves," in David J. Bodenhamer and James W. Ely, eds., Ambivalent Legacy: A Legal History of the South (Jackson: University of Mississippi Press, 1984): 147-70; John E. Stealey, "The Responsibilities and Liabilities of the Bailee of Slave Labor in Virginia," American Journal of Legal History, 12 (October 1968): 336-53; Mark V. Tushnet, The American Law of Slavery, 1810-1860: Considerations of Humanity and Interest. Princeton: Princeton University Press, 1981.

[3] Womack v. Smith & Tinsley, 30 Tenn. 329 (1850); Henderson v. Vaulx and Wife, 18 Tenn. 28 (1836). Loftin v. Espy and others, 12 Tenn. 74-75 (1833); Whitmore v. Parks and Jackson, 22 Tenn. 85 (1842).

[4] Loftin v. Espy and others, 12 Tenn. 75 (1833).

Justice Nathan Green underscored the Tennessee Supreme Court's recognition of the slave's human rights. "A slave is not in the condition of a horse or an ox," Green wrote.

> He is made after the image of the Creator. He has mental capacities, and an immortal principal in his nature, that constitute him equal to his owner but for the accidental position in which fortune has placed him.

These characteristics did not make the slave less a bondsman, but, according to Green, "the laws" under which the slave was held did not "extinguish his high-born nature nor deprive him of many rights which are inherent in man."[5]

One of the slave's "rights of humanity" which the Tennessee Court recognized involved manumission. Actually, the Tennessee Supreme Court considered emancipation to involve three different sets of rights, that is, the interest of three different parties. First, there were the property rights of the master. Emancipation rested upon the property owner's right to relinquish his property. Second, the slave had a right to receive freedom once it had been granted. Finally, the state itself was interested in manumission.

---

[5] Ford v. Ford, 26 Tenn. 75 (1846). Tennessee was not unique in this stance. As Orlando Patterson has written, "as a legal fact, there has never existed a slaveholding society, ancient or modern, that did not recognize the slave as a person in law." Patterson, Slavery and Social Death: A Comparative Study (Cambridge, Massachusetts, and London, England: Harvard University Press, 1982), p. 22.

For a detailed description of the Ford case, see Howington, "Not in the Condition of a Horse or an Ox," pp. 249-63.

The public had a right to regulate the introduction of new members into its community.

In practice, these three sets of rights were inextricable, but the Tennessee Court viewed them discretely, and they can be separated for purposes of analysis.

First, there was the right of the master to his property. In essence, all manumission flowed from this right, and the Tennessee Court gave masters great latitude in their exercise of it. In the absence of statutory regulation, the owner of a slave "had complete control over the question of emancipation" and could free his chattel "at pleasure."[6] The Tennessee Court required only that an owner "show his intention to emancipate.[7] This could be done by deed or by will, "by any species of instrument" that would "completely evince" the master's "intent and volition" to free the slave.[8] The court would even honor

---

[6] Hartsell v. George, 22 Tenn. 247 (1842); Fisher's Negroes v. Dabbs and others, 14 Tenn. 104 (1834); Ann Hope v. David Johnson and others, 10 Tenn. 114 (1826); Lewis and others v. Daniel, Administrator, 28 Tenn. 206 (1849); Charles C. Trabue, "The Voluntary Emancipation of Slaves in Tennessee as Reflected in the State's Legislation and Judicial Decisions," Tennessee Historical Magazine 4 (March 1918): 50-51; John W. Patton, "The Progress of Emancipation in Tennessee," The Journal of Negro History 17 (January 1932): 75.

[7] Lewis and others v. Daniel, Administrator, 28 Tenn. 206 (1849); Ann Hope v. David Johnson and others, 10 Tenn. 114 (1826).

[8] Ann Hope v. David Johnson and others, 10 Tenn. 114 (1826).

an oral declaration of emancipation.[9]

In the case of an oral declaration of emancipation, the Court would establish freedom only when the owner's intention was clear. In 1859, Isaac, a Washington county slave, claimed his freedom on the basis of the verbal declarations of his owner, Henry Sliger. Sliger had not emancipated Isaac in his will, and, according to the testimony at the trial, his comments about emancipating Isaac were inconsistent. On one occasion, Sliger had said he would free Isaac at his death; another time, he had said that he would emancipate Issac when his wife died. One witness testified that Sliger simply said "if Isaac was a good boy he would free him."[10]

The lower court thought these statements sufficient to free Isaac, but the Supreme Court did not agree. Because Sliger's intention was unclear, his comments failed to establish Isaac's "legal right to freedom," and he remained in bondage.[11]

This decision underscores one of the fundamental limits to the Tennessee Court's generosity and sympathy toward bondsmen. Because of its respect for the rights of

---

[9] McCloud and Karnes, Executors, v. Chiles et al., 41 Tenn. 168 (1860); Isaac (a man of color), by next friend, v. Henry Farnsworth, et al., 40 Tenn. 207-11 (1859).

[10] Isaac (a man of color) by his next friend, v. Willigm Sliger et al., 40 Tenn. 161-64.

[11] Ibid.

the master, the Court would not extend freedom to a slave whose owner's emancipatory wish could not be interpreted as unequivocal.

Still, when the owner's intention was clear, the Tennessee Court did reach out to effectuate manumission. It would do this even in the absence of written or oral declarations. In cases where such an indication was lacking, the Court would imply manumission "from the acts and conduct of the master."[12] One poignant example should suffice.

Elias, a free black, was married to Tenor, a slave owned by Phelps Read. Elias and Read had agreed that Tenor and her children would live with Elias and be supported by him until the children became ten years old. At that time, the children would be returned to Read, but Tenor would continue to live with her husband. When Phelps Read died, Elias and Tenor had one son, "lately born," living with them. After Read's death, the administrators of his estate allowed Elias to buy his family "at a trifle."[13]

Some time later, one of Elias's creditors tried to force the sale of Tenor and the child to satisfy a debt owed

---

[12] Greenlow v. Rawlings, 22 Tenn. 80, 83 (1842); Lewis v. Simonton, 27 Tenn. 150 (1847); Abram, a Man of Color, v. T.J. Johnson, et al., 38 Tenn. 76 (1858); McCullough v. Fanny Moore, etc. 17 Tenn. 234 (1836).

[13] Elias paid ten dollars for them. He chose to "own" his family in order to evade a law which required a $500 bond on each emancipated slave as indemnification against disorderly behavior or indigency.

him by Elias. Elias asked the courts to prevent such a sale "on the ground that the title to the slaves was vested in him for the purpose of emancipating them, and that they were entitled to their freedom, and not subject to his debts."

The Supreme Court supported Elias and halted the sale of his wife and child. Justice William Reese wrote the decision. Acknowledging that Tenor and her son were slaves, he nevertheless insisted that the Court would look "at the substance of things, . . . and will not suffer mere legal forms, the dress and drapery of a transaction, to alter the nature of things, and baffle the end aimed at." The circumstances surrounding Elias's purchase of his family clearly demonstrated that his wife and child were meant to be free. It was the "duty" of the Court to "interpose" to "prevent their sale."[14]

<u>Elias</u> not only underscores the Tennessee Court's recognition of slave humanity, but it makes clear the great latitude that the Court allowed master in emancipating slaves. Read had never freed Tenor. She and her

---

[14] Reese said that a court would have prevented even Elias from selling his wife and child, "if he, stifling the voice of nature, and severing the paternal tie had been such a barbarian and monster as to have meditated a sale of them for his pecuniary advantage, upon the strength of his mere legal title." To allow a creditor to sell them would have been "little short" of that "enormity." <u>Elias et al. v. Smith et al.</u>, 25 Tenn. 18-21 (1845). Also see, <u>Abram, a Man of Color, v. T.J. Johnson et al.</u>, 38 Tenn. 76 (1858) and <u>McCullough v. Fanny Moore, etc.</u>, 17 Tenn. 232-34 (1836).

children were purchased by Elias and legally were slaves, pure and simple. However, the Court believed that by their "acts and conduct," Read and his heirs had meant Tenor to be free, and the Court supported that wish.

Acts of emancipation, then, in the Tennessee high court's view, rested first upon the property rights of the master class. However, the Court also held that manumission involved a second set of important interests, those of the slave. Manumission involved, what Justice John Catron called, the "rights of humanity," one of which was the right of the slave to claim his liberty.

Throughout the antebellum period, the Tennessee Court ruled that an owner's act of emancipation conferred upon the slave "a moral right to freedom."[15] "Within the meaning of the law," Justice Robert McKinney wrote, a freed bondsman ceased "to be in the state and condition of slavery; [ceased] to have an owner, or master."[16] According to Justice Green, the master's act of emancipation "discharged the persons so emancipated from all obligations of service."[17] As late as 1854, Robert Caruthers saw the law on the subject as "settled"; no person could question

---

[15]<u>Fisher's Negroes v. Dabbs and others</u>, 14 Tenn. 104 (1834).

[16]<u>Lewis v. Simonton</u>, 27 Tenn. 150 (1847).

[17]<u>Laura Jane v. Hagen, Administrator</u>, 28 Tenn. 223 (1849).

an emancipated slave's "perfect right to liberty."[18]

To be sure, this right of humanity flowed from the right of property. For the right of the master to free his slave to have any meaning, the slave had to have the right to receive that freedom. However, it would be inaccurate to interpret the Tennessee Supreme Court's concern for the slave's right to freedom merely as a reflection of its concern for the property rights of the master class. Such a view misrepresents the tone and emphasis of the Court's jurisprudence in this area. Manumission converted an owner's right of property to a slave's right to liberty, a right which the Court then would protect on its own merits.[19]

---

[18] William Boon v. Samuel Lancaster, next friend etc., 33 Tenn. 395 (1854).

Most of the manumission cases concerned slaves emancipated in Tennessee, but the Court also dealt with the question of slaves claiming their freedom under the laws of other states. In such cases, if the slave had been freed according to the laws of the other state, the Court would protect that freedom, even if it the slave had been liberated in another state to circumvent restrictions on emancipation in Tennessee. Paul Finkelman has argued that, in the late antebellum period, throughout the South, "the trend was moving away" from recognizing freedom claims based on the laws of other states. There is no evidence of this trend in Tennessee. In fact, the Tennessee cases used by Finkelman to support his contention actually offer strong support for the opposite conclusion. See Blackmore and Hadley v. Negro Phill, 15 Tenn. 305-307 (1835); Reuben et al. v.Parrish, 25 Tenn. 108-110 (1845); Nancy et al. v. Wright et al., 28 Tenn. 404-408 (1848); Laura Jane v. Hagen, Administrator, 28 Tenn. 221-24 (1849). Paul Finkelman, An Imperfect Union: Slavery, Federalism, and Comity (Chapel Hill: The University of North Carolina Press, 1981), pp. 189-90.

[19] Mark Tushnet, who did not include Tennessee in his study, ignores this element of the law of manumission. Tushnet, American Law of Slavery, pp. 191-228.

The slave's right to freedom took hold the instant it was granted. The Court permitted a master to give a slave "an immediate right to present freedom" and also allowed an owner to give a slave freedom "dependent on the happening of some future contingency." In this latter case, the Court distinguished between the time the right to freedom "accrued" to a slave and and the time of its "final consumation." In the Tennessee Court's view, although a slave might not exercise his freedom until its "final consumation," the slave actually became legally free when the right accrued.[20]

In part, this view explains the Tennessee Court's stance on what David B. Davis has called "one of the most troublesome questions" in the law of emancipation, "whether children born of a female slave who had been promised freedom were entitled to the same benefit."[21] The issue came before the Tennessee Court in 1834. Justice John Catron delivered the Court's opinion, asserting that in such a case, where the effective date of emancipation was "doubtful," the Court should act in the "spirit of the laws of all civilized nations, which favor liberty" and "resort" to the rule that a grant of emancipation should be

---

[20] Lewis v. Simonton, 27 Tenn. 151-52 (1847). Also see Isaac (a man of color), by next friend, v. Henry Farnsworth et al., 40 Tenn. 209 (1859).

[21] David Brion Davis, The Problem of slavery in Western Culture (Ithaca: Cornell University Press, 1956), p. 270.

"liberally construed in favor of liberty." Therefore, Catron said, although a grant of freedom might take effect at a future date, the grant itself conferred a "present right to freedom," changing the slave into a "person bound to service for a term of years, who has a general right to freedom." A child born to such a person was born free.[22]

In contending that this decision "seems . . . highly libertarian," Nash goes too far.[23] The decision demonstrates only that the Tennessee Court was generous and sympathetic, sensitive to the humanity of the slave and unafraid to demonstrate those feelings in particular cases. It does not indicate support for the principle of absolute, unrestricted, universal liberty.

In fact, in Sidney, a Man of Color v. Thomas and Newton White, the Court sacrificed its doctrine in deference to the federal courts and the federal fugitive slave law. Sidney was born to a Knox county slave who had been promised freedom. Sold into Alabama, Sidney escaped back to Tennessee, where he was captured by agents of his Alabama master. He sued for his freedom in the Knox county circuit court. His captors argued that Sidney had been delivered to them as a fugitive slave by the federal

---

[22]Harris v. Clarissa and others, 14 Tenn. 164-65 (1834). The Court continued to support this position during the antebellum period. See Hartsell v. George, 22 Tenn. 245-47 (1842).

[23]Nash, "Negro Rights," p. 222; "Reason of Slavery," pp. 157, 164, 171.

district court and that this federal court action barred any action by the state circuit court, removing its jurisdiction to try a suit for freedom. The Supreme Court agreed. Although the Court admitted that Sidney "was free-born, according to the uniform course of decision in this state," it turned him over to his captors, leaving him in bondage.[24]

The slave's right to freedom was meaningless unless he or she could protect it. The Tennessee Court upheld the slave's right to use the courts to protect freedom as integral to the right to receive that freedom. According to Nathan Green, a grant of freedom conferred upon slaves " a right to invoke the action of the proper tribunal" to the end that "evidence of their freedom might be afforded." Otherwide, said Green, "the right of the owner to emancipate, and the right of the slave to receive his freedom, might alike be frustrated . . . a conclusion which would shock humanity, and be an indelible stigma on our jurisprudence."[25]

Some slaves used legal actions such as <u>habeas corpus</u>, trespass, assault and battery, and false imprisonment to secure a judicial determination of their

---

[24] <u>Sidney, a Man of Color, v. Thomas and Newton White</u>, 33 Tenn. 63-65 (1853); Knox County, Circuit Court, <u>Minutes</u>, February 1849, p. 24; October 1849, p. 159; February 1850, pp. 190, 214, 223; June 1850, p. 234; February 1851, pp. 330, 331, 381; June 1851, p. 407; "Thomas & Newton White v. Sydney, a Man of Color," Case Files, Eastern District, Tennessee Supreme Court, TSA.

[25] <u>Ford v. Ford</u>, 27 Tenn. 75 (1846).

freedom. On the whole, however, the Tennessee slave's standing in court rested on a 1829 statute.[26] This law provided that if a slave received his freedom in a will and the administrator or executor failed to have that freedom established, the slave by "next friend" could "file a bill in equity" to have that freedom secured. Thus, Justice Catron wrote, the slave was "entitled, independent of his color or his civil condition, to have justice administered in the due course of law, without denial or delay."[27]

The Supreme Court itself had little patience with recalcitrant or derelict executors.[28] For example, in Wilson county, an executor conspired with a widow to

---

[26] Clarissa v. Edwards, 1 Tenn. 409 (1809); Matilda v.Crenshaw, 12 Tenn. 249 (1833); Harris v. Clarissa and others, 14 Tenn. 158 (1834); Blackmore and Hadley v.Negro Phill, 15 Tenn. 297 (1835). Stewart v. Miller & Moore, 19 Tenn. 572-73 (1838); Hartsell v. George, 22 Tenn. 572-73 (1852); James v.Jones, 28 Tenn. 255 (1849); and Sidney, a Man of Color v. Thomas and Newton White, 33 Tenn. 64-65 (1853).

John Catron observed that prior to the passage of the 1829 statute, "the slave had no power to cause his right to be enforced by the courts of justice." This is not accurate. In particular, see Ex Parte, Rebecca Renny v. John Mayfield, 5 Tenn. 154-56 (1817); Abraham Vaughn v. Phebe, a Woman of Color, 8 Tenn. 15 (1827). Catron's comment is in Fisher's Negroes v. Dabbs and others, 14 Tenn. 105 (1834).

[27] Law of Tennessee, ch. 29; Fisher's Negroes v. Dabbs and others, 14 Tenn. 106 (1834).

[28] Hinklin v. Hamilton, and Hinklins v. Hinklin, 22 Tenn. 560 (1842); Howard et al. v. Clemmons et al., 24 Tenn. 361 (1844); Isaac et al. v. McGill, 28 Tenn. 418-19 (1848); and Laura Jane v. Hagen, Administrator, 28 Tenn. 223 (1849).

overturn her husband's will that freed his slaves. The slaves asked to have the order voiding the will annulled. The Supreme Court found the circumstances conclusive of fraud and ruled that the slaves were entitled to their freedom.[29]

The slave's standing in court was an area in which the Tennessee Supreme Court extended the rights of slaves. The 1829 statute touched only freedom bequeathed in a will, but the Court permitted the "next friend" benefit to give slaves access to the courts to protect freedom granted in other ways.[30] The Court also allowed the use of the "next friend" in tribunals other than the chancery courts. The Court upheld slaves who, "by next friend," contested wills in the circuit courts.[31] In 1842, the Court upheld the action of a Jackson county slave who had used his "next friend" to have his freedom established by the county court. The Court in this decision admitted that the 1829 statute limited the use of the "next friend" to the chancery court, but, Justice William Turley wrote, "it is the substance

---

[29] John et al., v. Tate et al., 26 Tenn. 316-20 (1846).

[30] Isaac (a man of color), by his next friend, v. William Sliger et al., 40 Tenn. 161 (1859); Isaac (a man of color),by next friend, v. Henry Farnsworth et al., 40 Tenn. 208 (1859); McCloud and Karnes, Executors, v. Chiles et al., 41 Tenn. 168-69 (1860).

[31] Ford v. Ford, 27 Tenn. 72 (1846); Jones v. Arterburn, 30 Tenn. 67-68 (1850).

of things, and not forms, which must control us in cases of this kind."[32]

In another area, when slaves had a "certain grant of freedom, to take effect in the future," the Court allowed them access to the courts through their "next friend" to protect property set aside for their use when liberated. There was no statutory provision for this, but, as Robert Caruthers wrote in 1859, to do otherwise, "would be entirely inconsistent with our liberal slave and emancipation Code, let others be as they may."[33]

Although the Tennessee Court was willing to extend the use of "next friend" access to the courts more widely than provided by statute, the requirement for a "next friend" was a legislative restriction on emancipation that the Court accepted. The Tennessee Supreme Court's emancipatory jurisprudence was not generous enough to challenge the legislature and extend protection of the courts to slaves who had no white sponsor.

The Supreme Court did not rule on the "next friend" requirement until 1852, when it heard a case that turned upon "the single question" of whether slaves could "sue

---

[32] Hinklin v. Hamilton, and Hinklins v. Hinklin, 22 Tenn. 562 (1842).

[33] Jeremiah Stephenson and Wife v. W. Harrison, Executor, et al., 40 Tenn. 555 (1859). Also see, Henry et al., by next friend, v. Hogan et al., 23 Tenn. 198-201 (1843); and Laura Jane v. Hagan, Administrator, 28 Tenn. 221-24 (1849).

for their freedom in their own names, and without a next friend."[34]

In deciding the case, the Court pointed out that the "next friend" rule was "not . . . an anomalous rule applying alone to slaves." It "extended, likewise, with but few exceptions, to all persons under the age of twenty-one, and femes covert." Furthermore, the Court explained:

> The experience of our country also demonstrated that no difficulty is ever found, where the claim is calculated to inspire the least confidence in its justice, in procuring the agency of responsible citizens to stand forth as next friend, in any suit which may be necessary to establish their claim to freedom.

However, "if this were otherwise," the Court insisted, its decision would have been the same. "A slave can have no status in court except by next friend. . . . They are property, and have no rights except such as are extended to them by some law."[35]

This description of the slave's rights departed from the central tendency of Supreme Court decision-making. More often, the Court extended judicial rights to a slave unless expressly denied him by statute. Still, the Doran decision clearly underscored the Court's acceptance of legislative limits on its generosity to slaves who claimed their freedom.

---

[34] Doran et al. v. Brazelton et al., 32 Tenn. 105-110 (1852)

[35] Ibid.

Recognition of Supreme Court acceptance of legislative limitations on manumission serves well to introduce the final set of interests which the Tennessee Court saw as integral to an act of emancipation. In the Court's view both the right of the master to free a slave and the right of the slave to receive that freedom had to be balanced against a third set of rights, the rights of society. According to the Court, society's interest in manumission came from its control over the composition of the citizenry. As Nathan Green wrote in 1842, "the State has an interest in the character of its citizens, and therefore has the right to regulate by law the manner in which new members may be introduced into its free community."[36]

To balance the rights of slaves and masters against those of the body politic, William Turley wrote in 1842, it was "well settled, and upon correct principles, that the state . . . possesses the undeniable right to regulate the manner in which manumission should be made, the extent or rights to be acquired under it, or to prohibit it altogether."[37] According to Justice Reese, the owner had property in the slave, but the government had "control

[36] Greenlow v. Rawlings, 22 Tenn. 83 (1842). Also see, McCullough v. Fanny Moore, etc., 17 Tenn. 234 (1836) and Fisher's Negroes v. Dabbs and others, 14 Tenn. 83 (1834).

[37] Hinklin v. Hamilton, and Hinklins v. Hinklin, 22 Tenn. 557-58 (1842).

over his social condition." Manumission, then, necessarily involved a "concurrent act by the owner of the slave and the government." The act of emancipation required not only the consent of the master but "the consent of the government" as well.[38]

The legislature determined how the government's agreement to a manumission was to be manifested and, throughout the antebellum period, the General Assembly assigned the responsibility of actually giving this assent to the county courts.[39]

In regard to how the county court carried out this duty, the Supreme Court showed concern for the substance of things; it did not insist that the legal technicalities be satisfied. Those who tried to void a judgment of freedom upon the basis of irregularities in the county court proceedings or in the record of those proceedings never received a sympathetic hearing from the Supreme Court. Jacob Peck wrote in 1835, it was a "constant course" that

---

[38] McCullough v. Fanny Moore, etc., 17 Tenn. 233-34 (1836); Hinklin v. Hamilton, and Hinklins v. Hinklin, 22 Tenn. 557-58 (1842); Fisher's Negroes v. Dabbs and others, 14 Tenn. 83 (1834); Ann Hope v. David Johnson, et al., 10 Tenn. 114 (1826).

[39] Act of North Carolina, 1777, ch. 6, in John Haywood, rev., A Revisal of All the Public Acts of the State of North Carolina and of the State of Tennessee Now in Force in the State of Tennessee (Nashville: Thomas G. Bradford, Printer, 1809), pp. 95-96; Return J. Meigs and William F. Cooper, eds., The Code of Tennessee, Enacted by the General Assembly of 1857-'8 (Nashville: E.G. Eastman and Company, State Publishers, 1858), p. 520.

when a "trial has been had upon the merits," the Court "will not determine the cause, perhaps against the justice of it, upon technicality, and especially in a case . . . where the matter to be settled is of more consequence to one of the parties than a mere right of property."[40]

The Supreme Court followed this "constant course" in upholding a Rutherford county court decision that had granted a slave Stewart his freedom. Those who claimed Stewart as a slave argued that his emancipation was void because the "report" of the county court chairman was not made according to the letter of the statute.[41] The Supreme Court disagreed. The Court, Nathan Green wrote, would accept the county court action as "sufficient to entitle [the slave] to his freedom," although "there may not be the most exact regularity" in the proceedings.[42] In an 1842 case, Green commented that when the county court granted a manumission the Supreme Court would "presume" that all the technicalities had been satisfied. The record might not show it, but, Green wrote, "all presumptions in favor of personal liberty and freedom ought to be made."[43]

The Supreme Court's refusal to allow technical

---

[40]Blackmore and Hadley, v. Negro Phill, 15 Tenn. 306 (1835).

[41]Law of Tennessee, 1801, ch. 27.

[42]Stewart v. Miller & Moore, 19 Tenn. 576 (1838).

[43]Greenlow v. Rawlings, 22 Tenn. 84 (1842).

errors to void county court decisions emancipating slaves can be described as sympathetic to affected bondsmen. However, in this area as in others, the Court's stance was limited and carefully hedged. The Court would protect the freedom of a slave when the county court had acted positively to support that freedom. If, on the other hand, the county court acted negatively, the Supreme Court would not overrule that decision. In fact, the Court would not allow a slave to appeal an unfavorable action of the county court on an emancipation petition. According to Justice McKinney, the county court's power to give the consent of the government to an emancipation was "a political, rather than a judicial, power." In emancipation cases, the county court had "exclusive and unlimited discretion" and was "not subject to the supervision or control of the superior judicial tribunals."[44]

The Tennessee Supreme Court recognized the right of the state to regulate manumission, but, in many of its rulings, the Court seemed to say that the slave's right to freedom was preeminent. The Court repeatedly held that the county court's refusal or failure to consent to an emancipation did not defeat the slave's right to freedom. This right to freedom, Justice Reece wrote in 1849, was "a substantive thing, whether it be recognized by the state or

---

[44]The Case of F. Gray, 28 Tenn. 347-49 (1848).

not."[45] Nathan Green pointed out that the Court had "uniformly held that a bequest of freedom discharged the persons so emancipated from all obligation of service . . . though the assent of the State may not have been obtained."[46] Justice McKinney observed in 1847 that, although the slave's right to freedom was "imperfect and incomplete" until the assent of the state had been obtained, "the legal character and condition of the slave . . . changed;" he was no longer "in the state and condition of slavery;" he no longer had an owner or master, "within the meaning of the law."[47] In short, the Supreme Court seemed to say that it would not allow the state's right to regulate manumission to abrogate the slave's right to receive that freedom. As late as 1854, Justice Robert Caruthers wrote that "whatever we might think of this doctrine, if it were an open question, it is now too firmly fixed, by a uniform series of decisions to be disturbed."[48]

By "this doctrine," the Supreme Court had created

---

[45]Lewis and others v. Daniel, Administrator, 23 Tenn. 209 (1849).

[46]Laura Jane v. Hagen, Administrator, 28 Tenn. 223 (1849).

[47]Lewis v. Simonton, 27 Tenn. 150 (1847). Also see, Lewis and others v. Daniel, Administrator, 28 Tenn. 209 (1849).

[48]William Boon v. Samuel Lancaster, next friend, etc., 33 Tenn. 393 (1854).

a gap in the structure of Tennessee society. It had created an interstitial position occupied by men free in the eyes of their former masters but not completely free in the eyes of their county courts and their communities. As Caruthers explained, "it is true" that the Court's stance "[seemed] to recognize a kind of intermediate state, between freedom and slavery, which it is difficult to manage and regulate."[49]

From the standpoint of public policy toward free blacks, this Supreme Court doctrine proved troublesome. The difficulty, as Caruthers put it:

> . . . [was] to devise some plan which would be just to the slave, and not inconsistent with the interests of society--that would sustain his right to liberty, and at the same time save the community from the evils of a free Negro population.[50]

---

[49] William Boon v. Samuel Lancaster, next friend, etc. 33 Tenn. 393 (1854).

Thomas R.R. Cobb in his 1858 treatise on slave law said that there was "no middle ground between slavery and freedom; no such thing as qualified freedom, or qualified slavery," but Catterall has pointed out that "the status of 'quasi slave' had no terrors for the logicians on the Tennessee bench, though scornfully rejected as impossible by those of other states." Thomas R.R. Cobb, An Inquiry Into the Law of Negro Slavery in the United States of America (Savannah: W. Thorne Williams, 1858), p. 283; Catterall, Judicial Cases, 2: 479. Also see England, "The Free Negro in Antebellum Tennessee," p. 53, and England, "The Free Negro in Antebellum Tennessee," Journal of Southern History 9 (February 1943): 46. This article is a condensation of England's dissertation. Unless otherwise indicated, all subsequent citations are to the dissertation.

[50] William Boon v. Samuel Lancaster, next friend, etc. 33 Tenn. 393 (1854)

Tennessee legislators attempted to devise some method to reconcile these conflicting goals. They never forbade emancipation or erased the slave's "right to liberty," but they did try to eliminate the problems attendant to a free Negro population. Their "plan" shifted in response to different magnitudes of free Negro "evils."[51]

To lawmakers considering slave emancipation, the "evils" of a free black population were twofold. First, they feared that free blacks, especially freed slaves, would not be productive members of society but would remain an idle poor parasitically drawing on the rest of society for their subsistence.[52] During the first three decades of the nineteenth century Tennessee's legislative regulation of emancipation was designed to provide protection against this eventuality. If a slave could provide assurances that he would not become an economic burden to the community, the

---

[51]For other treatments of the Tennessee legislation concerning emancipation, see England, "The Free Negro in Davidson County," pp. 38-39; England, "The Free Negro in Tennessee," pp. 53-72; Van Dyke, "The Free Negro in Tennessee," pp. 27-38; Patton, "The Progress of Emancipation," pp. 75-78; Patterson, The Free Negro in Tennessee, pp. 153-58; Trabue, "Voluntary Emancipation," pp. 50-68.

[52]Edmund S. Morgan, The Challenge of the American Revolution (New York: W.W. Norton & Company, 1976), pp. 146-52; Winthrop D. Jordan, White Over Black: American Attitudes Toward the Negro, 1550-1812 (Chapel Hill: University of North Carolina Press, 1968), pp. 406-10, 577.

state would consent to his emancipation.[53] Then, at the end of 1831, the Nat Turner insurrection intensified fears of racial conflict, a higher order of free Negro "evil" that demanded a more extreme safeguard.[54] After 1831, the state would consent only to those emancipations in which the newly freed black would be "immediately removed" from Tennessee.[55] In 1833 and again in 1842, this repressive legislation was modified to permit certain categories of freed slaves to remain in the state.[56] However, as sectional and racial tensions increased, the General Assembly, in 1849, reinstated the restrictive legislation and, five years later, expanded on it by requiring that

---

[53]Law of Tennessee, 1801, ch. 27. Tennessee's leniency in this regard was part of an Upper South trend. Ira Berlin, Slaves Without Masters: The Free Negro in the Antebellum South (New York: Pantheon Books, 1974), pp. 29-31.

In the early years of statehood, Tennessee slaves could be freed only "for meritorious services." This restriction came from a North Carolina statute passed in 1777, when the revolutionary legislature, during an "alarming and critical time," sought to guard against the "evil and pernicious practice of freeing slaves." This statute was in force in Tennessee until 1802. Law of North Carolina, 1777, ch. 6, in Haywood, Public Acts, 1809, pp. 95-96.

[54]England, "The Free Negro in Tennessee," pp. 57-60; Van Dyke, "The Free Negro in Tennessee," pp. 16, 30.

[55]Law of Tennessee, 1831, ch. 102.

[56]Law of Tennessee, 1833, ch. 81; Law of Tennessee, 1842, ch. 191. The 1833 statute exempted slaves who had contracted for their freedom prior to the passage of the 1831 legislation. The 1842 statute allowed those slaves residing in Tennessee prior to 1836 to petition for permission to remain in the state upon emancipation.

freed slaves be transported to western Africa.[57] Throughout the last years of the antebellum era, then, the state would agree to an emancipation only upon the condition that the freed slave leave Tennessee, and, after 1854, leave the country.

The Supreme Court accepted and enforced these legislative restrictions with all their antipathy to emancipation and the free black. In a number of cases, when the Court upheld the manumission of a slave, it also stipulated that, as directed by law, the newly freed black emigrate from Tennessee.[58] A slave's grant of freedom might be "substantive," but until the freed slave satisfied legislative requirements, his liberty was imperfect. He might have no legal master, but his freedom was held in abeyance until he agreed to leave the state.[59]

---

[57] Law of Tennessee, 1849, ch. 107; Law of Tennessee, 1854, ch. 50. States throughout the South enacted similar repressive measures. Berlin, _Slaves Without Masters_, pp. 138-40; Eugene D. Genovese, _Roll, Jordan, Roll: The World the Slaves Made_ (New York: Pantheon Books, 1974), pp. 51, 399, 400, 406; Kenneth M. Stampp, _The Peculiar Institution: Slavery in the Ante-Bellum South_ (New York: Vintage Books, 1956), pp. 234-35.

[58] _Fisher's Negroes v. Dabbs and others_, 14 Tenn. 84, 86-87 (1834); _Jacob v. Sharp_, 19 Tenn. 115,118 (1838); _Lewis and others v. Daniel, Administrator_, 28 Tenn. 210 (1849); _Abram, a Man of Color, v. T.J. Johnson, et al._, 38 Tenn. 77 (1858); _McCloud and Karnes, Executors v. Chiles et al._, 41 Tenn. 170 (1860).

[59] For example, the Court ruled that when an freed slave whose liberty had not been accepted by the county court committed a crime, he should be punished as a slave rather than as a free man. _James v. the State_, 28 Tenn. 209-11 (1848).

In evaluating the emancipation jurisprudence of the Tennessee Supreme Court, its willingness to enforce legislative restrictions on manumission without equivocation must be taken into account. Furthermore, the only manumission cases the Supreme Court could hear originated in an owner's alleged desires to liberate a bondsman. No decision of the Court could free a slave a master did not want freed. Therefore, A.E. Keir Nash is incorrect in asserting that the Tennessee Court approached "full-fledged pro-freedom libertarianism."[60] There is nothing in the record of that Court to suggest that is used manumission litigation to attack slavery or even to uphold the principle of universal liberty.

On the other hand, slaves with legitimate claims to their freedom did receive a serious hearing at the appellate level. The Supreme Court did not attempt to defeat a <u>bona fide</u> emancipation, and, as Robert Van Dyke states, it was "manifestly decisive in protecting freedom" when freedom had been "reasonably conferred."[62] Statistically, the record of the Supreme Court supports this view. The Supreme Court decided thirty-six cases in which the freedom of slaves was a central issue. In

[60]Nash, "Reason of Slavery," pp. 164, 171; Nash, "Negro Rights," pp. 188, 204, 233-34, 244, 247, 250. Also see, England, "The Free Negro in Tennessee," p. 53; Trabue, "Voluntary Emancipation," p. 54.

[61]Van Dyke, "The Free Negro in Tennessee," p. 52.

three-quarters of those cases, the Court ruled in favor of freedom.[62]

With good reason, then, Justice Robert Caruthers could point to the "liberality and humanity" of the Court in dealing with slaves who had claim to their freedom.[63] Yet, however, liberal and humane, generous and sympathetic, the emancipation jurisprudence of the Tennessee Supreme Court was completely compatible with and supportive of the Peculiar Institution.

---

[62]In thirty-three cases, slaves opposed whites in the original litigation. In fifteen of these, the slave appealed to the Supreme Court. Whites appealed in the other eighteen. The slaves won twelve (80%) of their appeals. The whites won only five (28%) of theirs. In the other three cases, whites were both plaintiff and defendant.

[63]Doran et al., v. Brazelton et al., 32 Tenn. 109 (1852).

CHAPTER II

MANUMISSION IN THE LOWER COURTS

David Brion Davis has observed that "from ancient times" slave regimes have "recognized that a man might be unjustly held in bondage, and that slaves should therefore be allowed the right to plead for freedom."[1] Tennessee courts accorded that right to its slaves.[2]

Bondsmen employed various legal means to secure their liberty. Some relied on the writ of habeas corpus. In 1820 and again in 1837, Davidson county slaves gained

---

[1] Davis, The Problem of Slavery in Western Culture, pp. 264-65.

[2] The data in this chapter come from a survey of the minutes of the county courts of fourteen counties (see Map 1), three in East Tennessee, four in Middle Tennessee, and five in West Tennessee. The counties include Davidson and Knox, which had the largest number of free blacks in 1860, and Fayette and Haywood, which had more slaves than whites in the same year. The counties also include Nashville, Knoxville, and Memphis, the cities that had the state's largest urban free black populations.

In addition to the minutes of county courts, those of eleven chancery courts were surveyed (see Map 2), two in East Tennessee, five in Middle Tennessee, and four in West Tennessee. Some chancery court heard cases for more than one county. For example, in 1858, the chancery court in Maury county also heard cases from Lewis county. The chancellor at Knox county also handled cases from Union county. Meigs and Cooper, The Code of Tennessee, pp. 93-97.

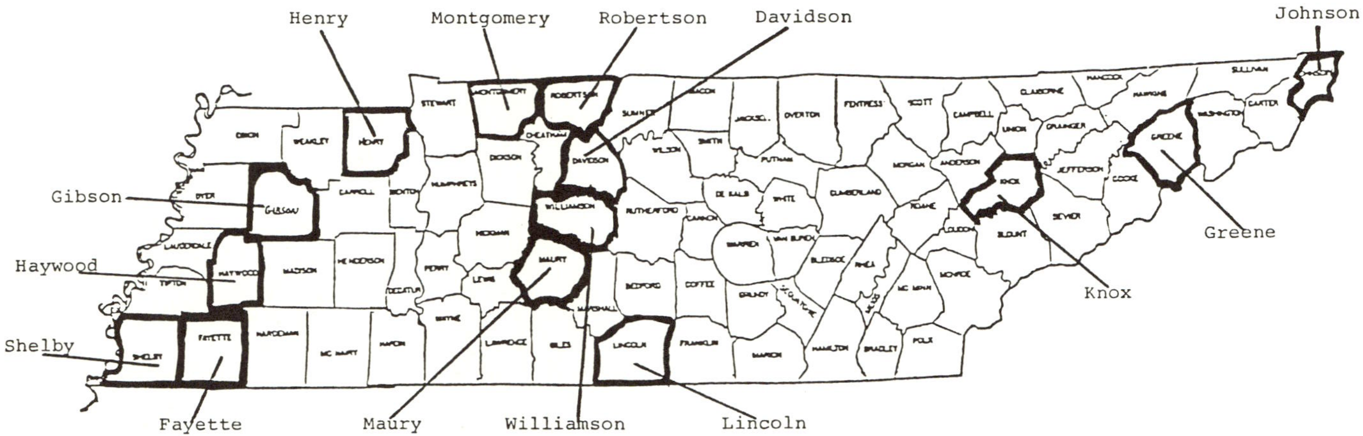

Map 1. Map of Tennessee, 1860; county courts surveyed.

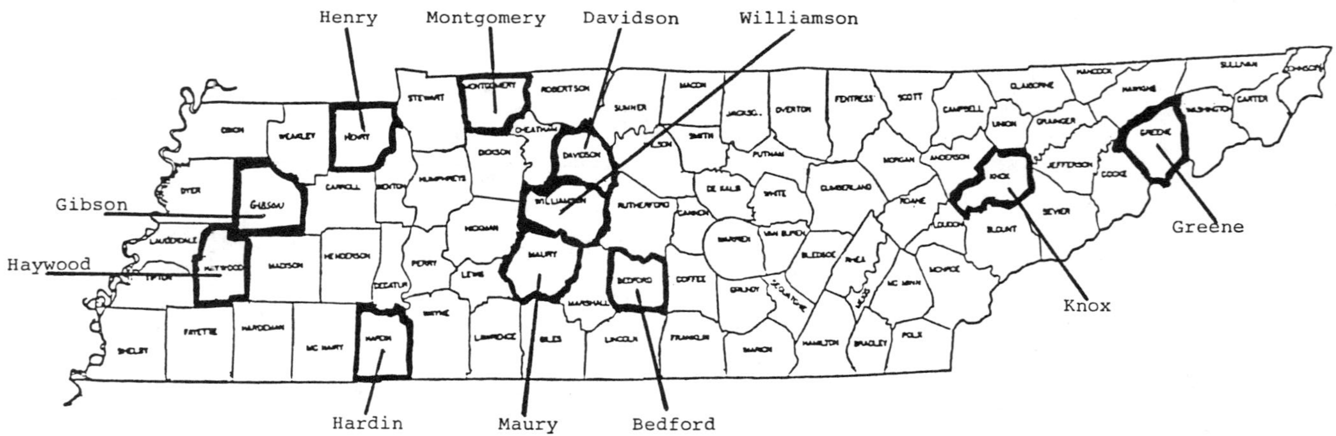

Map 2. Map of Tennessee, 1860; chancery courts surveyed

freedom using the Great Writ.[3] Slaves also successfully pleaded for freedom in actions of trespass _vi et armis_, assault and battery, and false imprisonment. The use of such actions was not great, but the evidence indicates that the courts considered these suits seriously, treating them with formality and fairness.

In the Maury county court in 1815, in an action of assault and battery and false imprisonment, Priscilla Gwin, a slave, sued her owner, Joel Burrow, for her freedom and for $3,000 in damages. Burrow was brought before the county court and required to sign a $6,000 bond for his release. He also had to enter into a $700 bond to produce Priscilla in court and "to treat [her] in a humane manner until the decision of said suit." The twelve-man jury that heard the case decided that Priscilla was "a free person born of a free mother" and awarded her damages of $465.[4]

Common law actions used by slaves "unjustly held in bondage" were not the primary form of emancipation proceeding in the local courts. Rather, most activity involved

---

[3]Davidson County, Circuit Court, _Minutes_, January 1820, p. 352; January 1837, pp. 35, 39, 44-45.

[4]Maury County, County Court, _Minutes_, September 1813, p. 49; August 1815, pp. 322, 359; November 1815, pp. 391, 392; April 1816, pp. 36-40. For other instances, see Davidson County, Circuit Court, _Minutes_, May 1828, p. 373; May 1829, pp. 86, 94; May 1834, pp. 13, 41; July 1834, pp. 60, 61; November 1834, p. 111; May 1837, p. 130; Knox County, Circuit Court, _Minutes_, February 1849, p. 24; October 1849, p. 159; February 1850, pp. 190, 214, 223; June 1850, p. 234. Also see James W. Ely, Jr., "Andrew Jackson as Tennessee State Court Judge, 1798-1804," _Tennessee Historical Quarterly_ 40 (Summer 1981), p. 149.

slaves who had been freed by their masters but who still needed the county court's consent to that manumission. It was the Tennessee legislature that determined the conditions which had to be met before the county court could agree to a slave being set at liberty.

Prior to 1802, legislative restrictions on emancipation were so severe that the county courts' power to accept an emancipation was extremely limited. Unless a slave had demonstrated "meritorious services," the county court could not agree to his manumission,[5] and the records of the counties under study contain only two manumissions granted while this restriction was in force. Moreover, "meritorious services" seem to have played little part, if any, in either case because both slaves had purchased their freedom.[6]

In November 1801, the legislature relaxed its restrictions on the county courts' power to consent to manumissions by permitting local officials to agree to any

---

[5]A slave freed in any other manner would be sold by the sheriff "to the highest bidder." This restriction came from a 1777 North Carolina statute which ran in Tennessee through 1801. Laws of North Carolina, 1777, ch. 7, in Haywood, Public Acts, pp. 95-96. Also see Laws of North Carolina, 1779, ch. 12; 1788, ch. 20, in Haywood, Public Acts, pp. 161, 234-35.

[6]Greene County, County Court, Minutes, May 1796, p. 445; Knox County, County Court, Minutes, July 1797, pp. 257-58; Laws of Tennessee, 1797, ch. 34. Also see, Tennessee, General Assembly, Senate, Journal, 2nd Gen. Ass., 1st sess. (1797), pp. 30-44, passim; House, Journal, 2nd Gen. Ass., 1st sess. (1797), pp. 151-68, passim.

emancipation in which the owner provided assurance that the freed slave would not become an economic burden to the community.[7]

---

[7]Law of Tennessee, 1801, ch. 27. If a slave liberated by this act did become "incapable of providing . . . the common necessities of life," that slave was to be provided for "by the county in which he or she was emancipated." The owner of the freed slave was required to put up bond "in such sum as the court may think proper to reimburse such damages as the county may sustain" in consequence of an eventuality.

According to the preamble of the 1801 legislation, the "meritorious services" requirement was relaxed because the large number of requests for special acts of emancipation tended "to involve the state in serious evils, but [were] also productive of great expense." The number of petitions actually does not seem to have been unusually large. I have found evidence of five between 1796 and 1802. Four of these, however, did occur in 1801. Petition of Sundry Inhabitants of Davidson County re: Emancipation of a negro man called Bob, #20-1-1801, Legislative Papers, Petitions and Memorials, Tennessee State Archives; Tennessee, General Assembly, Senate, Journal, 4th Gen. Ass., 1st sess. (1801), pp. 43, 49 80, 89, 157-58; House, Journal, 4th Gen. Ass., 1st sess. (1801), pp. 43, 48, 78, 80, 88; Tennessee General Assembly, Acts Passed at the First Session of the Fourth General Assembly . . . (1801), p. 198; Petition of Elisha Baker, #7-2-1801, Petition of William Nodding #5-2-1801, Legislative Papers, Petitions and Memorials, Tennessee State Archives; Petition of James Ford and others for the Emancipation of Ruben Ford, Tennessee, General Assembly, Senate, Journal, 4th Gen. Ass., 1st sess. (1801), pp. 52, 60; House, Journal, 4th Gen. Ass., 1st sess. (1801), pp. 54, 57-58, 86. Also see, Tennessee, General Assembly, Senate, Journal, 4th Gen. Ass., 1st sess. (1801), pp. 35, 36, 78, 89, 166; House, Journal, 4th Gen. Ass., 1st sess. (1801), PP. 37, 54, 56, 59, 87.

The number of petitions may have posed problems, but, in 1833, John Catron pointed out that since "every man had his own ideas of meritorious services," the notion was "abandoned" as "too uncertain" to ground a judicial opinion. However, most scholars have accepted Catron's 1835 observation that the General Assembly was concerned that emancipation for "meritorious services" would divide slave families. Since meritorious conduct was likely to be individual, the stipulation "usually precluded the manumission of both parent and child or husband and wife."

During the thirty years this statute remained in force, the minutes of the county courts surveyed for this study contain 118 manumission petitions involving the freedom of 192 slaves (see Table 2). Even during this period of minimum restrictions on legal manumission, then, it did not occur frequently. The 118 petitions represent a rate of only 3.9 petitions per year for all fourteen counties involved. (See Table 3).

The period of relaxed restrictions on emancipation ended in 1831. That December, as part of the reaction to the Nat Turner insurrection, the Tennessee legislature tried to halt the manumission of slaves if that manumission would add to the free black population of the state.[8] Beginning in 1832, county courts were authorized to consent only to those emancipations in which the newly freed black would be "immediately removed from Tennessee.[9]

This requirement governed manumission for two years, during which time its repressive impact was dramatic. In the counties under study, the courts agreed to only three

---

Loftin v. Espy and others, 12 Tenn. 75 (1833); Fisher's Negroes v. Dabbs and others, 14 Tenn. 83 (1834); Trabue, "Voluntary Emancipation," pp. 50-51; Patton, "Progress of Emancipation," p. 75; Van Dyke, "The Free Negro in Tennessee," p. 28.

[8] England, "The Free Negro in Tennessee," pp. 57-60; Van Dyke, "The Free Negro in Tennessee," pp. 16, 30.

[9] A person wishing to free a slave had to enter into bond "in a sum equal to the value of such slave or slaves so to be emancipated" that the slave or slave would leave Tennessee. Laws of Tennessee, 1831, ch. 102.

manumission petitions, all of which rested upon special acts of the legislature.[10]

The legislature, however, soon undermined its own restrictions. That body proved quite willing to pass private acts of emancipation and, in November 1833, it modified the 1831 law by exempting slaves who had contracted for their freedom or who had been freed in a will prior to the passage of the 1831 act.[11]

During the decade following the passage of the 1831 emigration requirement, this 1833 amendment and special acts of the legislature accounted for the bulk of the emancipation petitions. For example, the three petitions in Montgomery county rested on the 1833 statute. In Greene county, four of the nine petitions heard rested upon acts of the legislature and three upon the 1833 exemption.[12] With a

---

[10]Greene County, County Court, Minutes, October 1832, p. 70; Davidson County, County Court, Minutes, October 1832, p. 86; January 1832, p. 217; Laws of Tennessee, 1832, ch. 2, ch. 136; Tennessee General Assembly, Private Acts, 19th Gen. Ass., Called Sess. (1832), pp. 1-2, 36, 197.

[11]Law of Tennessee, 1833, ch. 81. The many requests for legislative exemption from the 1831 act may have prompted this 1833 modification. Tennessee, General Assembly, Private Acts, 19th Gen. Ass., Called Sess. (1832), pp. 1-107, passim; Private Acts, 20th Gen. Ass., 1st Sess. (1833), pp. 24-168, passim.

[12]Greene County, County Court, Minutes, October 1832, p. 70; January 1836, p. 163; February 1838, pp. 372-74; July 1839, pp. 42-44; May 1837, pp. 305-307; September 1839, pp. 65-66; July 1841, p. 246; Tennessee, General Assembly, Private Acts, 19th Gen. Ass., Called Sess. (1832), pp. 1-2, 123, 150.

single exception, every petition heard by the Davidson county magistrates rested either on a special act of the legislature or the 1833 enactment.[13]

The exception involved the will of John Donelson and, in this case, it appears that the county court tried to enforce the 1831 law. Donelson's will freed twenty of his slaves. The county court consented to the emancipation but directed that the slaves be sent "to the colony of Liberia," declaring that any bondsman who did not go "shall be and remain a slave" and that anyone who returned "shall be considered a slave."[14]

---

[13]Davidson County, County Court, Minutes, October 1832, p. 86; January 1833, p. 217; January 1834, pp. 265, 266, 281; April 1834, p. 335; July 1834, p. 55; October 1835, pp. 33, 66; January 1839, pp. 398-99; July 1840, pp. 539-40; Laws of Tennessee, 1832, ch. 45, ch. 136; Laws of Tennessee, 1833, ch. 106, ch. 126, ch. 152, ch. 173, ch. 175, ch. 229, ch. 258; Tennessee General Assembly, Private Acts, 19th Gen. Ass., Called Sess. (1832), p. 36, 197; Private Acts, 20th Gen. Ass., 1st sess. (1833), pp. 54-142, passim.

The single emancipation in Gibson county rested upon a special act of the legislature, but the records of the two emancipation petitions granted in Shelby county contain no reference to any of the aforementioned exceptions. Tennessee, General Assembly, Private Acts, 20th Gen. Ass., 1st sess. (1833), p. 153; Gibson County, County Court, Minutes, June 1834, n.p. Shelby County, County Court, Minutes, July 1835, p. 224; November 1837, p. 373.

[14]The slaves agreed to go and the county court allowed them a year to make the arrangements, requiring bond for twice each slave's value. After a year, the executor of Donelson's will petitioned for an extension of the deadline because of "unavoidable delays" and because the slaves had trouble finding the required security. The court granted the delay and reduced the necessary security to the value of each slave. Davidson County, County Court, Minutes, January 1835, p. 257; January 1836, p. 77.

After the passage of the 1833 amendment, the number of emancipations increased and the rate of emancipation remained substantial. In the 1832-1841 period, as a whole, the county courts heard thirty-four petitions involving ninety slaves. The average annual rate of petitions was almost exactly the same as during the 1802-1833 period, and the number of slaves affected by these petitions was actually higher in the period after 1831.

In February 1842, the legislature widened the loophole of 1833 by giving county courts power to permit an emancipated slave to remain in the state if that slave had been born in Tennessee or had become a Tennessee resident prior to 1836. However, even as the legislators liberalized the law for the overwhelming majority of the state's bondsmen, the stipulations they placed on county courts reflected intensified racial tensions. Before local magistrates could free a slave, they had to be satisfied not only that the slave would not become indigent but that he would "keep the peace and be of good behavior towards all free white citizens of this state."[15]

---

[15]The penalty bond was $500. If the bond was violated, the freed slaves were "liable to all penalties imposed" by the 1831 legislation. Also, they could live only in the county where the privilege of residence was granted. However, if they moved, they could petition for the same privilege in the new county.

The 1831 regulations could not be imposed until the freed slave had been given "twenty days notice of the existence of said act; and that it would be put in force against them unless they departed from the State within that time." The $500 bond had to be renewed every three years, "at which

This statute remained in effect until 1850. During that time, the county courts under study heard sixty-five emancipation petitions involving eighty-seven slaves. This represented the highest average annual rate of petitions during the antebellum era.

During this period, Davidson county was outstripped for the first time by Knox and Greene counties in East Tennessee and even by Maury county in Middle Tennessee with regard to the number of manumission petitions. The evidence strongly indicates that around 1843, as one slave suggested, the Davidson county court "set its fact against" granting petitions for freedom.[16]

In 1842, the Davidson magistrates had granted seven emancipation petitions and allowed the newly freed slaves to remain in the state.[17] However, in 1843, only two petitions were recorded in the minutes, and both were disallowed.[18] Then, no emancipation petitions were recorded in the minutes of the Davidson county court for

---

time the county court may again institute an enquiry into the character and conduct of the applicant." The county court could refuse to continue the privilege, whereupon the applicant had twenty days to leave the state. Laws of Tennessee, 1842, ch. 191.

[16]See below, pp. 41-42.

[17]Davidson County, County Court, Minutes, April 1842, pp. 50, 51, 55, 56; October 1842, pp. 93-94, 95, 96-97, 98-99.

[18]These were the only petitions disallowed in any of the counties during the period. Ibid., April 1843, pp. 145-46; July 1843, pp. 159-61.

the next seven years.

In 1849, the Tennessee legislature closed the loopholes it had shaped in 1833 and 1842, loopholes that had allowed emancipated slaves to remain in Tennessee. The legislature directed that "hereafter no slave shall be emancipated in this State, except upon the terms and conditions imposed by the Act of 1831, ch. 102."[19]

This 1849 law only partially achieved its goals. In East Tennessee, the number of petitions did drop significantly, only eight being recorded during the 1850s.[20] In Middle Tennessee, as well, the rate of manumission declined. However, Davidson county did act on twelve petitions, achieving its highest annual rate since 1831.[21] In West

---

[19] Law of Tennessee, 1849, ch. 107.

[20] Johnson County, County Court, Minutes, July 1850, p. 327. This was the only manumission petition in the minutes of the Johnson county court. The evidence seems clear, however, that in 1854, two other slaves were emancipated, but the court refused to assent to their freedom. The magistrates appointed a trustee for the two slaves under an 1852 law aimed at eliminating quasi-slaves. Apparently the magistrates were unaware that this statute had never gone into effect. (See below, p. 45.)

Knox County, County Court, Minutes, April 1850, pp. 461-64; July 1852, pp. 275-76; Greene County, County Court, Minutes, October 1851, p. 188; April 1852, p. 265; March 1852, pp. 243-44; November 1852, p. 329; July 1851, pp. 161-62; June 1855, pp. 180-81; January 1861, pp. 310-12.

[21] Davidson County, County Court, Minutes, July 1850, pp. 9-10; October 1850, p. 58; September 1851, p. 192; October 1850, p. 54; March 1851, pp. 134-35, 135-36, 137, 138-39; November 1853, p. 61; October 1853, pp. 51-52, 563-64; January 1853, p. 429; April 1854, pp. 192-93, 203-204; October 1855, p. 498.

Tennessee, no manumission petitions were recorded in the rural counties, but in Shelby county, the home Memphis, magistrates heard twenty-one petitions involving forty-one slaves.[22] For West Tennessee, then, the 1850s saw the largest number of petitions involving the largest number of bondsmen for the entire antebellum period.

In sum, the Tennessee legislature determined the conditions that masters and slaves had to satisfy before a county court could accept an emancipation. Prior to 1831, the court had only to safeguard against the freed slave becoming a financial burden to the community. After 1831, the legislature stipulated basically that a freed slave had to leave the state before the county court could consent to manumission, and, for the two-year period when this requirement was unamended, almost no petitions for emancipation were presented to the county courts for their approval. However, the General Assembly itself enacted so many exceptions to its 1831 emigration requirement that during the last decades of the antebellum era, the volume of emancipation petitions in the county courts never really diminished.

---

[22]Shelby County, County Court, Minutes, January 1850, pp. 333-34, 334-35, 337-38; April 1850, pp. 375-76; July 1850, pp. 446-47, 447-48, 449-50, 451-52; January 1851, pp. 559-60; June 1851, pp. 656-57; July 1851, pp. 665-66; September 1851, pp. 702-703, 703-704; April 1853, pp. 259-60; October 1853, p. 338-39; February 1854, p. 407; August 1855, p. 237.

In addition to the legislature, the Tennessee Supreme Court, through its opinions in emancipation cases, also decisively influenced the county court's role in manumission. Tennessee appellate court decisions created the potential for "a kind of intermediate state" between slavery and freedom[23] which contained "nominal" slaves who had been freed by their masters but whose freedom had not been confirmed by the county court. As one "man of colour" explained, emancipated bondsmen in Tennessee "might claim a sort of middle station between the slaves and free men of this state."[24]

The county court could refuse to confirm an emancipation, but this would not return the slave to bondage. Regardless of the action of the county court, a freed slave had no owner or master.[25] Therefore, if a slave, or slave owner, expected the county court to refuse to accept a manumission, it might be preferable simply to go one about one's business. For example, in 1843, a Davidson county slave named Dick was emancipated in his master's will. "A trusted and favoured slave" during his owner's lifetime, Dick

---

[23]<u>William Boon v. Samuel Lancaster, next friend, etc.</u> 33 Tenn. 393 (1854).

[24]Davidson County,County Court, <u>Minutes</u>, January 1824, p. 716

[25]<u>Lewis v. Simonton</u>, 27 Tenn. 1850 (1847); <u>Lewis and others v. Daniel, Administrator</u>, 28 Tenn. 209 (1849); <u>Laura Jane v. Hagen, Administrator</u>, 28 Tenn. 223 (1849).

had been "chiefly employed in personal attentions to his master," an occupation which allowed him time also to labor "for himself, and to enjoy the proceeds of that labour and to acquire and hold property."

When freed, Dick did not petition to have his freedom confirmed by the county court because he wanted to live in Tennessee, and the Davidson court, he believed, had "set its face against" granting manumission petitions unless the freed slave left the state. Hoping that in time the court "might be induced to change its policy," Dick chose, instead, to remain in Tennessee, working for wages for Horace Blackman, the executor and principal heir of Dick's former owner.

This strategy had its dangers. When Blackman moved to Mississippi, he put Dick "in irons" and tried to take him along "as a slave." Dick, however, turned to the chancery court in Williamson county for relief. That court, following Supreme Court doctrine, declared that "although not actually emancipated according to the forms of law," Dick, had "a vested right to his freedom," and was "entitled to emancipation." The court enjoined Blackman from taking Dick out of Tennessee and "from interfering with, or restraining his personal liberty in any manner."[26]

---

[26]Blackman had been the "trustee" for Dick's emancipation, but since he had violated that trust the Court replaced him with another "next friend" who was authorized to "procure" Dick's freedom. Williamson County, Chancery Court, Minutes, October 1848, pp. 162-64.

Dick's status as a nominal slave brought him other troubles. He had loaned his former owner money that had not been re-paid; Blackman had not given him his wages, and had also taken a mule and some hogs from him. The court ruled that, "by realm of his not having been actually emancipated," Dick was "incapable of maintaining a suit at law for the recovery" of his money and property. On the other hand, the court did declare that Dick was entitled to that property and that it should be his "whenever his emancipation shall take place."[27]

According to James Merton England, Tennessee did, in fact, have "a large number" of "*quasi* slaves, released from the dominion of the master but whose freedom had not been sanctioned by the state."[28] A singular entry in the Shelby county court minutes captures the existence of the class in that vicinity. In July 1850, Benjamin McClellan successfully petitioned for his own freedom. McClellan was "slave" enough to need the county court's consent to his liberty, but he was so "free" that the court allowed him,

---

[27]Ibid. In 1857, Dick dropped his suit against Blackman for his property, and there is no record of his ever having the Davidson county court confirm his freedom. Ibid., October 1848, pp. 162-64; April 1857, p. 22.

In Montgomery county in 1852, magistrates ordered two freed slaves out of the state but ruled expressly that regardless of whether they left, they were "freed from servitude." Montgomery County, County Court, *Minutes*, May 1852, pp. 345-46.

[28]England, "The Free Negro in Antebellum Tennessee," p. 53; Van Dyke, "The Free Negro in Tennessee," pp. 37-38; Trabue, "Voluntary Emancipation," p. 52.

as a "free man of color," to confirm his emancipation on his own behalf.[29]

In Nashville, some of the city's most notable free blacks were among the *quasi* slaves. James P. Thomas, the famous Nashville barber, was "freed" in 1834, but it was 1854 before his freedom was sanctioned by the Davidson county court. Frank Parish, perhaps Nashville's most prominent free black, was also a member of this class. Although Parish was a slave, Thomas remembered him "as free to do as he pleased as a man could be." Not until 1853, late in Parish's life, however, did he secure confirmation of his freedom by the Davidson county court.[30]

This apparant ability of freed slaves in Tennessee to live in the "middle station" between slavery and freedom helps to explain one significant aspect of the record of emancipation in the minutes of the county courts. We must surmise that only petitions whose confirmation was

---

[29] Shelby County, County Court, *Minutes*, July 1850, pp. 451-52.

[30] Loren Schweninger, ed., *From Tennessee Slave to St. Louis Entrepreneur: The Autobiography of James Thomas* (Columbia: University of Missouri Press, 1984), pp. 1-8, 18-31, 91-92, 197-98; Davidson County, County Court, *Minutes*, March 1851, pp. 134-35; October 1853, pp. 563, 564

On Thomas also see Schweninger, "The Free-Slave Phenomenon: James P. Thomas and the Black Community in Ante-Bellum Nashville," *Civil War History* 22 (December 1976): 305-14; "A Slave Family in the Ante Bellum South," *Journal of Negro History* 60 (January 1975): 29-44; and "Thriving Within the Lowest Caste: The Financial Activities of James P. Thomas in the Nineteenth-Century South," *Journal of Negro History*, 63 (Fall 1978): 353-64.

expected were presented for action because only rarely was a petition regarding emancipation refused.[31]

Prior to the imposition of the 1832 stipulation that freed slaves leave the state, county courts granted all but three of the petitions recorded in their minutes, and in two of those cases the slaves eventually gained judicial consent to their liberty. In his will, a Maury county master, Parninas Williams, freed a slave woman, Rachael, and her children. In October 1822, when Williams' executor petitioned for the freedom of those slaves, the county court turned him down although he had agreed to the required bond against the slaves' indigency. It is not entirely clear why the Maury county court rejected this petition. The magistrates seem to have been concerned that the debts against the Williams estate had not been settled. Seven years later, when Williams' executor petitioned a second time for the court's consent to Rachael's emancipation, he expressly pointed out that the estate had been "distributed and settled." This time the county court consented to the manumission.[32]

---

[31]In 1852, lawmakers tried to re-enslave freed bondsmen. According to the statute, when a slave was freed without the state's consent, the county court was to appoint a trustee for the slave. This trustee was tantamount to a master. The law was repealed, however, before it ever took effect. Law of Tennessee, 1852, ch. 300; Law of Tennessee, 1854, ch. 50.

[32]Maury County, County Court, <u>Minutes</u>, October 1822, n.p.; October 1829, pp. 228-29, 429-30.

In 1822, in Davidson county, the court refused to agree to the freeing of nineteen slaves emancipated in the will of David Beaty.[33] The minutes contain no explanation, but there was little chance of David Beaty's slaves becoming an economic burden on Davidson county. Beaty had left his plantation to his slaves. It was to be sold and the proceeds "laid out in land in the Indiana Territory," which was to be given to the freed slaves.[34]

After the Davidson county court refused the manumission petition, the executor of Beaty's will secured an act of the Tennessee General Assembly authorizing him to petition for the freedom of Beaty's slaves in a county adjoining Davidson. He went to Sumner county and secured the state's consent to the freedom of the slaves.[35]

During the first decade after the 1831 emigration

---

[33] Davidson County, County Court, Minutes, July 1822, p. 210.

[34] One suspects that the Davidson county court refused the petition because Beaty's sister, Ann Hope, claimed both the slaves and the plantation. Ann Hope v. David Johnson and others, 10 Tenn. 111 (1826).

[35] Ann Hope v. David Johnson and others, 10 Tenn. 111-14 (1826); Laws of Tennessee, 1822, ch. 198; Tennessee, General Assembly, Acts of a Local or Private Nature . . ., 14th Gen. Ass., 2nd sess. (1822), pp. 156-57. Beaty's sister appealed her case to the Supreme Court. The Court upheld the decision of the Sumner magistrates, and David Johnson executed Beaty's will to the letter.

Little is known about the third case in which the county court refused to consent to the manumission of two slaves, Sterling and Harvey, who had been freed by the will of James Hamilton. Davidson County, County Court, Minutes, July 1820, p. 375.

restriction was enacted thirty-seven of the thirty-eight petitions heard by the county courts were granted.[36] Only five of those petitions were accompanied by directions that the freed slaves leave Tennessee,[37] and, in two cases, the evidence is clear that the slaves did not leave the state, choosing instead to live in Tennessee in the "middle station" between slavery and complete freedom until the legislative climate improved and they could petition to have their liberty perfected without having to take up residence elsewhere.[38]

Likewise, between 1842 and 1850, when slaves freed prior to 1836 were allowed to petition to remain in the state, most emancipation petitions were granted and were accompanied by a successful request to remain in the state.

---

[36] The petition that was dismissed was filed in Knox county. In 1834, Duke Howell attempted to emancipate "a negro woman called Edy." The county court, "after hearing argument of counsel," dismissed Howell's petition. He appealed to the circuit court, which upheld the action of the county court. He also appealed to the Supreme Court, but the high court's decision was not reported. Knox County, County Court, Minutes, April 1834, p. 382; Circuit Court, Minutes, August 1834, p. 431.

[37] Knox County, County Court, Minutes, March 1841, p. 62; August 1842, p. 148; Greene County, County Court, Minutes, January 1840, pp. 100-101; January 1842, pp. 300-301; June 1846, p. 253; January 1847, pp. 306-307; March 1847, pp. 308-312; Davidson County, County Court, Minutes, January 1835, p. 257; January 1836, p. 77; Robertson County, County Court, Minutes, September 1840, p. 344.

[38] Knox County, County Court, Minutes, March 1841, p. 62; August 1842, p. 148; Greene County, County Court, Minutes, June 1840, pp. 100-101; June 1846, p. 253; January 1847, pp. 306-307; March 1847, pp. 308-312.

In West Tennessee, every slave freed was permitted to remain in the state.[39] The same was true in Middle Tennessee in Davidson, Maury, Robertson, and Williamson counties.[40]

However, in Lincoln county, in two instances, and in Montgomery county in one case, newly freed slaves were required to emigrate. In Lincoln county, in July 1848, Edward Luke was emancipated by his owner. Luke indicated that he was "willing to remove," and the county court consented to his emancipation on condition that he do so.[41] That October, the Lincoln magistrates consented to the emancipation of Frankey Gray, a "free woman of color" who had purchased herself. The court then refused her petition to remain in Tennessee.[42] Similarly, in Montgomery county,

---

[39]Henry County, County Court, Minutes, April 1847, p. 394. Shelby County, County Court, Minutes, October 1844, p. 149; Janury 1848, pp. 523-25; July 1848, pp. 58-59; January 1849, p. 166; April 1849, pp. 198, 199; July 1849, pp. 250-52; October 1849, p. 294.

[40]Davidson County, County Court, Minutes, April 1842, pp. 50, 51, 55, 56; October 1842, pp. 93-94, 95, 96-97, 98-99; Maury County, County Court, Minutes, April 1844, p. 410; January 1843, pp. 494-95; January 1847, pp. 172-74; April 1847, pp. 216-17; July 1847, pp. 255, 256; October 1847, pp. 295-96, 297-98, 298-300; January 1848, pp. 337-38; April 1848, pp. 375-76; January 1849, pp. 514-15; "Petition of Dyer Johnson," Garrett Scrapbook, TSLAmd; Robertson County, County Court, Minutes, October 1846, p. 261; January 1847, p. 265; February 1849, p. 393.

[41]Lincoln County, County Court, Minutes, July 1848, pp. 493-94.

[42]Gray appealed, unsuccessfully, to the Supreme Court. See above, pp. 26-27. Ibid., October 1848, April 1843, pp. 395-96; January 1844, pp. 436-39; July 1845, pp. 131-32; October 1845, pp. 157-59; April 1847, pp. 357-58.

the local magistrates allowed James B. Reynolds to emancipate "his negro man George," but they refused Reynold's request that George be allowed to remain in Tennessee.[43] In all the counties under study, these are the only decisions of this type on record.

In East Tennessee, twelve of the fourteen manumission petitions granted in Knox county were accompanied by successful petitions to stay in the state,[44] and all the slaves freed in Greene county were allowed to remain in Tennessee.[45] This was true even in the case a fifty-two-year-old slave named Solomon, who was owned by agents of the "Colonization Society." Solomon's previous owner had sold him to the agents, who were to free him and send him to

---

[43] Montgomery County, County Court, Minutes, October 1849, p. 449.

[44] Knox County, County Court, Minutes, October 1846, p. 53; April 1847, pp. 111-12. For the other Knox county cases, see ibid., October 1842, p. 158; January 1843, p. 174; October 1844, p. 302; April 1847, pp. 112-13; January 1848, pp. 177-79, 180; April 1849, pp. 344-46, 346-48, 349-52; July 1849, pp. 373-75, 375-77.

[45] I am including the somewhat confused petition by Hugh Carter, the executor of Jesse Davis. Apparently, Davis had freed a "certain family" of slaves on his estate, and the executors had failed to carry out Davis' wishes. Carter was the "surviving executor." Unsure as to how many slaves his petition covered, he mentioned seven by name. Only one of those was named in the emancipation decree. Since that was so singular an occurrence, I strongly suspect it was an oversight. Greene County, County Court, Minutes, June 1848, pp. 460-61. For the other Greene county cases, see ibid., September 1842, pp. 359-60; August 1843, pp. 454-55, 455-57; October 1845, pp. 188-89; October 1847, pp. 367-69; January 1847, pp. 306-307; March 1847, pp. 308-312; August 1849, pp. 38, 51.

Liberia "as soon as he may be in readiness to go there." Instead, upon Solomon's petition, the county court allowed him to remain in Tennessee.[46]

The story is much the same during the last decade of the antebellum period even though the legislature had tightened its restrictions on the county courts' ability to consent to a manumission. Declaring its legislation of 1831 again to be in full force, the General Assembly renewed its stipulation that newly freed bondsmen leave the state.[47] Nevertheless, every petition recorded during the 1850s was granted, and many magistrates apparently either did not understand the law or disregarded it because county courts continued to give freed slaves permission to remain in Tennessee. In nine of the twelve petitions recorded in Davidson county, for example, and in nineteen of twenty-one in Shelby county, the slaves were allowed to remain in the state.[48]

Also, during the last antebellum decade, the

---

[46] Ibid., March 1847, pp. 317-318.

[47] Law of 1849, ch. 107.

[48] Davidson County, County Court, Minutes, July 1850, pp. 9-10; October 1850, p. 58; March 1851, pp. 134-135, 136, 137, 138; September 1851, p. 192; October 1853, pp. 51-51, 563, 564; April 1854, pp. 192, 193, 203; October 1855, p. 498; Shelby County, County Court, Minutes, January 1850, pp. 333-35, 337-38; April 1850, pp. 375-76; July 1850, pp. 446-52; January 1851, pp. 559-60; June 1851, pp. 656-57; July 1851, pp. 665-66; September 1851, pp. 702-704; April 1853, pp. 259-60; October 1853, pp. 338-39; February 1854, p. 407; August 1855, p. 237.

Tennessee legislature enacted a final modification of its emancipation law. In 1854, the state's lawmakers directed that slaves acquiring a right to freedom "shall be transported to the western coast of Africa."[49] In the records of the courts surveyed for this study, there is only one instance of a freed slave being sent there. By his owner's 1835 will, a young Maury county slave named Powhattan was to be freed at age twenty and was given $150 to be "put at interest" until that time.[50] When Powhattan was freed, the circuit court declared that his trust fund, then about $400, was adequate to transport him to Liberia and support him for six months, and ordered him "removed to the western coast of Africa."[51]

---

[49] Law of Tennessee, 1854, ch. 50.

[50] Maury County, Chancery Court, <u>Enrollment Docket</u>, Book F, pp. 328-31; <u>Minutes</u>, March 1853, p. 632; March 1854, p. 241.

[51] Ibid., Circuit Court, <u>Minutes</u>, January 1858, pp. 597-98, 606. The 1854 statute stipulated that a slave not be sent to Africa until there was a "fund sufficient" to pay for transportation and to support the slave for six months. If the slave did not have such a fund when freed, he was hired out until the fund was raised. When enough money was available, it was transferred to the state treasury, and the governor made "the necessary arrangements" for conveying the slave to Africa.

State treasury records show only two disbursements from the "emancipation fund," $908.66 during the October 1856-September 1857 fiscal year and $1,439.00 in December 1859. On both occasions, this represented all the funds on deposit, indicating that, at the state level, the 1854 "Liberia" law was enforced only twice. Tennessee, General Assembly, "Controller's Report," <u>Appendix to the Senate and House Journals, 1855-56</u>, pp. 5-6; <u>Appendix . . . 1857-58</u>, pp. 133-34, 136, 137; <u>Appendix . . . 1859-60</u>, pp. 12-13, 14-15; Tennessee, Treasurer, "Journal 1856-61," Record Group 23, Treasurer, 1796-1869, TSA, p. 112.

The courts exempted some freed slaves from the requirement to go to Liberia. In the 1859 Greene county case of Mrs. DeWitt's Isaac, the chancery court upheld his freedom and stipulated that he had to go to Liberia, but a year later it reversed that decision and allowed Isaac to remain in Tennessee. The reason given was that Isaac, a "man of good character," was married to a slave woman and had several children. He was "much attached" to his family and wanted to continue living with them.[52]

The 1854 legislation provided that emancipated slaves "who from age or disease were unable to go with safety" would not be required to emigrate to Africa.[53] Joseph Jones, a sixty-seven year old man who had "purchased his freedom," petitioned for the Davidson county court's consent to his freedom and explained that "from his age he could not go to Liberia with safety." Freeing Jones, the Davidson court "permitted [him] to remain unmolested in the city of Nashville or any place in Davidson county" and declared "that any interference with him [would] be a contempt of court."[54] Harry Turk, a fifty-nine year old slave, had

---

[52]Green County, Chancery Court, <u>Minutes</u>, May 1859, pp. 102-103; November 1860, pp. 262-63. In two other cases, chancery courts signalled their willingness to enforce the Liberia provision, but there is no evidence that the slaves ever were sent. Ibid., May 1855, p. 553; Knox County, Chancery Court, <u>Minutes</u>, January 1861, pp. 275-76.

[53]Law of Tennessee, 1854, ch. 50.

[54]Davidson County, County Court, <u>Minutes</u>, October 1855, p. 498.

purchased his freedom "from his own earnings and savings," and his owner had freed him "as far as he could do under the laws of Tennessee."[55] Turk asked the Knox county court to confirm his manumission and to allow him "to reside for the residue of his days in Knox county where he alone hopes to find the comfort and enjoyment he set before himself as an incentive to his exertions to obtain his freedom." Furthermore, Turk said, he believed that "at his advanced age a removal to Liberia or any portion of Africa would be tantamount to a sentence of speedy death from the effect of the climate." Turk produced six witnesses to testify to his good character, four of whom also testified to the lethal effects of the Liberian climate on elderly American slaves. The county court dismissed Turk's petition because the magistrates believed that they did not have jurisdiction, but, on appeal, the circuit court emancipated Turk and declared itself "satisfied that from the age . . . it would be dangerous and hazardous for him to be removed to the western coast of Africa."[56]

---

[55] Knox County, County Court, Minutes, August 1857, p. 108.

[56] Knox County, County Court, Minutes, August 1857, pp. 103-105, 108-109; Circuit Court, Minutes, October 1857, p. 77. The Knox circuit court exempted two other "very aged" slaves from deportation. Knox County, Circuit Court, Minutes, June 1854, p. 669; October 1857, p. 78. The legislature also exempted freedmen from the 1854 act, thus undercutting its own policy. For example, in 1856, the General Assembly made exceptions for nine slaves and ordered that all funds "accumulated" in their behalf be turned over to them. Law of Tennessee, 1856, ch. 126.

In summary, almost all the manumission petitions recorded in the minutes of the fourteen county courts under study were granted. Likewise, these courts seldom required a freed slave to leave the state. This is not to say that the Tennessee county courts consented to the emancipation of every freed slave within their jurisdiction. Indeed, the evidence seems clear that they did not. On the other hand, the evidence seems equally clear that the Supreme Court doctrine regarding the "substantive" nature of freedom completely undercut, if it did not eliminate, the county courts' ability to keep freed slaves in bondage.

Other aspects of the record of emancipation in the county courts deserve emphasis. First, for most of the antebellum period, legal emancipation was concentrated in Middle Tennessee and East Tennessee. Prior to 1832, only a single manumission petition was recorded in the West Tennessee counties.[57] It was not until the 1840s that a West Tennessee county, Shelby, recorded enough manumission petitions to average one a year. However, during the 1850s, Shelby county recorded more manumission petitions and accepted the emancipation of more slaves than any of the other counties under consideration.

Shelby county, of course, was the home of Memphis, the major city in West Tennessee, which supports the view

---

[57] In 1830, the Haywood county court allowed William Downs to emancipate his slave, William. Haywood County, County Court, <u>Minutes</u>, September 1830, pp. 161-62.

that legal emancipation was predominately an urban phenomenon. Indeed, the county courts of Knox, Davidison, and Shelby counties, the homes of Knoxville, Nashville, and Memphis, accounted for sixty per cent of the manumission petitions and fifty-nine per cent of the emancipated slaves in this entire study.

Another interesting facet of the record of emancipation in the county courts is that testamentary manumission was not the primary source of petitions. In his study of the free Negro in Tennessee, Raymond Van Dyke wrote that "in most cases, slaves were manumitted in Tennessee by wills. . . . Hence, the most common procedure under the 1801 act was for the executor, rather than the master, to file the petition and give bond."[58] This statement is simply not accurate. In Davidson county, for example, only nine of the fifty-two petitions recorded between 1802 and 1832 were filed by an executor seeking to confirm freedom bequeathed in a will. Most of the petitions were filed by owners emancipating their own chattel.

Many of these manumission petitions involved initiatives by blacks.[59] One petition was filed by

---

[58]Van Dyke, "The Free Negro in Tennessee," p. 29. Van Dyke, like England, "passed over" the "usually dry court records of emancipation." England, "The Free Negro in Davidson County," p. 40.

[59]Laurence J. Kotlikoff and Anton J. Rupert found a similar pattern in New Orleans. Kotlikoff and Rupert, "The Manumission of Slaves in New Orleans, 1827-1846," Southern Studies (Summer 1980): 172-81.

a slave himself. In 1812, the General Assembly authorized the Davidson county court to emancipate George Barnet. The next year, Barnet filed his petition, which was granted.[60]

Twelve of the Davidson county petitions involved owners freeing slaves who had purchased themselves.[61] In the same vein, four petitions involved owners freeing slaves who had been purchased by other blacks. For example, in 1820, Oliver Hays freed a female slave named Aggy. She was the wife of a free black named Philip Thomas, who had paid Hayes "a stipulated price" for her.[62] A decade later, Charles Duncan, a free black, freed a slave, Jane, whom he had purchased "with the intention of having her emancipated."[63] On another occasion, Randolph McGavock freed three slave children who, indirectly, had been purchased by their free black father, Thomas Wright. While a slave, Wright had purchased himself and his wife Clara. Since a slave could not hold property, the bill of sale to Clara had been given to McGavock. The three children

---

[60] Laws of Tennessee, 1812, ch. 62; Tennessee, General Assembly, Acts, 9th Gen. Ass., 2nd sess. (1812), p. 37; Davidson County, County Court, Minutes, July 1813, p. 1106.

[61] Davidson County, County Court, Minutes, January, 1810, pp. 77-78; July 1813, p. 1098; January 1813, pp. 967, 975; October 1823, p. 643; April 1828, p. 376; July 1828, p. 427; April 1829, pp. 740, 741, 798; July 1829, p. 904; April 1831, p. 199.

[62] Ibid., July 1820, p. 436.

[63] Ibid., January 1830, pp. 149-50.

children were born to Clara while she was owned by him.[64] In nine instances, one member of a family emancipated another. For example, Samuel Hart, a "free man of colour," freed his son Henry Hart, whom he had bought from Thomas Talbot; Ned Needy freed his wife, "a certain negro woman slave called Jenny Needy"; and Frank Curtis freed his sister Dilsey and her son.[65]

The focus of this chapter is on emancipation per se, but one related aspect of county court activity should, at least, be mentioned. After the passage of the 1842 legislation allowing free blacks to live in Tennessee if they had been emancipated in Tennessee or had moved to the state prior to 1836, the county courts received petitions not only to consent to manumission but petitions from free blacks seeking simply to reside in the state.[66]

---

[64] Ibid., July 1813, p. 1098; April 1819, p. 72.

[65] Ibid., October 1827, p. 330; October 1819, p. 209; July 1825, p. 256. Also see, ibid., July 1817, pp. 298-99; October 1831, p. 437.

Petitions stemming from black initiative made up a significant part of the emancipation "business" of all the county courts under study. For example, see Montgomery County, County Court, <u>Minutes</u>, July 1812, pp. 117-19; July 1834, pp. 45-46; June 1848, pp. 252-56; Shelby County, County Court, <u>Minutes</u>, January 1850, pp. 337-38; July 1849, pp. 250-252, 449-50, 451-52; Williamson County, County Court, <u>Minutes</u>, July 1812, pp. 12-13; October 1842, pp. 210-211; July 1843, pp. 263-64; January 1850, pp. 143-44.

[66] A few petitions for permission to reside in the state came under an 1846 law that allowed a free black to be a Tennessee inhabitant if the free black had "married a slave in another state" and that spouse had been brought to Tennessee. Fayette County, County Court, <u>Minutes</u>, April

In Gibson county, in West Tennessee, for example, where only one emancipation petition was recorded throughout the antebellum period, the county court received and granted petitions from twenty-seven free blacks requesting "benefit" of the 1842 legislation.[67] Likewise, in the October 1843 term of the Shelby county court, magistrates received and granted petitions from eleven free blacks wishing to live within the state.[68]

As with emancipation petitions, requests to be allowed to remain in the state seem to have been routinely granted. In fact, all of those discovered in the minutes of the county courts under study received a favorable response.[69]

1847, p. 369; Greene County, County Court, Minutes, December 1860, p. 292; Lincoln County, County Court, Minutes, June 1846, pp. 232-34; Shelby County, County Court, Minutes, July 1850, p. 438; June 1857, p. 656.

The 1846 law did not apply if marriage had taken place "with a view on the part of [the] free person of color to become an inhabitant" of Tennessee, and, if the free black was a male, the owner of his slave wife had to give bond for the husband's good character and behavior. Law of Tennessee 1846, ch. 184.

[67] Gibson County, County Court, Minutes, September 1842, pp. 380, 381; October 1842, p. 391.

[68] Shelby County, County Court, Minutes, October, 1843, pp. 53-54, 56. Also see Fayette County, County Court, Minutes, September 1856, pp. 567-68; Haywood County, County Court, Minutes, August 1843, p. 154; June 1848, p. 412; December 1850, p. 26; April 1853, p. 342.

[69] For example, see Davidson County, County Court, Minutes, October 1842, pp. 94, 96, 97; January 1843, p. 429; Greene County, County Court, Minutes, October 1848, pp. 494-95; March 1849, p. 13; December 1860, p. 292; Lincoln County, County Court, Minutes, May 1846, pp.

With regard to free blacks being permitted to remain in the state one incident in Montgomery county is worthy of note. In August 1849, the county court ordered each constable to "make a list" of every free black in his district and to notify them that they were required to leave Tennessee within twenty days "or comply with the requisitions of the law."[70] The next month, the court explained officially what it understood the "requisitions" of the law to be: that no free black in the county was excused, either by the 1831 legislation or any subsequent act, from entering into bond for good behavior and against indigency, regardless of when, where, or how that individual became free.[71]

This was a misreading of the law, and it was quickly tested. In November 1849, James Scott, a free black, asked the county court to be permitted to remain in Montgomery county without being required to give bond. And "upon a full hearing of the case," the court reversed itself, ruling that

---

224-25; October 1848, p. 526; April 1849, pp. 18-19; May 1852, p. 382; September 1852, p. 414; Maury County, County Court, Minutes, February 1849, pp. 535-36; October 1849, p. 12; May 1850, p. 93; Montgomery County, County Court, Minutes, October 1843, p. 172; December 1846, p. 23; March 1847, p. 60; April 1847, p. 74; September 1847, p. 152; January 1848, p. 179; June 1848, p. 256; March 1849, p. 373; November 1851, pp. 268-69.

[70] Montgomery County, County Court, Minutes, August 1849, p. 428.

[71] Ibid, September 1849, p. 442.

since Scott had been a Tennessee resident prior to 1831 there was "no law in force" making it necessary for him "to apply . . . for the privilege of remaining within" Montgomery county, the county court "having no jurisdiction of his person more than any free white person of this state."[72]

Montgomery magistrates continued to try to enforce the statutes, requiring the county's free blacks to give bond "according to law or leave the county." However, it seems that, after the James Scott case, they no longer believed requirements for legal residence to be the same for everyone. Many Montgomery county free blacks did make their "free bond," but others did not, and continued to live, apparently undisturbed, as residents of the county.[73]

In addition to the county courts, the local chancery courts took cognizance of some manumission questions, and in the actions of these courts we can see most clearly the influence of Supreme Court opinion at the local level.

An 1829 statute gave the chancery courts concurrent jurisdiction in cases of testamentary manumission where the executor failed to act in the county court. If the executor

---

[72]Ibid, November 1849, pp. 463, 465.

[73]Ibid, September 1849, pp. 431, 433, 438, 439, 440, 441, 442; October 1849, pp. 455-56; November 1849, p. 463; November 1851, pp. 268-69; May 1853, p. 105; June 1853, pp. 115-16, 117; August 1853, p. 140; December 1856, pp. 82-86; February 1857, pp. 115, 122-24, 126-27; March 1857, pp. 132, 133, 134, 138.

did not act, slaves "by their next friend" could file a bill in equity to have their freedom confirmed.[74] The slaves' recourse to the chancery courts did not produce a large number of cases. In the eleven chancery courts surveyed for this study, only twenty-nine bills in equity involving emancipation were discovered. As with most of the county court cases, the complainants resided either in East or Middle Tennessee.

Also, as with county court cases, most of the chancery bills were granted; only six were dismissed. These dismissals, however, demonstrate one of the central points of this study; that for all their sympathy and protectiveness of slaves who claimed their freedom, the Tennessee courts would not release a slave whose manumission could not be proved. The courts were protective of a slave's right to freedom if it was genuine; they were willing to give a slave a chance to present his case. However, this was not an anti-slavery position. If the emancipation did not prove _bona fide_, the Tennessee courts unhesitatingly left the slave in bondage.

One example should suffice. In 1842, in Greene county, John, "a man of color," filed a bill in equity to enforce a verbal contract in which his alleged owner, William Ripley, had agreed to free him after five years

---

[74] Law of Tennessee, 1829, ch. 29.

service.[75] Ripley had sold the slave to John Hise "upon the positive agreement and condition" that the slave "should have his liberty" at the end of five years. Instead, John stayed with Hise for eleven years and was then sold to David Brumley, who had possession of the slave when he sought to establish his freedom.[76]

The chancery court went to great lengths to insure John a hearing. He had begun his action without a "next friend," but the court permitted him to correct that omission. John also petitioned as a "pauper" and without an attorney. The court appointed Robert J. McKinney as his counsel. The court issued an injunction against Hise and Brumley, ordering them to post $5,000 bond not to take John out of Greene county, and, finally, upon John's request, the court placed him in the hands of a receiver while the suit was pending.

Yet the chancery court did not grant John his freedom. One fact made his complaint fatally defective.[77] William Ripley, with whom John had allegedly contracted for

---

[75] According to John's complaint, William Ripley had allowed him to choose his master. Greene County, Chancery Court, <u>Enrolling Docket</u>, vol. 7, pp. 194-95.

[76] John said that he had remained in servitude for nineteen years because "he knew not how to obtain his rights, and was afraid to assert them lest his condition might be made worse. Ibid., p. 196.

[77] John Hise and David Brumley both vehemently denied the facts stated in John's bill of complaint, Brumley calling it "a tissue of falsehood and misrepresentation from the beginning to the end." Ibid., pp. 198-99.

his freedom, had never been his owner. John had been owned by Thomas Ripley, William Ripley's brother, and had been bought by Hise when Thomas Ripley's estate was sold at his death in 1822. On the basis of the evidence, it is hard to deny either that John received a fair hearing or that the chancellor was correct when he ruled that John was "not entitled to the relief prayed for."[78]

The chancery courts were not merely careful of procedure. Following the Supreme Court's lead, they treated a slave's right to freedom as a "substantive thing" and went to great lengths to see that the substance of a slave's freedom was established. When David and Moses appealed to the chancery court of Davidson county to confirm their freedom, the chancellor refused jurisdiction on the basis of a recent Supreme Court decision that denied slaves access if they were freed by a will dated prior to 1829.[79] David and Moses then turned to the Davidson county court to have their freedom sanctioned.[80] They were opposed by the administrator of the estate, and the county court by a

---

[78]Greene County, Chancery Court, Minutes, May 1842, pp. 474, 476, 486; May 1843, p. 514; November 1843, p. 525; May 1844, pp. 547-48; Enrollment Docket, vol., 7, pp. 194-204.

[79]Davidson County, Chancery Court, Minutes, May 1848, p. 206; Hinklin v. Hamilton, and Hinklins v. Hinklin, 22 Tenn. 559 (1842).

[80]They based their move on the same Supreme Court decision that denied them access to the chancery court. Ibid.

sixteen to seventeen vote refused to assent to their emancipation.[81]

Regardless of the chancery court's lack of jurisdiction in the case, it continued to intervene. The chancellor declared David and Moses entitled to their freedom and the administrator of the estate "guilty of a gross violation of his duty." The chancellor then appointed a trustee for the slaves and ordered him to continue to apply for the state's assent to their emancipation.[82] The chancellor further decreed that the administrator of the estate "shall not under pain of contempt of this court resist said application directly or indirectly." The chancellor also retained the case on his docket until it could be concluded to his satisfaction. It remained there until 1852, when David and Moses were finally set at liberty.[83]

Another illustrative case involved a Greene county slave named Delilah. In 1839, she was emancipated by her owner's will. At the executor's request, the county court

---

[81] Davidson County, County Court, Minutes, July 1843, pp. 159-61. Five witnesses testified to the good character that the two slaves had maintained for thirty years.

[82] The slaves had appealed the county court action to the circuit court. The trustee was empowered to pursue that circuit court appeal or reapply to the county court. Davidson County, Chancery Court, Minutes, May 1848, pp. 206, 207.

[83] Ibid., May 1852, pp. 510-11.

consented to the emancipation, but required Delilah to leave Tennessee. Instead, Delilah, "to evade the law," went to North Carolina where she "executed a bill of sale of herself without consideration." Then she returned to Tennessee.

Later, when her owner threatened to sell Delilah, she filed a bill in the chancery court to establish her freedom. The chancery court could easily have avoided jurisdiction. This was not a case where an executor had failed or refused to act. His petition to emancipate Delilah had been granted, but she had refused to meet the statutory conditions for the emancipation to take effect. The chancery court hear the case, however, and declared Delilah "entitled" to her freedom. Because she had not complied with the law, the county court decision accepting her emancipation was "inoperative." This meant that Delilah was "incapable of making a contract" and that her sale of herself was void. The chancellor directed the executor of the will to reapply to the Greene county court for its consent to Delilah's emancipation and to apply as well for permission for her to remain in Tennessee.[84]

---

[84]Delilah had three children. The chancellor declared all of them entitled to their freedom, and Delilah quickly secured the county court's consent to their emancipation as well as permission for them to remain in Tennessee. Greene County, Chancery Court, Minutes, May 1846, pp. 83-84, 90; November 1846, pp. 111-12; May 1847, p. 133.

Clearly, the chancery courts did not narrowly construe their jurisdiction. They decided manumission cases involving circumstances other than the failure of an executor to establish a direct testamentary legacy of freedom. For example, the chancery courts enforced contracts for manumission. A Greene county slaveowner, Mrs. Dewitt, told her slave, Isaac, that he could purchase his freedom. Isaac contracted with a third party, Michael George, to pay Mrs. Dewitt the sum she wanted. In return, Isaac agreed to work for George for eight years. Mrs. Dewitt gave George absolute title to Isaac with a "verbal agreement" that Isaac would be emancipated after eight years service. Before Isaac's term expired, Mrs. Dewitt and George attempted to sell him. Isaac filed a bill in equity to have the verbal contract for his freedom carried out, and the chancellor ruled in his favor.[85]

In addition to cases seeking to establish freedom, the chancery courts also had jurisdiction in cases where

---

[85] Greene County, Chancery Court, Minutes, November 1856, p. 604; May 1857, p. 631; May 1859, pp. 102-103; November 1859, p. 172; May 1860, p. 202; November 1860, pp. 262-63. This case was appealed to the Supreme Court, which upheld the lower court decision. In his opinion, Justice Robert Caruthers decried "the picture of depravity and the perversion of truth" that this case presented. "It is revolting to see to what extent some men will go against the rights of the weak in eager pursuit of gain." Isaac (a man of color), by next friend, v. Henry Farnsworth et al., 40 Tenn. 209 (1859). For other examples of chancery court enforcement of a contract for emancipation, see Williamson County, Chancery Court, Minutes, October 1844, p. 222; May 1845, p. 291; October 1845, p. 378; October 1846, p. 624.

slaves claimed property as a result of their emancipation. For example, in a Knox county case in 1848, an executor had refused to carry out a will which emancipated four slaves. The slaves still managed to obtain the county court's consent to their freedom. Then they filed a bill in chancery court, claiming the value of their services between the death of their master and their release from the custody of the executor. The chancellor declared them entitled to the compensation that they sought.[86]

Twice in the Davidson chancery court, former slaves received remarkably large property settlements. Both of these cases, which occurred in the 1850s, seem to demonstrate that the chancery courts' concern for the "rights" of slaves did not diminish as sectional tension heightened during the decade before the Civil War.

The first case involved the slaves David and Moses discussed above. In the will emancipating them, their owner had bequeathed all his slaves "a certain portion of a tract of land . . . together with all his household and farming utensils and stock of every kind." The tract of land

---

[86]Knox County, Chancery Court, Minutes, January 1848, pp. 177-79; December 1850, pp. 41, 80; January 1851, p. 91; April 1851, pp. 101, 136, 157, 175-76.

Also see, Greene County, Chancery Court, Minutes, November 1842, p. 494; May 1843, p. 514; Henry et al., by next friend, v. Hogan et al., 23 Tenn. 198-201 (1843); Davidson County, Chancery Court, Minutes, November 1849, pp. 534-35; December 1849, p. 541; Laura Jane v. Hagen, Administrator, 28 Tenn. 221-24 (1849); Maury County, Chancery Court, Minutes, March 1853, p. 632; March 1854, p. 241; Enrollment Docket, Book F, pp. 328-31.

contained 495 acres.

The slaves became entitled to their legacy in 1808. However, the administrator of the estate did not free the slaves; he "kept them in slavery and ignorant of the provisions of said will in their behalf." The slaves did not learn of their legacy for over thirty years. By this time, only two of the slaves, David and Moses, were still alive and in Tennessee.[87] David and Moses immediately "quitted" the services of the administrator and filed a bill in equity in chancery court to have their freedom established and to secure the other benefits of the will.[88]

It required a decade of legal maneuvering before the chancellor could act, but in 1852 he decreed that David and Moses were entitled to all that was left them in the will. Furthermore, the chancellor ruled that the two slaves were entitled to all the rents and profits of the real estate and to the value of their hire since 1808.

---

[87]There were three other slaves included in this bequest. The chancery court tried to find them, but, by the time the case came to court, two were dead, and one had been "sent off into South Alabama many years ago, and [had] not been heard of for many years." Davidson County, Chancery Court, <u>Minutes</u>, May 1852, pp. 511-112; December 1852, pp. 133-34.

[88]A principal actor in this case seems to have been a man named William Gleaves. When he learned of the bequest to the slaves, he informed them of their legacy and became their "next friend." Davidson County, County Court, <u>Minutes</u>, April 1843, pp. 145-46; Chancery Court, <u>Minutes</u>, May 1848, p. 207.

The total cash value of the real estate, the personal property, the hire of the slaves, and the rents on the property came to $37,184.[89]

The second case involved the will of David M. Harding. Harding left one-half of his estate to his wife and the other half to a slave named Priscilla and her children. Priscilla had to file a bill to get the chancery court to enforce the provisions of the will. The share that she was awarded amounted to $38,340.27.[90]

One ironic aspect of this case clearly demonstrates that the chancery court could extend generous treatment to some slaves without being anti-slavery. The Harding estate included slaves other than Priscilla and her children. In order for Priscilla to obtain her legacy, the chancellor directed that those other slaves be sold and Priscilla given one-half of the proceeds.[91]

The examination of the law of manumission as manifested in statutes, appellate court opinions, and lower court action permits the drawing of certain conclusions.

---

[89] Davidson County, Chancery Court, Minutes, May 1848, pp. 205-207; May 1852, pp. 510-11; December 1852, pp. 133-34; May 1853, p. 218; November 1854, pp. 371-72; County Court, Minutes, April 1843, pp. 145-46; July 1843, pp. 159-61.

[90] Davidson County, Chancery Court, Minutes, December 1858, pp. 363-64; May 1859, pp. 427-28, 573-78. Also see ibid., June 1851, p. 218; May 1853, pp. 161-62, 218, 231-32.

[91] Ibid., May 1859, p. 577.

Slaves were property in man. Tennessee law and the courts gave primacy to the property aspect of the slave's nature, but they unhesitatingly accepted the humanity of the slave as well. This humanity conferred certain rights of which the law and the courts took cognizance. Manumission involved one such right. Tennessee was a slave regime of racially distinctive bondsmen, a society whose white masters feared the presence and influence of the black man and did not want to admit him to any position of equality. Against this background, nevertheless, Tennesseans erected a law of manumission that was favorable to the rights of slaves who had claim to their liberty and astonishingly considerate of rights of specific slaves in individual cases. At times, however, racial fear and prejudice came to the fore, and, when they did, white Tennesseans revealed their willingness to abridge--but not to eliminate--those rights in the name of peace, safety, and order.

CHAPTER III

THE TENNESSEE COURTS AND THE PROTECTION OF THE SLAVE AGAINST PERSONAL VIOLENCE

Tennessee courts weighed the rights of slaves not only when they had been liberated by their masters, but also when they had been victims of personal violence. Issues relating to violence against slaves came before the Tennessee Supreme Court in a number of forms. The focus of this chapter will be on those issues involving slaves as victims of personal violence at the hands of whites. However, bondsmen were subject to violence from other blacks, both slave and free. Tennessee courts never seem to have had any question about punishing slave or free blacks who killed slaves. The Supreme Court heard appeals in four cases where slaves had murdered fellow bondsmen, affirming one conviction. The courts' cognizance of such an offense was not an issue in any of the appeals.[1] In the circuit and criminal courts under study twenty-three

---

[1] _Jim, a slave, v. The State_, 23 Tenn. 279 (1843); _Jim, a slave, v. The State_, 24 Tenn. 137 (1844); _Nelson v. The State_, 38 Tenn. 169 (1852); and _John (A Slave) v. The State_, 38 Tenn. 31 (1858).

slaves were charged with killing other slaves. Only two were convicted on the capital charge, but five were convicted of manslaughter, a non-capital offense.[2]

The Supreme Court heard one appeal in a case of a free black murdering a slave. The Court reversed the conviction but did not question the lower court's right to punish the free black for the crime. In the lower courts, eight free blacks were charged for either murder or felonious assault on bondsmen. Three were convicted.[3]

In regard to white violence against slaves, one issue involved the question of how much violence a slave had to endure before he could defend himself and not have his life exacted as a penalty if that resistance resulted in the death of his assailant. The statutes made no provision for this eventuality. However, the common law, as it applied to whites, provided that felonious homicide provoked by violence was manslaughter, not murder. Therefore, the question became whether this principle applied to a slave who killed a white person.

The case which first posed this problem to the Supreme Court was <u>Jacob v. the State</u> (1842).[4] Jacob

---

[2] See below, pp. 212, 259.

[3] <u>Young v. The State</u>, 30 Tenn. 138 (1850); Davidson County, Circuit Court, <u>Minutes</u>, November 1819, pp. 259, 261, 279, 282; May 1835, pp. 253-56; Criminal Court, <u>Minutes</u>, April 1858, pp. 312, 337-49; <u>Nashville Daily Gazette</u>, 16 April, 17 April, 18 April 1858.

[4] <u>Jacob v. The State</u>, 22 Tenn. 501 (1842).

was convicted in Davidson county for the murder of his master, Robert Bradford. Jacob had stabbed Bradford during a struggle that occurred when Bradford had tried to whip the slave. The crucial question at Jacob's trial was whether a master in punishing a slave could so provoke the slave that if he killed his master the killing would be manslaughter, not murder.[5]

That slavery was not recognized by the common law did not deter Justice William Turley, who wrote the majority opinion in Jacob upholding the conviction. The common law, Turley argued, was "not like the statute law, fixed and immutable"; it could "be modified and extended by analogy, construction, and custom, so as to embrace new relations, springing up from time to time, from an amelioration or change of society." The common law "by analogy and construction" could embrace the "new" relationship of master and slave and "give security and protection to all rights arising under it."

Turley looked for analogy to other authoritarian relationships: master and apprentice, teacher and pupil,

---

[5]The murder actually occurred on August 17, 1840, the day of the Whig Convention. James P. Thomas recalled the incident in his autobiography: the slave "was not inclined to go to work that morning. . . . Everybody was going to town to drink hard cider, wear a coontail in his hat, and Yell for Tippicanoe and Tyler too, and likely Jake wanted a holliday." Also, according to Thomas, on the scaffold, Jacob confessed to another murder which had taken place ten years earlier. Schweninger, ed., From Tennessee Slave to St. Louis Entrepreneur, pp. 58-59.

guardian and ward, parent and child, officer and prisoner. In these relationships, personal injury, "if it exceeds not the bonds of moderation, is lawful correction" and "necessary for the proper organization and due discipline of society." In these relations, lawful personal injury was not sufficient grounds to reduce murder to manslaughter. When resistance resulted in homicide, it was murder because "the law can not admit of the provocation." Similarly, Turley maintained, a master had no right to kill or to maim his bondsman, but if the master inflicted punishment which did not affect life or limb, the slave had no right to resist, no right to protect himself. If he did so and killed his master, the slave had committed murder "because the law [did] not recognize the violence of the master as a legitimate cause of provocation."[6]

Justice Turley went further than one other member of the Supreme Court was willing to go in limiting the slave's right of resistance to those situations where life or limb were endangered. Justice Nathan Green filed a separate opinion that underscored his difference with Turley. Green insisted that

> . . . there may exist cases in which the killing of a master by his slave would be manslaughter. What circumstances of torture, short of endangering life or limb, would so reduce a homicide, it is not easy to indicate. Every such case must rest upon its own peculiar facts.

---

[6] <u>Jacob v. the State</u>, 22 Tenn. 5Ø1-5Ø9 (1842).

However, Green's difference with Turley was not sufficient for him to argue with the verdict in Jacob. As Green put it, the "peculiar facts" of the case were "destitute of a single mitigating circumstance"; it was "most clearly one of murder."[7]

In 1850, in Moses, a slave v. The State, the Supreme Court again faced the issue posed in Jacob. In Moses, the defense actually based its case upon the Jacob ruling. Moses' attorneys argued that the defendant was "alarmed at the character of the preparation for his punishment and under the fear and apprehension of death, or great bodily harm" when he killed his master, John Lauderdale.[8] According to defense testimony, Moses has been whipped by his master one year before the crime. One witness testified that "from the middle to the knees he was whipt all to pieces."[9] The defense pictured Lauderdale as "a violent man" and a person who "when mad struck with anything and anywhere." The defense argued that Moses was, indeed, in fear for his life when the previous whipping and the master's character combined with the circumstances of the day of the crime.

---

[7]Ibid., p. 509.

[8]Moses, a slave, v. The State, 30 Tenn. 166 (1850); "State of Tennessee v. Moses, a slave," Case Files, Tennessee Supreme Court, Middle District, TSA, pp. 11-12, 14-15, 21 (hereinafter referred to as "Moses" Transcript).

[9]"Moses" transcript, p. 18.

On the day of the homicide, Lauderdale's slaves were working at a stone quarry. Moses twice seemed responsible for trouble with the ox cart used in hauling the stone. Lauderdale tied Moses, struck him multiple blows with the ox bow, tied a heavy chain to his leg, and then whipped him with the ox switch for about fifty yards as he marched the slave back to work.[10] Lauderdale then went to his house and prepared a "thick leather" paddle. The defense pointed out that this "instrument of correction" was new to Lauderdale and to the neighborhood, thereby intensifying Moses' fear. Therefore, when Lauderdale came back to the quarry with the paddle and called to Moses, the slave thought that he was obliged to take his master's life to save his own.[11]

The prosecution argued that Moses really had little to fear. Among his neighbors, Lauderdale was reputed to be a stern master but not an inhumane one. The instrument prepared for Moses' punishment "was not calculated to inflict wounds, or in any way to disable the party to be chastised." Furthermore, Moses had already threatened to kill Lauderdale. According to the testimony of witnesses, he had stated that "if his master got him in a close place and he could not get out he would knock him down and kill

---

[10] Ibid., pp. 14, 18, 21.

[11] Moses, a slave, p. 166; "Moses" Transcript, pp. 12, 14, 15, 17-21.

him before he would be beaten as he had been." Finally, Moses had been armed with a mattock and a knife, the instruments of Lauderdale's death. There was no evidence that Lauderdale had actually struck moses with the leather paddle, and one witness testified that Moses had attacked Lauderdale from the rear.[12]

Circuit Judge Maney's charge to the jury certainly could not be faulted. Maney instructed the jury that the "prisoner stood charged with a high crime and like every other person was entitled to a fair and impartial trial," and that there "must be a decided preponderance" of evidence as to leave "no reasonable doubt of the guilt of the prisoner." Maney pointed out that Moses could be convicted of murder or manslaughter or be acquitted. He explained clearly that "the master had no right to kill or maim his slave, and if he attempted either, the slave has a right to resist to the last extremity . . . to kill his master to prevent such injury to himself." Maney then went even further. He said that, if a slave killed his master "from emotions or terror or resentment excited by the cruelty of the master," the slave's offense "would not exceed "manslaughter." Maney also stated that if a slave killed his master because the slave thought his life in danger or because he thought that he was in danger of being maimed,

---

[12]Moses, a slave, pp. 165-67; "Moses" Transcript, pp. 12-18.

the slave should be acquitted by reason of self-defense.[13] Quite accurately, this charge was characterized by Justice Green as "in every respect favorable to the prisoner's defence."[14]

In Moses, the Supreme Court upheld the slave's conviction for murder, a decision, like Jacob, that seems to support Daniel Flanigan's view that southern judges "worked within the confines of the proslavery mentality."[15] The Moses and Jacob decisions clearly indicate that the Tennessee Supreme Court would not easily or quickly question the power and authority of masters over their chattel and the use of physical violence to maintain that power and authority. It would not easily or quickly countenance the slave's resistance to the physical violence of the master and would exact the slave's life as penalty when that resistance resulted in the master's death.

---

[13] "Moses" Transcript, pp. 21-23. In his remarks on self-defense, Maney went well beyond the reduction of murder to manslaughter. However, Justice Green noted Maney's "instructions as to the law" on the "question, whether the killing was murder or manslaughter, or excusable self-defense," and ruled that "there is no error in the charge of the court to the jury." In another case involving a slave accused of murder, Maney made a similar charge regarding self-defense, which, upon appeal, also was accepted by the Supreme Court. Moses, a slave, v. The State, 30 Tenn. 167 (1850); "Henry a Slave v. The State of Tennessee [1850], Case Files, Middle District, Tennessee Supreme Court, TSA; Henry v. the State, 30 Tenn. 160 (1850).

[14] Moses, a slave, p. 167.

[15] Flanigan, "Criminal Law of Slavery,", p. 105.

In Nelson v. the State(1850), the Court confronted the issue of a slave's right to defend himself and kill a white man who was not his owner. Nelson was convicted in Hardin county for the murder of David Sellers. At a corn-husking, some slaves quarreled. In breaking up the quarrel, Sellars struck one of them. Nelson "thereupon spoke in an abrupt manner to Sellars," and Sellars struck the slave two or three times with "a hickory stick as large as a chair post." After this incident, Nelson started to go home but was called back to get his super. When he returned, Sellars returned, Sellars confronted him, saying, "you have come back again, have you?" To which Nelson replied, "yes, and if you will give me a white man's chance, I will whip you like damnation." Sellars struck Nelson several times with the hickory stick, knocking the slave to his knees. As Nelson tried to rise, Sellars struck him again, whereupon the slave fatally stabbed his white assailant.[16]

Justice Green wrote the Nelson decision. He overturned the lower court conviction because the circuit judge's instructions to the jury were "vague and indistinct," excluding altogether "the consideration of a case of manslaughter."[17] However, Green explained that the rule permitting violent provocation to mitigate murder to mansaughter did not apply in the same way when a slave

---

[16] Nelson (1850), pp. 344-45.

[17] ibid., pp. 348, 349.

killed a white man as it did when one free man killed another.

Green's Nelson opinion deserves quoting if only to balance the egalitarianism in his manumission opinions. Where slaves killed white men, Green was not so willing to countenance equality. He argued that "the influence of enlightened reason" showed that

> . . . the same indignity which would excite the passions of a white man, would not have a like effect upon a slave. That which would be grievous provocation to the one, would provoke the other but slightly. This difference arises from the different habits of feeling, and modes of thought of the two races.

To treat the slave and white man alike, Green wrote,

> . . . would be a perversion of the principles of the common law by sticking to its letter. It would be to disregard entirely the character and condition of this portion of our population, and would be as repugnant to reason, as it would be mischievous in practice.

At the same time, Green did not draw the line completely against the slave. "It does not follow," he stated, "that a provocation may not be so grievous as that, if the slave slay the white man, it will be but manslaughter, although the life or limb of the party killing is not endangered." Repeating his opinion in Jacob, the jurist declared that he had "no doubt but that cases may exist, where the slave committing the homicide . . . cannot be deemed to have done the act with malice aforethought."[18] Green again relied

[18] Ibid., p. 351

on the doctrine of reasonable punishment. If a slave misbehaved and "provoked merited chastisement," and the punishment "be reasonably inflicted upon him," it was the slave's "duty to submit." If the slave resisted and killed the person punishing him, it was murder. However, if the chastisement was "unreasonable and excessive, the killing will only be manslaughter." Green again insisted that the Supreme Court would not indicate "with precise accuracy, what particular extent of provocation will reduce such homicide to manslaughter." Each case would "depend very much upon its own circumstances, and . . . the enlightened judgment of the jury."[19]

Taken together, the *Jacob*, *Moses*, and *Nelson* decisions demonstrate that the Court carefully hedged its position. The Court would not deprive the slave of the benefit of the law governing grades of homicide, but neither would it demand that the rules mitigating murder to manslaughter be applied equally to slave and free. The Court would leave it to the local circuit jury to decide when punishment short of danger to life or limb was improper chastisement and when a white man had so exceeded the bounds of propriety that the law would not demand the slave's life

---

[19] *Nelson* (1850), p. 352. As Mark Tushnet has observed for the North Carolina Supreme Court, upon which Green depended heavily in forming his *Nelson* opinion, this stance kept the issue of what constituted provocation "from becoming an element of articulated law." Tushnet, *American Law of Slavery*, p. 107.

for committing homicide. This position severely limited the slave's right to defend himself against personal violence if that violence took the form of punishment.

Overall, the Supreme Court heard seven cases involving slaves accused of murder or attempted murder while resisting punishment. Two cases, Moses and Jacob, involved slaves killing masters. In both instances the Supreme Court upheld the lower court convictions and the slaves went to the gallows. The other five cases involved one instance of murder and four instances of attempted murder of whites who did not own the accused slaves. Slaves fared better in these cases. Only once did the Supreme Court uphold the conviction and sentence of death.[20] In the four other cases, the Court reversed the trial court convictions and awarded the slaves a new trial. These cases actually involved only two slaves. Both had their cases before the Supreme Court twice. In one case, because the pertinent records have not survived, the final outcome is unknown. In the other the slave eventually was acquitted.[21]

---

[20] This case involved a Maury county runaway slave who show a man he thought was going to try to capture him. He was convicted of attempted murder and eventually went to the gallows. Tom, a Slave, v. The State, 27 Tenn. 68 (1847).

[21] "Elijah, a slave, v. the State," Case Files, Middle District, Tennessee Supreme Court, TSA; Smith County, Circuit Court, Minutes, April 1942, p. 26; Hardin County Circuit Court, Minutes, January 1848, pp. 458-59; Perry County, Circuit Court, Minutes September 1950, p. 422.

In the trial courts in the counties under study, there were eight trials of slaves who murdered or attempted to murder their masters. There were fifty trials of slaves who murdered or attempted to murder whites who were not their masters. The nature of the evidence does not permit us to know whether the slaves were resisting punishment. However, the outcome of these cases seems clearly to demonstrate that slaves who killed masters, for whatever reason, were far more likely to go to the gallows than if their victims had been "strangers." In the eight prosecutions against slaves who killed or attempted to kill their masters, there were six convictions, seventy-five percent of the cases. In the fifty-four prosecutions of slaves who killed or attempted to kill whites other than their masters, there were only eight convictions, fifteen percent, for the capital offenses. There were four other convictions, seven percent, for lesser, non-capital offenses. Thus, the total conviction rate when the white victim was not the owner of the slave was only twenty-two percent.[22]

A second form in which the issue of the slave's protection from physical assault or murder came before the courts involved whites accused of violence against slaves. Here, Tennessee statutes provided a limited degree of protection. Under Tennessee law, anyone who was alleged to have "wantonly and without sufficient cause" beat or abused

---

[22] See below, pp. 213, 260.

the slave "of another person" was subject to indictment. The person accused of committing the offense was tried in the county court, "subject to the same pains and penalties for the commission of similar offenses on the body of any white person."[23] However, there was no statutory provision making the wanton abuse of a slave by his owner an indictable offense.

Tennessee law also provided that killing a slave would be treated as murder "as if such person so killed, had been a free man." Those who killed slaves, then, were subject to the death penalty. However, the law provided for three significant exceptions: the law did not apply to a slave "outlawed" by the General Assembly, to a slave who was "in the act of resistance" to his lawful owner, or to a slave "dying under moderate correction."[24]

As Andrew Fede has written, the "terrible texture" of these exceptions meant "paltry protection" for the slave against the violence of the master.[25] And, in addition to such limitations written into the law itself, the statutory protection of slaves was undermined further by what Eugene

---

[23]Law of Tennessee, 1813, ch. 56; Meigs and Cooper, <u>The Code of Tennessee</u>, p. 513.

[24]Law of North Carolina, 1771, ch. 31, in Scott, <u>Laws</u>, 1: 134-35; Law of Tennessee, 1799, ch. 9; Meigs and Cooper, <u>The Code of Tennessee</u>, pp. 512-13.

[25]Andrew Fede, "Legitimized Violent Slave Abuse in the American South, 1619-1865: A Case Study of Law and Social Change in Six Southern States," <u>The American Journal of Legal History</u>, 29 (April 1985): 120-21.

Genovese has called "the fatal weakness of the law," the prohibition on black testimony against white defendants.[26]

The Tennessee Supreme Court went well beyond these narrowly drawn statutes in upholding convictions of whites who killed or assaulted slaves. Where the killing of a slave was concerned, the Court relied upon the common law.[27] The issue of the common law protecting a slave's life generated considerable discussion on other southern appellate benches, but the Tennessee court "with much less ado" and "with little concern for logical niceties" decided the issues in favor of the bondsman.[28]

The Court established its position in 1829 in William Fields v. State of Tennessee. Fields had been charged in Maury county with the murder of another man's slave. The circuit court jury acquitted Fields of murder but convicted him of manslaughter. He appealed on the grounds that he could not be convicted of manslaughter when the victim was a slave because the crime did not exist in the statute law. Manslaughter was a common law offense

---

[26]Genovese, Roll, Jordan, Roll, p. 38.

[27]Nash has written that whether the slave came "under the protection of the common law" or had "to rely on the more flimsy armor of statutory law" was "the first and most fundamental question" in guarding the slave against unlawful physical violence. Nash, "Fairness and Formalism," p. 67; "More Equitable Past," p. 203.

[28]Nash, "More Equitable Past," p. 212; Fairness and Formalism," p. 76; also see, Flanigan, "The Criminal Law of Slavery," pp. 155-57.

and because "slavery never existed in England" that law did not apply in the killing of a slave in Tennessee.[29]

The Tennessee Supreme Court did not support Fields. Justice Robert Whyte and Jacob Peck both wrote opinions. Whyte simply argued that serfdom and slavery exhibited "a strong resemblence." The "principal features of both are the same, and differing only in some minutiae, which do not require to be noticed." Therefore, the common law was as applicable to the slave as to the serf, and the "offense of manslaughter, when a negro or mulatto slave is the subject of it . . . exists by common law; because it is the unlawful killing of a human being."[30]

Peck agreed, but his guiding principle seemed to be religion. "I have been taught," he wrote, "that Christianity is part of the law of the land. The four gospels upon the clerk's table admonish me so every time they are used in administering oaths."[31] Peck concluded that "the law which says thou shall not kill, protects the slave; and he is within its very letter. Law, reason, Christianity and common humanity, all point out one way."[32]

---

[29] William Fields v. State of Tennessee, 9 Tenn. 141-42 (1829).

[30] Ibid., pp. 144-45.

[31] Ibid., p. 148.

[32] Ibid., p. 150. In 1851, the Court upheld the second degree murder conviction of a man accused of killing a slave. The victim having been a slave was not a factor in the decision. Rowe v. The State, 30 Tenn. 337-39 (1851).

The Supreme Court never heard a criminal appeal involving the law against the wanton abuse "of another's slave," but the Court protected slaves against physical abuse, even at the hands of their masters, by extending to slaves the protections of the regular criminal law. In 1850, in Giles county, an owner was convicted of maiming his slave by castration. Upon appeal, the defense argued that the conviction should be overturned because the crime was "not within the provisions of the penal code." Justice A. W. O. Totten, who wrote the Court's opinion, did not agree. The code did not apply to offenses committeed by slaves, but, he wrote, "it does not follow" that offenses committeed by whites "upon the persons of slaves, shall not be punishable under this code." The slave, Totten continued,

> . . . is to be regarded as a reasonable creature in being, in the sense of the code, and as a person upon whom the offense . . . may be committeed. We consider that this view of the subject not only accords with the reason and humanity of the law, but with the obvious intention of the code.[33]

---

[33]Werley v. The State, 30 Tenn. 119-22 (1850).

Mark Tushnet has portrayed antebellum southern law as ensnared in the contraditions generated by dependance upon a slave-labor mode of production in a free labor, bourgeois capitalist world. Tushnet's "primary conclusion" is that the "general solution" to the tension created by such contraditions was "the development of a distinct category of slave law," that is, "bracketing slave law off from other areas of the law." Tushnet uses North Carolina appellate cases involving interracial violence in support of this argument. Justice Nathan Green, in 1850, observed that in Tennessee "it is unquestionably true, that the difference between the two races, and the nature of our institutions, must greatly modify the rules of law, in

The defense in this case also contended that there was an "absence of malice" in the incident, without which no crime had been committeed. On the one hand, the slave was "of a most wicked and turbulent disposition . . . in the constant habit of running away . . . lewd and incontinent, and in other respects of a very bad morals and character." On the other hand, the defendant was "remarkable for his kindness and humanity towards his slaves" and had "never given the slave . . . any cause or excuse for his turbulent and vicious conduct." Furthermore, before resorting to castration, the master "had used mild and reasonable means to reform him."

The Court would not allow these circumstances to remove the implication of malice. The act was unlawful and was done "on preparation, wilfully and deliberately." It was therefore malicious. "We utterly repudiate,"

---

relation to criminal offenses, committed by a party of the one race upon a person of the other." However, the picture from Tennessee regarding this area of law is mixed. There was some "bracketing" off of cases where slaves killed whites. On the other hand, in cases involving white violence against slaves, the movement clearly was in the opposite direction. Tushnet, himself, acknowledges that the development of categorization was incomplete and that it "moved haltingly, and at different rates in different geographic and legal areas." The Tennessee experience suggests that, even with this nearly fatal cavaet, Tushnet has hypothesized a development that simply may not have existed. Tushnet, American Law of Slavery, pp. 8-10, 90-121. Green's comment is in Walker v. Brown, 30 Tenn. 126 (1850). Thomas D. Morris has reached a similar conclusion regarding another area of slave law. See Morris, "'As if the Injury Was Effected by the Natural Elements of Air, or Fire,'" p. 595.

Totten continued,

> . . . the idea of any such power and dominion of the master over the slave, as would authorize him thus to maim his slave for the purpose of his moral reform. Such a doctrine would violate the moral sense and humanity of the present age.[34]

The Tennessee Supreme Court's willingness to punish whites for murder and mistreatment of slaves penetrated to the lower courts to some degree. The law against wanton abuse of another's slave was enforced in all the counties under study, but not with great frequency. In Maury county, for example, between 1810 and 1860, a mere twenty-six such cases were brought before the circuit court; only ten of

---

[34]Ibid. Also see Fede, "Legitimized Violent Slave Abuse," pp. 146-47. In addition to upholding the criminal prosecution of whites who abused slaves, the Supreme Court also upheld the right of the slaveowner to recover damages when a bondsman was victim of wrongful violence from another white man. This was a "property" right of the master, but there was protection for the slave contained within it. On one occasion, the Court seemed to explicitly acknowledge this connection, asserting that "to deny the owner's right . . . would be justly esteemed a reproach to humanity in any condition of civil society above the level of barbarism." Jane G. James v. Sampson Carper, 36 Tenn. 244-29 (1857). Also see, Puryear v. Thompson, 24 Tenn. 389-92 (1844); Walker v. Brown, 30 Tenn. 125-27 (1850); James M. Tomlinson, et al., v. William Darnall, 39 Tenn. 341-43 (1859); Flanigan, "The Criminal Law of Slavery," pp. 169-71.

In a similar fashion, the Court sought to protect slaves from lynch law and vigilantism. It could not bring back the life of the slave, nor could it independently prosecute whites who, in the exercise of lynch law or vigilantism, unlawfully killed slaves, but the Court could award damages to the owner of the slave so destroyed. Here, the Court seemed motivated as much by its concern for the life of the slave as by its regard for the property of the master. As Justice Robert Caruthers wrote, "no man, whether bond or free" should be condemned to death "without a hearing--a fair and impartial trial." Polk, Wilson & Co. v. Thomas H. Fancher et al., 39 Tenn. 214 (1858); J. M. Kirkwood et al., v. George Miller, 37 Tenn. 297 (1858).

them resulted in convictions. The fines in those cases ranged from one cent to twenty-five dollars.[35]

The statute itself required that wanton abuse of a slave be treated like "similar offenses on the body of any white person." The courts treated the offense like simple assault and battery, a misdemeanor. For example, in 1834, in the Davidson county court, Judy Young pleaded guilty to abuse of a slave and was fined six cents. That same term, the court fined John Reddick the same sum for assault and battery on another white man.[36] It seems safe to assume that such penalties for assault and battery did little to reduce the level of violence between whites or to protect slaves from abuse and physical assault by whites.

More serious violence against slaves also led to prosecutions. In the counties under study, there were fifty-four felony prosecutions against forty-seven individual whites for either killing of physically assaulting slaves. Thirty-three (sixty-one percent) of those prosecutions were for murder. With one exception, the others were for felonious assault, either attempted murder malicious stabbing, or malicious shooting. (See Tables 4

---

[35]For example, see Maury County, Circuit Court, Minutes, January 1844, pp. 490, 494; January 1848, p. 422; August 1850, p. 500; May 1852, p. 425; January 1854, p. 323; August 1857, p. 543; January 1861, p. 242.

[36]Davidson County, County Court, Minutes, April 1834, pp. 379, 436.

and 5.) The exception was the 1854 indictment in Shelby county of a white man, James Keyton, for the rape of a young slave girl. The girl's owner was the prosecutor, and the grand jury indicted Keyton. Howver, he was acquitted.[37]

Only three of the cases involved owners of the slave victims. All three were murder cases in which the owner was indicted for whipping or beating his slave to death. None of the owners accused of murdering their slaves ever came to trial. In each case, the cause eventually was "stricken" because the defendant "was not to be found."[38]

One of these slaveowners, Hugh C. Hurst of Bedford county, was indicted on the basis of the findings of a coroner's inquest. The jury of inquest in this case actually ordered the body of his slave, a woman named Almira, exhumed for examination.[39] Tennessee law required that a coroner's inquest be held when any person died "accidentally or by unlawful violence, or other suspicious cause" and directed that an indictment was to be filed if

---

[37]Shelby County, Circuit Court, Minutes, January 1855, pp. 400-401, 425-27, 428.

[38]Ibid., May 1856, pp. 331-35; May 1858, p. 294; Bedford County, Circuit Court, Minutes, April 1860, p. 380; Tipton County, Circuit Court, Minutes, May 1858, p. 224.

[39]Bedford County, Circuit Court, Minutes, August 1858, pp. 67-68; Nashville Republican Banner, 23 July 1858; Nashville Daily Gazette, 25 July 1858. There is much in this data from Tennessee to support Andrew Fede's ideas regarding the importance of the "class identity" of those who committed violence against slaves. Fede, "Legitimized Violent Slave Abuse," p. 117.

it appeared that some person had been guilty of "wilful homicide or murder."[40] Tennesseans routinely included slaves within this provision. In the counties under study, three whites, other than Hurst, were indicted for the murder of slaves based on the report of a coroner's inquest.[41]

---

[40] Law of Tennessee, 1812, ch. 41; 1825, ch. 36; Meigs and Cooper, The Code of Tennessee, pp. 935-38.

[41] Bedford County, Circuit Court, Minutes, August 1858, pp. 199-200; Davidson County, Criminal Court Minutes, March 1844, pp. 447-48; Shelby County, Circuit Court, Minutes, June 1843, pp. 100-101. Also see, Nashville Republican Banner, 3 June 1858.

The coroner's inquests were not courts of record. The references to them and their activities are usually sketchy entries in the county or circuit minutes directing that certain fees be paid. In the counties surveyed for this study, there were scores of such entries dealing with the death of slaves. For example, see Greene County, County Court, Minutes, January 1814, p. 227; July 1817, p. 222; Henry County, County Court, Minutes, October 1845, p. 332; Haywood County, County Court, Minutes , January 1858, p. 37; Knox County, County Court, Minutes, October 1857, p. 125; Gibson County, County Court, Minutes, September 1829, p. 128; February 1838, p. 8; Lincoln County, County Court, Minutes, August 1852, p. 399; Maury County, Circuit Court, Minutes, January 1848, p. 452. Also see, Nashville Daily Gazette, 30 March 1856; Nashville Republican Banner, 4 August 1859; 11 October, 14 October 1859; 6 July 1860.

Occasionally the cause of death was indicated. In Fayette county, for example, coroners reported that one slave was killed "by falling off limb," another "murdered," and another "axed to death by another slave." Fayette County, County Court, Minutes, July 1845, p. 142; February 1851, p. 343; October 1857, p. 345.

In Robertson County, five coroner's reports on slave deaths gave suicide as the cause of death, two gave exposure, two accidental drowning, and one "by a fit" because the jury counld "find no bruise or any other sign of violence." Robertson County, County Court, Minutes, June 1841, p. 390; October 1856, p. 588; January 1854, p. 228; May 1857, p. 101; March 1858, p. 302; February 1850, p. 461; May 1850, p. 487; June 1853, p. 41; September 1857, p. 135; May 1850, p. 486.

Over one-half (53 percent) of the individuals charged with murder or felonious assault on slaves did go to trial. This suggests that the authorities were generally diligent when the victim was a slave. However, one revealing incident should be cited. In Williamson county in 1855, Ellen Bolton, "exasperated by jealousy," the Nashville Republican Banner reported, murdered a female slave owned by her husband in a fashion "without parallel in atrocity in the criminal annals of the State." As Representative William Ewing of Williamson later stated on the floor of the Tennessee General Assembly, she "took three days to study out the most inhuman manner" to kill her servant. In her "inhuman butchery," not only did she beat the slave with a shovel, but she hung her and scalded her entire body with boiling water. However, after her preliminary examination before two justices of the peace, Mrs. Bolton was released on what Ewing called "nominal bail," and she never appeared for trial.[42]

Regardless of the apparent willingness to bring

---

[42]The bail was $1,000. Williamson County, Circuit Court, Minutes, November 1855, pp. 304-305; July 1856, p, 378; Nashville Republican Banner, 21 September 1855, 21 December 1859; Nashville Daily Gazette, 22 September 1855.

One example in the other direction should be cited. In 1858, a Maryville grand jury, acting upon a coroner's inquest, indicted a master for the death of his slave, "a small negro boy," killed by "cruel treatment." The court set the master's bail at $10,000. Nashville Republican Banner, 3 June 1858.

whites to trial for the murder of slaves, only three of the whites so accused were convicted. Two of those cases occurred in the 1820s. Both white defendants were convicted of a lesser degree of homicide than murder and both were branded with the letter "M" as punishment.[43] One case did take place late in the antebellum era. In Shelby county in 1849, Benjamin Rowe "shot a negro through the back of the head and instantly killed him . . . without the least provocation." According to a newspaper report, "so exasperated were the neighbors at the unprovoked murder, that they erected a gallows and hung a rope to it for the purpose of hanging the murderer." Better judgment, however, prevailed, and Rowe was tried before the Shelby county circuit court, convicted of murder in the second degree, and sentenced to ten years in the penitentiary.[44]

Of fifteen individuals accused of felonious assault on slaves, only five were convicted. One of these, John Munds, convicted in Shelby county in 1851, for the malicious stabbing of a slave, was granted a new trial and

---

[43] "State v. William Fields," Case Files, Middle District, Tennessee Supreme Court, TSA; Maury County, Circuit Court, _Minutes_, June 1821, pp. 502-13; December 1821, pp. 41, 42; Williamson County, Circuit Court, _Minutes_, August 1828, pp. 122, 132, 163, 165-66.

[44] _Memphis Daily Eagle_, May 1849; Shelby County, Circuit Court, _Minutes_, September 1850, pp. 285-87, January 1851, pp. 200, 206, 317-18. Also see the _Nashville Daily Gazette_, 16 May 1858, for the conviction of a Murfreesboro man, William Hagar, for killing a slave. Hagar was sentenced to three years in the penitentiary.

acquitted.[45] In the other cases, DeWitt C. Clark was convicted of malicious stabbing of a slave and sentenced to two years for a similar offense; Nathaniel Wills received a two year sentence for the malicious stabbing of a slave; and Richard Sevier was sentenced to six years for the malicious shooting of a slave.[46] In five cases of felonious assault, the felony charge was dismissed and the defendants pleaded guilty to or were convicted of a misdemeanor, either assault and battery or wantonly abusing a slave. One fine was suspended; the others ranged from five to fifty dollars.[47] Overall, then, only seven of the forty-seven whites accused of either murder or felonious assault were convicted of those crimes. Even taking into those who were convicted of lesser offenses, only twelve of the forty-seven received any punishment at all.

---

[45] Shelby County, Circuit Court, Minutes, September 1851, pp. 401, 406, 442; January 1852, p. 16. On his first trial, Munds was sentenced to two years in the penitentiary.

[46] On the Clark, Gay, Wills, and Sevier cases, see, respectively, Williamson County, Circuit Court, Minutes, November 1847, pp. 310, 314, 319; Shelby county, Circuit Court, Minutes, January 1858, pp. 212-213; September 1858, pp. 400-402; Lincoln County, Circuit Court, Minutes, July 1853, pp. 557, 561-62, 565-66; Davidson County Criminal Court, Minutes, August 1859, pp. 336, 348, 353, 367.

[47] Shelby County, Circuit Court, Minutes, September 1854, p. 305; Williamson County, Circuit Court, Minutes, February 1836, 165; July 1837, p. 542; Knox County, Circuit Court, Minutes, October 1854, pp. 458-59, 624; February 1855, pp. 32-33; Davidson County, Circuit Court, Minutes, September 1838, pp. 43, 80; Maury County, Circuit Court, Minutes, January 1842, pp. 68-69; May 1843, p. 302.

In their statutes and court decisions, Tennesseans recognized the humanity of their bondsmen. However, Tennesseans proved unwilling to establish and enforce significant safeguards to protect their slaves from violence. Slaves who retaliated against white violence, especially that of the master, shouldered a heavy burden of proof that the bounds of proper punishment had been exceeded. According to statute and Supreme Court opinion, whites could not murder or physically assault slaves with impunity. However, the trial courts did not follow through, and the actual conviction of a white man on such charges occurred rarely.

In 1970, A.E. Keir Nash wrote a seminal article in which he argued that an analysis of the protection provided the antebellum Negro by the southern supreme courts revealed a "more equitable past" than had traditionally been portrayed. Nash cited the Tennessee Supreme Court as the court "of all the Southern courts" which "seemed persistently the most inclined to find on behalf Negroes."[48] Nash's work was a necessary and fundamental corrective. Those who read him should never again accept uncritically the traditional picture of an antebellum South "given to speedy and violent settlement of Negro-white imbroglios with scarcely a nod to the formal law's delays."[49]

---

[48]Nash, "A More Equitable Past," pp. 200, 213, 217.

[49]Ibid., pp. 199-200.

That being said, the analysis in this chapter of the Tennessee experience at both the appellate and trial court levels, suggests that, in this area of slave law, Nash was perhaps too positive, that he took his argument too far.[50] Instead, for Tennessee, Nash's ultimate example, the findings more nearly bear out Daniel Flanigan's observation that in "the slim protection" afforded slaves against white violence, the law and the courts "failed miserably."[51]

---

[50] I would not go so far in criticizing Nash as Bertram Wyatt-Brown who asserts that "some legal historians have tended to treat appeals cases as typical instead of exceptional, thus giving a benign cast to slave jurisprudence that simply distorts the picture." The Tennessee experience suggests that, on the whole, appellate court decisions were, indeed, more typical than exceptional. Bertram Wyatt-Brown, <u>Southern Honor: Ethics and Behavior in the Old South</u> (New York/Oxford: Oxford University Press, 1982), pp. 18, 561-62.

[51] Flanigan, "The Criminal Law of Slavery," pp. iii, 146.

CHAPTER IV

THE SLAVE DEFENDANT: "TRIVIAL" OFFENSES, 1796-1860

We now turn to a consideration of the slave as a criminal defendant. The late Herbert L. Packer developed two models as a "convenient way to talk about the operation" of the modern criminal process.[1] According to Packer, the administration of modern criminal justice systems can be said to follow either a Due Process Model or a Crime Control Model. These models also afford an framework within which to "talk about" the treatment of slave defendants in antebellum Tennessee.

According to Packer, the Due Process Model rests on a vital concern for protecting the defendant from the coercive power of the state. The accused is presumed to be innocent and can be found guilty "if and only if" that factual determination has been made in a "procedurally regular fashion." Therefore, the Due Process Model resembles "an obstacle course" with "each of its successive stages . . . designed to present formidable impediments to

[1]The following discussion is based on Herbert L. Packer, The Limits of the Criminal Sanction (Stanford: Stanford University Press, 1968), pp. 149-246.

carrying the accused any further along in the process."

The Crime Control Model rests on the "proposition that the repression of criminal conduct is by far the most important function" to be performed by the criminal justice system. The accused is presumed to be guilty and the factual determination is "not cluttered up with ceremonious rituals that do not advance the progress of a case." A premium is placed on efficiency, speed, and finality. Procedures are informal, routine, and stereotyped. The Crime Control Model resembles an "assembly-line," rather than an "obstacle course."[2]

Tennessee slave defendants were tried according to both the Due Process Model and the Crime Control Model. The most common use of the Crime Control Model, and one that lasted throughout the antebellum period, involved the trial of slaves for minor, "trivial," crimes.

Such slave crimes fell into two groups. First, slaves were liable for most of the crimes for which whites were liable. Many of the statutory provisions concerning slave crime were merely provisions indicating the number of

---

[2]Other scholars have found Packer's models to be helpful. See, Richard Maxwell Brown, "Lawless Lawfulness: Legal and Behavioral Perspectives on American Vigilantism," in _Strain of Violence: Historical Studies of American Violence and Vigilantism_ (New York: Oxford University Press, 1975), pp. 143-79; David Jackson Bodenhamer, "Crime and Criminal Justice in Antebellum Indiana: Marion County as a Case Study" (Ph.D. dissertation, Indiana University, 1977), pp. 3-5.

lashes to be levied when the offender was a slave.[3]

In addition to being liable for these general crimes, Tennessee slaves were subject to special laws regulating the Peculiar Institution itself. Slaves, except household servants, were forbidden to leave the premises where they were "appointed to live" unless they possessed a "written certificate of leave." Slaves were forbidden to carry weapons except one slave "employed by the master in each district plantation, to hunt in the woods on his own land, to preserve his stock, or kill game for his family." Slaves could not "hunt or range in the woods with a dog or

---

[3]For example, see, Law of North Carolina, 1741, ch. 13; Law of North Carolina, 1784, ch. 33; Law of North Carolina, 1777, ch. 25, in Haywood, Public Acts, pp. 37-38, 130-31, 103; Law of Tennessee, 1809, ch. 5; Law of Tennessee, 1838, ch. 114; Meigs and Cooper, The Code of Tennessee, pp. 835-36.

The criminal law that Tennessee received from colonial North Carolina subjected both slaves and whites to severe corporal punishments: castration, branding, whipping, having ears nailed to the pillory and then cut off. Tennesseans gradually turned away from such sentences. For whites, the move was complete; the 1829 penal code prescribed only hanging and imprisonment. Tennessee legislators did not ignore slaves in their retreat from brutal punishment. In 1831, they repealed all laws that authorized the punishment of slaves "by nailing them to the pillory and cutting off their ears." This left other relics of colonial brutality, such as branding, on the books, but the evidence suggests that they fell into disuse. By 1858, Tennessee divided most slave crimes between those "punished by death" and those "punishable by stripes." A few offenses were "punishable discretionally," but the sentence could not extend "to life or limb." In effect, then, the discretion was limited to the number of stripes to be applied. Scott, Laws, 1: 253, 366; Haywood, Public Acts, pp. 33-36, 94, 462-65; Law of Tennessee, 1829, ch. 23; Law of Tennessee, 1831, ch. 103; Meigs and Cooper, The Code of Tennessee, pp. 507-509.

dogs" without written permission. Tennessee law prescribed lashes for selling spirituous liquor and for possession of spirituous liquor "at any other place than his own house." Slaves could be whipped for failure or refusal to disperse an unlawful assembly, for "going about the country under the pretext of practicising medicine or healing the sick," and for offering to sell goods "not of his own manufacture" without written authorization from his master. The number of stripes to be laid on varied from crime to crime but never exceeded thirty-nine.[4]

A few slave crimes did not carry specific punishments. Disorderly behavior, unlawful assemblies, seditious speeches, and "insulting or provoking language used by a slave to any white person" was "punishable by stripes, at the discretion of a Justice of the Peace."[5] The malicious or willful burning or attempted burning of any valuable property could be punished "in such manner, not extending to life or limb, as the jury in their discretion may affix." If lives were endangered by such burning, this offense carried the death penalty.[6]

State statutes were not the only slave laws. In towns and cities, slaves also had to abide by municipal

---

[4]Meigs and Cooper, The Code of Tennessee, pp. 502, 506, 507-508.

[5]Ibid., pp. 508-509.

[6]Ibid., p. 509.

ordinances. Charters of incorporation routinely empowered city officials to enact ordinances "deemed necessary to control and regulate" slaves.[7] This "web of restraints" included ordinances forbidding slaves to hire their own time, regulating where and with whom slaves could live, restricting slave movements, setting slave curfews, and preventing slave gatherings.[8]

Bondsmen could also be punished for violating regular municipal ordinances, and many specifically indicated the punishment for slave offenders.[9] Some gave officials discretion in determining the punishment. A number of Memphis ordinances simply stated that the slave offender "shall receive such corporal punishment at the workhouse as the [court] may determine."[10] Other

---

[7] L.J.Dupree, comp., A Digest of the Ordinances of the City Council of Memphis, From the Year 1826 to 1857 (Memphis: Memphis Bulletin Company, 1857), pp. 32, 45; John Hugh Smith and John M. Lea, comps., The Revised Laws of the City of Nashville, with the Various Acts of ncorporation and Laws Applicable to the Town and City of Nashville, and a List of the Different Boards of Mayor and Aldermen, and other Officers of said City from the Year 1806 to 1850, Inclusive (Nashville: Harvey M. Watterson, Printer, 1850), p. 43.

[8] Richard C. Wade, Slavery in the Cities: The South 1820-1860 (New York: Oxford University Press, 1964), pp. 80, 106; Dupree, Ordinances of Memphis, pp. 124-25; Smith and Lea, Laws of Nashville, pp. 124-26; Chace C. Mooney, "Slavery in Davidson County, Tennessee" (M.A. thesis, Vanderbilt University, 1936), p. 96.

[9] Dupree, Ordinances of Memphis, pp. 109, 161; Smith and Lea, Laws of Nashville, pp. 155-56.

[10] Dupree, Ordinances of Memphis, pp. 184-85.

ordinances set limits on the punishment. In Nashville, for instance, a slave who put trash in the streets or who "put any dead carcass into the Cumberland River" was subject to from ten to thirty lashes, unlike a free offender who faced a fine.[11]

Cities passed ordinances to regulate vehicular traffic within their limits. A free Nashville driver violating the speed limit was fined from one to five dollars. A slave driver received five to ten lashes. Dragging a log across a macadamized thoroughfare brought a white driver a one dollar fine, a slave "not more than five lashes." In Memphis, all traffic violations by slaves carried the same punishment, ten to thirty lashes.[12]

Even when an ordinance failed to specify the punishment for slave offenders, slaves could still be punished for a violation. A Nashville ordinance stated that when a slave violated an ordinance which did not specify punishment, the offenders was "to be whipped . . . not exceeding twenty-five lashes."[13]

Urban ordinances differed from state laws in that the former generally provided that if the owner or employer of a slave was willing to pay the fine "attached" to the

---

[11]Smith and Lea, Laws of Nashville, pp. 97-98.

[12]Ibid., pp. 134-36; Dupree, Ordinances of Memphis, pp. 114-16.

[13]Smith and Lea, Laws of Nashville, pp. 126-27.

offense for white offenders, the slave could escape the lash. Indeed, in Nashville, a slave accused of violating a city ordinance could not be brought to trial "until due notice" had been given to his owner or employer.[14]

Tennessee received its court structure and its procedure for trying slaves from colonial North Carolina.[15] For minor crimes, the court structure was not elaborate, and it changed little during the antebellum period. Also, as Packer described for his Crime Control Model, its procedures were informal, swift, and relatively certain.

In rural areas, county Justices of the Peace had control of the initial stages of the trial process. In what came to be called a "committing trial," an accused slave, like an accused free man, underwent a preliminary examination before a local magistrate.[16] If he decided that the slave was accused of an offense "so trivial"

---

[14] Ibid., pp. 97-98, 126-27; Dupree, Ordinances of Memphis, pp. 74-75, 109, 184-85.

[15] Mooney, "Slavery in Tennessee," pp. 10-11.

[16] Specific legislation for slave defendants was not enacted until 1741, but a 1715 statute required that "no person . . . shall be committed to prison for any criminal matter until examination thereof be first had before some magistrate." Law of North Carolina, 1715, ch. 16, in Scott, Laws, 1: 13;; Law of North Carolina, 1741, ch. 24, in Haywood, Public Acts, p. 54. Also, the law instructed that upon the trial of a slave before a Justice of the Peace, "any other of the justices of the county . . . may, if they think proper, . . . assist in the examination and trial." Law of North Carolina, 1783, ch. 14, in Haywood, Public Acts, p. 122.

that it deserved no punishment greater than forty lashes, the single Justice could "proceed immediately" to try the accused slave "in a summary way." The Justice could "issue subpoenas, if necessary to compell the attendance of witnesses" and could "pass sentence and award execution."[17]

Violations of city ordinances were deemed misdemeanors, "trivial" offenses for which slave offenders were tried by "a single magistrate."[18] This magistrate could be a regular Justice of the Peace. In Nashville, for example, the Mayor and Aldermen appointed a particular Justice of the Peace for Davidson county as "city justice." This "city justice" was empowered "to open and hold a court for the trial of all such persons as shall be brought before him charged with violations of the city ordinances." Throughout the last two decades of the antebellum era, the Nashville "city justice" held trials of slaves who had allegedly violated municipal ordinances.[19]

The police court, presided over by the Recorder, provided another tribunal for those who violated city

---

[17]Law of North Carolina, 1783, ch. 14, in Haywood, _Public Acts_, pp. 121-22; Caruthers and Nicholson, _Compilation of the Statutes of Tennessee_, pp. 675-76; Meigs and Cooper, _The Code of Tennessee_, pp. 510-11.

[18]Smith and Lea, _Laws of Nashville_, p. 19.

[19]Ibid., pp. 42-45, 91-93; _Nashville Daily Gazette_, 13 February 1850; 1 February, 2 February 1855; _Nashville Republican Banner_, 4 April 1860.

ordinances. In both Memphis and Nashville, the Recorder was given "concurrent jurisdiction with justices of the peace in all cases of violation of the criminal law of the state or of the ordinances of the Mayor and Aldermen."[20] Quite often, it was in the Recorder's Court that urban slaves were tried for transgressing municipal regulations.

Local magistrates left few records, and, as Daniel Flanigan has lamented, "it is difficult to determine the quantity and quality of justice they dispensed."[21] This is particularly true for rural Justices of the Peace. Still, bits and pieces of evidence do exist. For Maury county, a local historial preserved some records produced by local magistrates who dealt with slave offenders. Literally scraps of paper, these documents afford only a sketchy picure of the activities of justices, but they are revealing nonetheless.[22]

---

[20]It is unclear who decided whether a case would be heard by a JP or by the Recorder. Smith and Lea, <u>Laws of Nashville</u>, pp. 51-52; Dupree, <u>Ordinances of Memphis</u>, pp. 45, 171, 173.

[21]Flanigan, "Criminal Law of Slavery," p. 89.

[22]Scrapbook of Slavery Material, Jill Garrett Collection, TSLmd (hereinafter cited as Garrett Scrapbook). A county historian, Jill Garrett of Maury, preserved these documents from a courthouse cleaning. Ms. Garrett put the records in a scrapbook. Some of the documents she glued in place, others she did not. Many of the pages of the scrapbook are not numbered. These factors make precise citation difficult; therefore, for this Maury county material, only the scrapbook itself will be cited.

Kenneth Stampp probably was right when he observed that "most minor offenses . . . were disposed of without resort to the court,"[23] but Maury county magistrates did arrest slaves, issuing formal warrants to bring them into custody. They ordered slaves arrested for crimes of violence against fellow blacks. In 1822, for example, Benjamin Welks complained to Justice of the Peace Isaac Bills that his slave Solomon "has had his lip bit off" by "Black Bob the Blacksmith." Based on the "evidence introduced in favour of the state," Justice Bills found Bob guilty and sentenced him to twenty-five lashes.[24]

Justices also dealt with cases of violence between slaves and whites. In 1826, Benjamin Sessunes complained to Justice Pleasant Nelson that he had been assaulted by Jacob, a slave owned by Thomas Jones. Nelson ordered the slave arrested and called two witnesses, one "in behalf of the State" and one "in behalf of the defendant." The trial was held the following day. "Testimony having been heard," Nelson sentenced Jacob to fifteen lashes.[25] In a fascinating 1850 episode, a justice asserted the power of the state to prevent violence by a slave against a white man, John Butler. Butler complained that he had

---

[23] Stampp, The Peculiar Institution, p. 224.

[24] Garrett Scrapbook, TSLmd.

[25] Ibid.

> . . . just cause to fear and does fear that King, a negro slave the property of Willian Chaffin, will kill or do hom some great bodily harm or procure it to be done, or destroy or injure his property.

A Justice of the Peace ordered King arrested, judged him "guilty as charged in this warrant," and ordered him to jail "to be dealt with as the law directs." A few days later, the circuit court released King when his master signed a one thousand dollar peace bond "to be void on the condition that the negro King keep the peace towards all the good citizens of the state of Tennessee and particularly towards John Butler."[26]

Local Justices also tried slaves for crimes against property. In September 1832, Anderson Glance complained that a slave, Weden, had stolen "divers goods" from him. The JP issued an arrest warrant and summoned four witnesses, including a "negro boy Mingo." The next day, the magistrate found Weden guilty and sentenced him to thirty-five lashes. In February 1849, a Justice of the Peace sentenced William, a bondsman, to fifteen lashes for "stealing." The following year, a magistrate tried George for "stealing meal & bags." In both of these trials,

---

[26] Ibid., Maury County, Circuit Court, Minutes, May 1850, pp. 378, 388. For a similar case in Williamson county, see Williamson County, Circuit Court, Minutes, July 1841, p. 383; July 1842, pp. 22, 72. In this case, a woman, Martha A.R. Owen, sought a peace warrant against a slave named Tom. Tom was kept in jail almost a year, presumably because no one would sign the five hundred dollar peace bond set on his good behavior.

officials subpoenaed witnesses to testify.[27] If the number of witnesses summoned to testify is any indication, one Justice took considerable pains in the trial of a slave. In December 1860, Spencer was tried for an unspecified offense before Justice W.R. Mack, who subpoenaed thirteen witnesses to testify.[28]

Justices in urban areas regularly tried slaves for minor violations. According to newspaper accounts, the City Justice in Nashville did so for unlawful gaming, breaking and entering, assault and battery, possessing stolen goods, and hiring their own time. Slaves convicted of hiring their own time were fined twenty dollars. In all other cases, the the slaves received lashes.[29]

Nashville newspapers reported on the activities of the Recorder's Court. They did so in a style that suggested that that court's business was considered both entertaining and newsworthy. Slaves were regularly brought before the Recorder for a variety of offenses, but they do not seem to

---

[27] Garrett Scrapbook, TSLmd. There is slim evidence that some slaves might have been acquitted. When the justices filed their bills of cost with the county, they listed the fees charged. In most of the cases involving slaves, a thirty-three cent fee for whipping was included. Occasionally, however, this fee was omitted. Admittedly, such omissions could have been accidental, but they might also suggest that a slave had not been convicted.

[28] Ibid.

[29] Nashville Daily Gazette, 13 February 1850; 1 February, 16 March, 30 June, 1 July 1855; Nashville Republican Banner, 12 August 1856; 20 February 1861.

have constituted an unusually large part of the Recorder's business. On December 20, 1858, for example, Recorder Glenn disposed of thirteen cases; two of the defendants were slaves, one charge with "being out without a certificate" and the other with "fast driving." For the latter offense, the slave received twenty-five lashes, a sentence which, the newspaper commented, "was not a lick too much for the occasion."[30] The next day, the Recorder disposed of eighteen cases, a docket which the newspaper called "heavy." Again, two of the defendants were slaves, one charged with being out without a certificate and the other with "stealing a kit of mackerel." The second slave was sentenced to twenty-five lashes. The slaves charged with being out with a certificate were fined for their offense.[31]

The lash was the principal means of punishment in urban areas, but, as the last two cases indicate, slaves were sometimes fined or given the opportunity to pay a fine to escape whipping.[32] For example, Nelson was arrested in November 1856 for "inhaling the fumes of bad whiskey." The offense, according to the Banner, required "a penalty in the shape of stern reality, or in current

---

[30] Nashville Daily Gazette, 21 December 1858.

[31] Ibid., 22 December 1858.

[32] Nashville Daily Gazette, 24 June 1853; Nashville Republican Banner, 12 August 1856; 20 February 1861.

funds. Nelson liquidated upon the latter plan, and went home with a whole cuticle." In December 1858, Peter Shields, a slave, was convicted of fighting with "a colored contemporary" and was allowed to pay a fine of eight dollars "to shield his cuticle from cutting."[33] Such sentences were not as frequent as those involving the lash, but slaves were allowed to pay fines for a variety of offenses. They were fined in instances of fighting, gambling, careless driving, creating a nuisance, selling liquor, selling rotten meat, selling in the marketplace, hiring their own time, and living off their master's premises.[34]

Occasionally the Nashville Recorder acquitted slaves. In April 1858, Samuel Stratton drive a hack over a small child. Stratton "was tried and discharged, there being no evidence to throw the fault upon him." In December 1859, Bob was brought before the Recorder for "stealing dry-goods." According to the Banner, "the proof not being sufficient to convict Bob of the charge, he was discharged, and 'Bobbed his way rejoicing.'" In April 1861, Alf was tried by the Recorder for "receiving a lot of coffee from

---

[33]Nashville Republican Banner, 11 November 1856; 30 December 1858.

[34]Nashville Daily Gazette, 24 June 1853; 8 July, 29 July 1856; 23 July 1858; 31 July, 4 September 1860; Nashville Republican Banner, 29 July, 12 August 1856; 11 June, 20 December 1857; 2 August, 7 August 1858; 11 August 1860; 20 February, 12 March 1861.

another negro who had stolen it." The other Negro testified that Alf was not aware that the "Java" was "contraband," and Alf was discharged.[35]

Newspaper accounts do not permit systematic analysis of police court activity. For that, records, dockets, and minutes are needed. Fortunately, five docket books for the Memphis Recorder's Court survive. These dockets cover the activities of that court for thirty-nine of the fifty-eight months between July 1856 and April 1861.[36] During that period, 834 slaves were brought to trial. The largest number were tried for unspecified misdemeanors. Occasionally, the particular offense might be noted. For example, in July 1858, Charles' misdemeanor was "stealing" and the following month Jerry's misdemeanor was "carrying concealed weapons."[37] The next largest group of crimes involved disorderly behavior. Broadly defined, this category included the specific offenses of fighting, drunkenness, disorderly conduct, and being drunk and disorderly. Smaller numbers of slaves were tried for violations of the slave code, traffic violatins, gaming, larceny, and miscellaneous

---

[35] Nashville Republican Banner, 17 April 1858, 30 December 1859, 13 April 1861.

[36] City of Memphis, Recorder's Court, Docket Books, July 1856-March 1857; July 1857-June 1858; July 1858-March 1859; August 1860-November 1860; December 1860-April 1861; Memphis/Shelby County Archives, Memphis, Tennessee

[37] City of Memphis, Recorder's Court, Docket Book, July 1858-March 1859, Case #327, Case #359.

other offenses.[38] (See Table 6.)

A random sample of white trials shows the configuration of offenses to have differed somewhat from that of slaves.[39] Disorderly behavior and misdemeanors constituted the majority of offenses for both whites and slaves, but the whites were tried more frequently for disorderly behavior. No slaves were tried for vagrancy, and no whites for larceny or for gambling violations.

In regard to verdicts and sentencing, the Recorder directed convicted whites to pay fines. If they could not do so, they were sent to the workhouse to work off the sentence at a rate of fifty cents per day. The Recorder sentenced most convicted slaves to lashes. The number of lashes that slaves received varied, but the most frequent sentence was the maximum, thirty-nine. Over three-quarters of those sentenced to lashes received at least twenty-five (see Table 8). It is interesting to note, however, that a sizable minority (twenty-six percent) escaped the lash by

---

[38] Most of the slave code violations (21) were for being out without a pass after curfew. The next largest category (9) was "acting as free." Other offenses were harboring a runaway, unlawful assembly, unlawfully entering a drinking house, and working in the city "contrary to ordinance."

[39] I drew the 1,000 case sample by randomly selecting 200 cases from each of the five docket books. Using a random number table to select the beginning pages, I selected all the white cases from every 16th page in the dockets with 8 cases per page and every 20th page in the dockets with 10 cases per page. If the page selected did not have the required number of white cases, I selected the number needed, in order, from the next page.

paying a fine (see Table 7).

Some defendants brought before the Memphis Recorder were declared not guilty, and about the same percentage of whites and slaves were acquitted. Still, criminal justice for slaves in the Memphis Recorder's Court did resemble the Crime Control Model "assembly-line." Slaves tried before the Memphis Recorder were likely to be convicted; if convicted they were likely to be sentenced to the whip; and, if sentenced to stripes, they were likely to receive the maximum number that the law allowed.

Late in the antebellum period, the legislature added an important "due process" element to its procedure for trying slaves accused of "trivial" offenses. In 1858, the General Assembly provided that a conviction of a slave for "any offence, now cognizable and punishable by justices exclusively" could be appealed to the circuit court, where the slave would be given a new trial. This gave the circuit court appellate jurisdiction over the most minor crime a slave could commit.[40]

Apparently, most owners were unwilling to make such appeals; only a few were entered. Some were unsuccessful. In 1855, in Lauderdale county, a slave, Boswell, was convicted by a Justice on a charge of larceny. On appeal, the circuit court jury also convicted Boswell and

[40] Law of Tennessee, 1848, ch. 50.

sentenced him to "forty stripes save one."[41] However, the procedure could work to the slave's benefit. In Knox county, in 1850, the attorney general dismissed larceny charged against Morgan, and, in 1857, a similar result occurred in Robertson county for Oliver, a slave accused of "drawing a knife."[42]

In conclusion, we might do well to underscore the intrustion of the State into this area of Tennessee criminality. In the cities, to be sure, but also in the countryside, bondsmen who committed "trivial" offenses might find themselves standing before a magistrate. The level of formality in such trials was low, but, on the whole, it does not seem to have been all that different for slaves than for whites. Also, the outcome, while fairly certain, was not absolutely ordained. Still, the thrust of such proceedings clearly was less to insure justice than it was to control crime by inflicting punishment. And, for slaves, unlike for whites, punishment routinely meant the lash, a distinction that no similarities should belittle.

---

[41] Lauderdale County, Circuit Court, Minutes, February 1855, n.p. Boswell's conviction was appealed to the Supreme Court, but the outcome of that appeal is unknown. He was not tried again, which suggests his appeal was unsuccessful.

[42] Knox County, Circuit Court, Minutes, October 1849, p. 140; June 1850, p. 256; Robertson County, Circuit Court, Minutes, June 1857, p. 18.

CHAPTER V

THE SLAVE DEFENDANT: THE SLAVE COURTS, 1796-1860

During Tennessee's first four decades, special slave courts had jurisdiction over bondsmen accused of crimes too serious to be handled by a single magistrate. Comprised of Justices of the Peace and slaveholders, these tribunals decided the fate of slave defendants "without the solemnity of a jury."[1] Dramatic illustration of Herbert Packer's Crime Control Model in operation, the slave courts were designed to foster control of the slave population, to facilitate "speedy verdicts and certain punishment" for

[1] A 1741 colonial North Carolina statute governed the composition, jurisdiction, and procedure of the early Tennessee slave courts. Laws of North Carolina, 1741, ch. 24; 1783, ch. 14, in Haywood, Public Acts, pp. 54, 121-22; Mooney, Slavery in Tennessee, p. 22.

Kenneth Stampp has observed that colonial "Negro courts" were "usually less concerned about the formality of traditional English justice than about speedy verdicts and certain punishments." For a description of the activities of the colonial North Carolina slave courts and one which supports Stampp's assertion, see Alan D. Watson, "North Carolina Slave Courts, 1715-1785," North Carolina Historical Review 60 (January 1983): 24-36; Also see, Ernest James Clark, Jr., "Aspects of the North Carolina Slave Code, 1715-1860," North Carolina Historical Review, 39 (April 1962): 148, 150-51; Stampp, The Peculiar Institution, p. 224.

slave criminals.[2] On the other hand, these slave courts courts did clothe their activities with some procedural

---

[2]This discussion does not touch on other examples of a Crime Control Model of criminal process, i.e., "plantation" justice, vigilantism, and lynch law. We will probably never know how many of slave defendants were dealt with by the informal or quasi-formal criminal law mechanisms established by masters within their households, in their churches, and on their plantations. Certainly, such mechanisms operated in antebellum Tennessee. For example, see See Mary C. Wagner, "The Settlement of Zion Community in Maury County, Tennessee, 1806-1860" (M.A. thesis, Vanderbilt University, 1945), pp. 75-77; Horace E. Orr, "The Tennessee Churches and Slavery" (M.A. thesis, University of Tennessee, 1924), pp. 41-43; and Robert E. Corlew, "Some Aspects of Slavery in Dickson County, Tennessee" (M.A. thesis, Vanderbilt University, 1949), pp. 77-78.

Tennessee slaves suffered from lynch law and vigilantism. The worst single episode was the 1856 insurrectionary scare. Six or seven slaves were executed in Stewart county, and four were hanged in Sumner county. Benjamin F. Allen to William Trousdale, January 8, 1857, William Trousdale Papers, Box 5, Folder 1, TSLmd; Nashville Daily Gazette, 7 December, 18 December, 21 December 1856; and Charles B. Dew, "Black Iron Workers and the Slave Insurrection Panic of 1856," The Journal of Southern History 41 (August 1975): 332.

At least seven "non-insurrectionary" lynchings of slaves occurred in the last ten years of the antebellum era. Nashville Daily Gazette, 10 October 1851; 9 October 1852; 30 September 1855; 24 February 1858; 21 December 1860; Diary of John Nick Barker, Entry for February 19, 1858, TSLmd; Polk, Wilson & Co. v. Thomas H. Fancher, et al., 38 Tenn. 213-16 (1858).

These figures hardly support the well-established notion that slaves were lynched infrequently prior to the Civil War. However, these incidents do support Clement Eaton's observation that "almost invariably the chief reason for lynching Negroes was the fear of servile insurrection or the brutal murder of a master or overseer by a slave." See James E. Cutler, Lynch-Law: An Investigation into the History of Lynching in the United States (n.p.: Patterson Smith Reprint, 1969), pp. 124, 128; W.J. Cash, The Mind of the South (New York: Alfred A. Knopf, Inc.,), p. 43; Genovese, Roll, Jordan, Roll, p. 32; Brown, Strain of Violence, p. 151; Clement Eaton, "Mob Violence in the Old South," Mississippi Valley Historical Review 29 (December 1943): 367.

formality. For example, only a Justice of the Peace could convene a slave court. Generally, this necessitated an official complaint, following which the Justice of the Peace issued a warrant for the arrest of the slave.[3] Then the magistrate would examine the evidence to determine if the slave should be charged with the crime. For example, in the case of Stephen Smith's Richmond, accused of beating and stabbing the "patroller" James Winn, Justice Rice issued the arrest warrant on August 5. The next day, Richmnd was brought before Rice and a second magistrate, Alex Johnson. Rice and Johnson found the charges to be "supported by the evidence" and bound Richmond over for trial on August 9.[4]

After being charged, a slave might be released on bail. Richmond was released when his master was "recognized" in a penal bond of $800, "to produce the boy" at the courthouse on the day of trial.[5]

A fine line separated the decision to arrest from the decision to charge a slave. Theoretically, a Justice could release a slave after arrest without charging him. However, it is doubtful that many magistrates exercised such

---

[3] Davidson County, County Court, Minutes, Book A, p. 411; "State v. Daniel, a Slave," "State v. Richmond," Garrett Scrapbook, TSLmd; "State v. Amos, a Slave," Case Files, Tennessee Supreme Court, Middle District, TSA.

[4] "State v. Richmond," Garrett Scrapbook, TSLmd.

[5] Ibid. Also see, Williamson County, County Court, Minutes, vol. 2, p. 255.

discretion. In some instances, the Justice did not even examine the slave before deciding he should be tried. In 1819, in Davidson county, William Jones found the body of William O'Briant. "Suspecting a murder to have been committed," Jones "arrested the slave Israel" and had him put in jail. With nothing more than the sheriff's official notification of Israel's incarceration, Thomas Claiborne, a Davidson county JP, ordered that the slave be tried for murder.[6]

After the magistrate decided to convene a slave court, he instructed the sheriff to summon the required number of Justices and slaveholders. Sometimes the Justice who committed the slave sat on the trial, but often he did not.[7]

With regard to the composition of the slave courts, we have the names of the Justices and slaveholders who made up such courts in eight trials in Williamson county between

---

[6] Davidson County, Circuit Court, _Minutes_, November 1819, pp. 271-73. Also see, "Harry, a slave of Robert Beard, Case of," Transcript of Trial, Petitions and Pardons, Papers of Governor William Carroll, 1827-27, TSA. (Hereinafter the collection of documents concerning this case will be referred to as Harry's Case, Carroll Papers.)

[7] "State v. Amos, a Slave," Case Files, Tennessee Supreme Court, Middle District, TSA; _Bob, a slave, v. The State_, 10 Tenn. 173-44 (1826); "State v. Richmond," Garrett Scrapbook, TSA; "State v. Daniel, a slave," ibid.; Transcript of Trial, Harry's Case, Carroll Papers; Davidson County, County Court, _Minutes_, Book A, p. 411; Circuit Court, _Minutes_, November 1819, pp. 271-73.

1804 and 1815.[8] This allows us to make some comparison with Michael Hindus's findings regarding the slave courts in Spartenburg county, South Carolina. According to Hindus, "a small cluster of men" repeatedly appeared as jurors in Spartenburg county slave court trials.[9] To some degree, this was true in the eight Williamson county cases. Eight of the Justices participated in more than one trial.[10] There was also some repetition among the slaveholders called to serve on the slave courts. In the eight trials, thirty-two different slaveholders could have been called, but only twenty-six were, because John Johnston, Sr. and Henry Cook sat on three of the slave courts and Nicholas Perkins and George Strambler sat on two.

Using last names as a guide, Hindus found Spartenburg county, South Carolina, slave trials "procedurally incestuous." They were "neighborhood events" and "family affairs" because the courts were convened at "the most convenient farms and plantations," and "fathers, sons, and other relatives" were summoned to sit on the trials. This

---

[8]Williamson County, County Court, Minutes, vol. 1, pp. 148, 200, 221, 222, 253-54, 276; vol. 2, pp. 179-80, 213, 255. In these eight trials, twenty-nine justices presided. Five of the trials had three justices, the minimum called for by statute; two trials had four justices and one had six.

[9]Hindus, Prison and Plantation, p. 155.

[10]John Spenser sat on one trial in 1805 and on three trials in 1806. Ewen Cameron sat on the three trials in 1806. Six other JPs sat on two trials

was not true of Williamson county. Slave courts convened at the courthouse, and only one of the eight trials involved individuals with the same last name. Hindus argues that repeated last names testified to the "informal organization" and the "local and private" nature of the South Carolina slave courts. By the same criteria, Williamson county slave courts seem to have been more formal in their organization, more open and public in their operation.[11]

The operation of the slave courts can be examined more closely by focusing on a series of cases in Williamson county. Between 1805 and 1823, the Williamson county court clerk made entries in his minutes for the trials of eleven slaves.[12] Three were on trial for murder--Harriet for the murder of her master's daughter, Molly for the murder of her child, and Gilbert for the murder of a fellow slave. Two slaves were tried for attempted murder, two for attempted rape, and one each for housebreaking, horse stealing, and larceny. One was tried for an unspecified felony.

Packer's Crime Control Model predicts a speedy trial. The Williamson county slave courts seem to have operated this way. For example, Harriet committed murder

---

[11]Hindus, Prison and Plantation, p. 155.

[12]Williamson County, County Court, Minutes, vol. 1, pp. 148, 200, 221,222, 253-54, 276; vol. 2, pp. 179-80, 213, 255; vol. 8, p. 225; Circuit Court, Minutes, vol. 4, pp. 67, 113; Transcript of Trial, Harry's Case, Carroll Papers. Also see, Margaret Kinard, "Frontier Development of Williamson County, Tennessee" (M.A. thesis, Vanderbilt University, 1948), pp. 60-61.

on August 17 and was convicted six days later.[13] The longest span between crime and trial seems to have been one and one-half months, when Harry and Jim were tried for the attempted murder of Robert Beard and his wife.[14] Further, most of the trials were one-day affairs. In a few instances, however, brief delays were granted by the courts. At the request of the prosecution, Sherwood's trial for attempted rape was delayed and the defendant admitted to bail.[15] In the case of Molly, accused of murder, the trial was delayed over the weekend so that a motion for arrest in judgment could be argued.[16] Again consistent with the Crime Control Model, sentences were usually carried out quickly. Sentences other than death were carried out the day of the trial.[17] Capital sentences were usually carried out within the month. Indeed, Harriet was sentenced to be hung thirteen days after her conviction.[18] At the other extreme, Jim was hung forty-three days after his

---

[13]Thomas Hart Benton, Report to John Sevier, Harriet's File, Petitions and Pardons, Papers of Governor John Sevier, 1803-1809, TSA. (Hereinafter referred to as Benton Report.)

[14]Transcript of Trial, Harry's Case, Carroll Papers.

[15]Williamson County, County Court, Minutes, vol. 2, p. 255.

[16]Ibid., vol. 1, pp. 253-54.

[17]Ibid., pp. 122, 148.

[18]Benton Report.

conviction.[19]

During the trials themselves, the state's case was handled by an attorney and the defendants had benefit of counsel. In an 1806 murder case, P.R. Barker "appeared as counsel in behalf of the state," and Thomas Hart Benton represented the slave. Although Benton's defense was unsuccessful, there is little reason to fault his effort or to regard his presence as cosmetic.[20] In at least one instance, a slave court appointed an attorney when an owner refused to provide one.[21]

The outcome of the slave court trial was a near certainty. Eight of the eleven trials produced convictions. One of these cases apparently was not regarded as capital. The slave, Bob, convicted of "larceny from the house of James McEwen," was not condemned to death. Nevertheless, his sentence was brutal. Bob was to receive fifty lashes at the Franklin whipping post and to stand in the pillory for two hours, his ears nailed to it; "at the expiration of which time both ears is [*sic*] to be cut off that is one half of each ear so as to include all the soft part of each." Finally, Bob was to be branded with the letter "R,"

---

[19] Transcript of Trial, Harry's Case, Carroll Papers.

[20] See below, pp. 127-30. Also see, Williamson County, County Court, *Minutes*, vol. 1, pp. 253-54.

[21] N.P. Perkins, Statement to Governor William Carroll, Harry's Case, Carroll Papers.

at least one inch long, on each cheek.[22]

The other ten trials involved capital crimes. The picture of the trial results in these cases is not totally bleak. One slave was acquitted,[23] and two were convicted

---

[22]Williamson County, County Court, Minutes, vol. 1, p. 148. Except for nailing ears to the pillory and cutting them off, sentences similar to Bob's were handed to white defendants in Williamson county. For example, two white defendants in November 1816 were convicted of larceny and were sentenced to lashes, six months in jail, six hours in the pillory, and branding. Williamson County, Circuit Court, Minutes, November 1816, pp. 812, 813.

Other slave courts handed down sentences similar to Bob's, and worse. In July 1793, in Davidson county, a slave convicted of burning a barn was sentenced to fifty lashes and "afterwards have both his Ears cutt off." Davidson County, County Court, Minutes, July 1793, pp. 119-20. On August 3, 1801, a slave court in Knoxville convicted Jack for the murder of Sarah Crawford. The Court sentenced Jack "to be burnt on the morrow." John Sevier, who attended the trial, recorded in his diary for Tuesday, August 4: "Negro Jack was agreeably to the sentence of yesterday executed in the presence of a great number of spectators." Diary of John Sevier, in Heiskell, Andrew Jackson, 2: 583. In 1807, a Montgomery county court handed down a sentence that was "medieval in its barbarity." The court ordered the executioner to hang a Negro named Moses, who had been convicted of murder and then to have his head off and "put upon a post" for public exhibition. Finally, in 1825, a Stewart county slave court convicted a slave of stabbing a white man and sentenced him to be whipped, to have his ears cropped, and to be "branded with hot wine under the armpits." Montgomery County, County Court, Minutes, March 1807, pp. 146-47; E. Bruce Thompson, "Reforms in the Penal System of Tennessee 1820-1850," Tennessee Historical Quarterly 1 (December 1942): 293, 299.

[23]The slave acquitted was Jack who was accused of housebreaking. Williamson County, County Court, Minutes, vol. 1, p. 200. Other slave courts handed down acquittals. In May 1798, in Greene county, Ben was acquitted of housebreaking. In June 1812, in Robertson county, Mary was acquitted of arson. In January 1813, in Maury county Daniel was acquitted of stealing, and in July 1827, in Hickman county, Amos was acquitted of attempted murder. Greene County, County Court, Minutes, April 1798, p. 90; Robertson County, County Court, Minutes, August 1812, p.

of lesser, non-capital offenses.[24] These three verdicts, however, only slightly soften the harsh reality of the slave court. Seven of the ten slaves charged with a hanging offense were convicted and sentenced to the gallows.[25]

95; "State v. Daniel," Garrett Scrapbook, TSLmd; "State v. Amos, a slave," Case Files, Tennessee Supreme Court, Middle District, TSA.

[24]Ned (1806), accused of horsestealing, was convicted of trespass and sentenced to twenty-five lashes. Sherwood (1815), accused of attempted rape, was convicted of assault and sentenced to thirty-nine lashes. Williamson County, County Court, Minutes, vol. 1, pp. 222; vol. 2, p. 255.

[25]By way of comparison, between 1812 and 1826, fourteen slaves were tried for capital crimes in the Inferior Court of Baldwin County, Georgia. Unlike Tennessee, Georgia provided no appeal from the verdict of the Inferior Court. Of those fourteen Baldwin County slaves, six were sentenced to hang. Three were convicted of lesser non-capital crimes and three were acquitted. The other two slaves were convicted but were not given the death sentence. Therefore, considering slaves who received executive clemency, over one-half the defendants in both Williamson and Baldwin counties escaped the death penalty. Royce Gordon Shingleton, "The Trial and Punishment of Slaves in Baldwin County, Georgia, 1812-1826," Southern Humanities Review, 8 (Winter 1974): 67-73.

Also see, Hindus, Prison and Plantation, pp. 146-50; "Black Justice Under White Law," pp. 586-90; Robert M. Saunders, "Crime and Punishment in Early National America: Richmond, Virginia, 1784-1820," The Virginia Magazine of History and Biography 86 (January 1978): 33-44; Mariane Buroff Sheldon, "Black-White Relations in Richmond, Virginia, 1782-1820," The Journal of Southern History 45 (February 1979): 27-44; Philip J. Schwarz, "Gabriel's Challenge: Slaves and Crime in Late Eighteenth-Century Virginia," The Virginia Magazine of History and Biography 90 (July 1982): 283-309; "Forging the Shackles: The Development of Virginia's Criminal Code for Slaves," in Bodenhamer and Ely, eds., Ambivalent Legacy, pp. 125-46; E. Merton Coulter, "Four Slave Trials in Elbert County, Georgia," The Georgia Historical Quarterly 41 (September 1956): 237-46; John C. Edwards, "Slave Justice in Four Middle Georgia Counties," The Georgia Historical Quarterly, 57 (Summer 1973): 265-73.

After conviction, the slave had one last official means of salvation. Under Tennessee's Constitution, the governor had the power "to grant reprives and pardons after conviction," and governors extended this protection to slaves.[26] In fact, three of the Williamson county slaves sentenced to death successfully appealed for executive clemency and avoided the hangman's noose.[27]

Even considering those slaves saved by the governor's mercy, bondsmen fared badly in comparison with white defendants. Between 1810 and 1823, ten Williamson county whites went on trial in the circuit court for capital offenses. Two were convicted and sentenced to hang.[28]

---

[26]Tennessee, Constitution, art. 2, sec. 19 (1796).

[27]See below, pp. 132, 138, and Williamson County, County Court, Minutes, vol. 1, pp. 253-54, 276.

Successful appeals for executive clemency were made from slave convictions in other counties. For example, see Petitions for Pardon--1826, Papers of Governor William Carroll, 1821-27, TSA. In this case, Carroll pardoned a Nashville slave, Henry, convicted of burglary on flimsy circumstantial evidence.

In regard to executive clemency, slaves seem to have been benefiting from a general trend in Tennessee criminal justice. According to E. Bruce Thompson, the solicitation of executive clemency by "sympathetic judges" and "influenctial citizens" was such a common practice that "even if convicted, the criminal had an excellent chance of escaping punishment." Thompson, "Reforms in the Penal System of Tennessee," p. 293.

[28]All but one of the ten cases were for murder in the first degree. The exception was the counterfeiting case of A. Edwards, convicted in May 1814 and sentenced to hang. The other defendant sentenced to death was charles Bennett. After his conviction in August 1819, he appealed. The outcome of the appeal is not know. However, Bennett was not tried again in Williamson county, which suggests that his sentence of death was affirmed. Williamson County, Circuit

Two were convicted of lesser non-capital offenses.[29] Six were released, one after a mistrial, the other five after verdicts of acquittal.[30] The comparison is stark. Six whites were released, only one slave. Seven slaves were convicted, only two whites. Four slaves and two whites were executed.

Detailed evidence regarding two of the Williamson county slave trials exists in the pardon papers of Tennessee governors. This documentation consists of petitions and correspondence to the governor and other influential persons regarding executive clemency. These documents detail many of the events surrounding the trials, allowing a partial reconstruction of the trials themselves. Beyond intrinsic interest as human drama, such reconstruction captures the flavor of a slave court trial in a way not permitted by the sketchy entries in the court records. The taste is bitter.

The first of these trials occurred in 1806. On Monday, August 17, John Record, a Baptist preacher, found

---

Court, Minutes, May 1814, pp. 625, 637; August 1819, pp. 1099, 1099-1100. For a general discussion of the Williamson county circuit court during this period, see Cornelia Ann Clark, "Justice on the Tennessee Frontier: The Williamson County Circuit Court, 1810-1820," Vanderbilt Law Review 32 (January 1979):413-45.

[29]Williamson County, Circuit Court, Minutes, November 1810, pp. 130-31; November 1816, p. 801.

[30]Ibid., November 1811, p. 320; May 1812, p. 405; May 1813, p. 508; November 1816, p. 804; August 1821, pp. 1355, 1360, 1373; February 1822, p. 1466.

his daughter, Polly, drowned in the West Harpeth river. He suspected that she had been murdered by one of his slaves, an eleven-year-old girl named Harriet. Record confronted Harriet; she "hesitated and appeared confused" but "recovered herself and firmly denied the murder."

John Record was "inclined to bury his suspicions and let the matter rest." His neighbors were not similarly inclined. They tied Harriet and carried her "into the woods" for a "more rigid examination."[31] During this sylvan interrogation, Harriet doggedly maintained her innocence until her inquisitors, frustrated by the slave girl's intransigence, turned to trickery. Hariet was "threatened with death," told that her guilt could be proved and that she would be executed even if she did not admit killing Polly. It would be best then for her to clear her conscience by telling the truth. Furthermore, her owner's family would be "contented" if they knew how their child had died.[32]

Harriet succumbed to this combination of threats and inducements. "As questions pressed upon her," the young slave "gave up one point after another, until a story was collected, which amounted in the eyes of her interrogators

---

[31] Benton Report; Charles Bailey to Chapman White, Harriet's File, Petitions and Pardons, Papers of Governor John Sevier, 1803-1809, TSA.

[32] Benton Report; Charles Bailey to Chapman White, 25 August 1806; Citizens of Franklin, Petition to Governor Sevier, ibid.

to a confession." Record's neighbors took Harriet to jail and "fastened [her] down to the back part of it with an iron chain" to await her trial.[33]

At the trial, Thomas Hart Benton, twenty-four years old and only recently admitted to the bar, defended Harriet.[34] When the prosecution introduced Harriet's confession, Benton objected on a number of grounds: the confession was "extrajudicial"; it had been "obtained by artifice . . . while the prisoner was in chains"; and it was "unsupported by corroborating circumstances." Such a confession was "abhorrent in its own nature and to common justice," "proscribed by common sense," and "condemned by the whole body of criminal law." However, the court decided that Harriet's confession was "proper."

A number of witnesses were introduced to support Harriet's confession. Under Benton's cross-examination, one witness testified that the young girl had been confined about twenty-four hours before she confessed. Benton observed that "the prisoner . . . held out well" and expressed "his horror and indignation at the idea of taking away the life of a child on such miserable evidence."

---

[33] Ibid. Also see, James Hicks to Abram Maury, 25 August 1806; P.R. Barker to John Sevier, 25 August 1806, ibid.

[34] Robert M. McBride and Dan M. Robison, <u>Biographical Dictionary of the Tennessee General Assembly</u>, vol. 1: 1796-1861 (Nashville: Tennessee State Library and Archives and the Tennessee Historical Commission, 1975), pp. 44-45; Barker to Sevier, 25 August 1804, Harriet's File, Sevier Papers, TSA.

The state continued with testimony to establish the motive for the killing. Harriet had been overheard saying that she did not like Polly as well as other children; Harriet had thrown stones at Polly and had been seen pushing and shaking the Record child. "To crown the scene," the State introduced the county jailer. He testified that he had questioned Harriet the night before the trial and that she had confessed to the murder a second time. During this confession, Harriet was still in jail and still fastened down "with an iron chain." When Benton questioned the admissability of the jailer's testimony--"Can you listen to such evidence as this?"--the court responded, "it was evidence proper to be attended to."

The trial was over soon after the State rested its case. Benton, "having read the fate of the unfortunate victim," gave up his client's defense and "rested her life with executive clemency." The seven-man tribunal reached a verdict of guilty; sentence of death "followed in rapid succession."

Immediately after the trial, a petition for pardon was prepared and sent to Governor John Sevier in Knoxville. Twenty-six Franklin citizens signed this petition; Benton's name topped the list. Among the other petitioners were two witnesses for the prosecution and the jailer. The petitioners described Harriet as an "unfortunate convict" who was "worthy of mercy." She had not yet reached "that age which renders her amenable to a criminal jurisdiction."

Furthermore, Harriet failed to demonstrate "that discretion which supplied the want of age." Her "indifference" at the trial and her "unconcern" with the sentence of death "evinces a disposition, either cruel and obdurate beyond conception, or a degree of simplicity incapable of being affected by the terrors of death in this world, or by the idea of punishment in that "which is to come." The petitioners also cited errors in the trial procedure. Harriet had been convicted on inadmissable evidence; before judgment was pronounced, she had not been asked the "usual question, 'what have you to say in arrest of judgment?" Finally, the petition concluded that the death of this "unhappy convict" would not serve any purpose "for which punishments have been ordained; but, in the language of Lord Coke, would be a miserable spectacle of extreme inhumanity, and shocking to the feelings of all who should see it."[35]

In addition to this petition to Governor Sevier, several Franklin citizens wrote personal letters to members of the General Assembly, asking them to intercede with the governor on Harriet's behalf. P.R. Barker, the prosecuting attorney, wrote directly to Governor Sevier himself: "I have no hesitation in communicating to your Excellency that from the apparent understanding, discretion, and age of Harriet which is eleven years, I conceive her to be an object more

---

[35]Citizens of Franklin, Petition to Governor Sevier, Harriet's File, Sevier Papers, TSA.

entitled to mercy than I have ever seen."[36]

Apparently, the petition and letters convinced the governor. John Sevier recorded in his diary for Sunday, August 31, 1806: "Went early into Knoxville. Granted a pardon for a negro girl named Harriet the property of John Record of Williamson county at Harpeth. The girl . . . for drowning her master's daughter named Po[lly]."[37]

This episode demonstrates the central flaw of the slave courts. They were designed to punish and to enhance social control, functions that undermined their ability to promote law and justice. Record's neighbors found themselves with a backward, perhaps mentally retarded, slave girl in their midst, a slave girl they feared capable of killing their children. The slave court provided little restraint on those fears. The informal nature of the court maximized its susceptibility to the pressures of the moment. Composed of laymen, the tribunal lacked the legitimacy even to turn down evidence such as a confession coerced from an eleven-year-old girl, evidence that ran counter to the canons of the law.

To underscore the incapacity of the slave court to promote justice, one has only to consider the trial during

---

[36]Barker to Sevier, 25 August 1806. Also see, Hicks to Maury, 25 August 1806; Bailey to White, 25 August 1806; Thomas Hart Benton to Senator Maury and Representatives White and Perkins, 25 August 1806, ibid.

[37]"Diary of John Sevier," in Heiskell, Andrew Jackson, 2: 589.

the same year of Mary Doherty for the axe murder of her father. At first glance, there are many interesting points of similarity between the cases of Harriet and Mary. Both were young girls. Harriet was a slave, but Mary was an outcast, "without education, decorum, a sense of religion, or the benefits of social intercourse." After her arrest, Mary Doherty displayed the same lack of expression and understanding that had characterized Harriet's behavior. Both girls were treated badly after being arrested, and both made self-incriminating statements under duress.

There were, however, significant points of difference. Before Mary Doherty came to trial, a coroner's inquest was necessary to determine the cause of death and a grand jury required to detemine whether sufficient evidence existed for an indictment. Because of these procedures, there were four months between Mary's arrest and her trial. On the trial itself, Mary could challenge jurors preemptorily and for cause. The judges ruled that her confession was inadmissable because "no confession obtained . . . by hope or fear should be given in evidence against her." Finally, in instructing the jury, the Court directed that unless "removed by circumstances," the "presumption of the law" was that a defendant of Mary's age [could] not discern between right and wrong." These differences were telling; Mary Doherty was acquitted.[38]

---

[38] <u>State v. Mary Doherty</u>, 2 Tenn. 85-88 (1806).

The second slave court trial under examination occurred in 1823, toward the end of the period during which the slave courts exercised exclusive jurisdiction over serious slave crimes. Between 1806 and 1823, the General Assembly modified the slave courts somewhat,[39] but, as this case demonstrates, these changes did little to enhance that tribunal's ability to produce justice.

This case involved two slaves, Jim and Harry, accused of the attempted murder of Harry's owner, Robert Beard, and his wife. The crime occurred on February 20; the slaves were arrested and jailed the next day. Their trial began on April 16 before a slave court comprised of three presiding Justices of the Peace and a twelve-man jury.[40]

Harry, tried first, was convicted on the basis of his confession.[41] At Jim's trial the next day, Harry was the principal prosecution witness. After he was sworn, the court warned him of the "dangers of false swearing;"[42]

---

[39]See below, pp. 140-46.

[40]Hudson Dawson, Statement to Governor William Carroll; Confession of Jim and Harry; Transcript of Trial, Harry's Case, Carroll Papers, TSA; Williamson County, County Court, Minutes, vol. 2, pp. 179-80.

[41]The state did try to establish the motive for the crime. "A close intimacy subsisted" between Jim and Harry, but Mr. Beard had forbidden Harry to associate with Jim because of Jim's "bad reputation." The two slaves determined to take "vengence" upon Mr. Beard by murdering him. Transcript of Trial; Dawson Statement of Governor Carroll; William Banks, Joshua Farrington, et al., Petition to Governor Carroll, Harry's Case, Carroll Papers, TSA.

[42]Statement of Stephen Childress, Harry's Case, Carroll Papers, TSA.

that is, both ears nailed to the pillory and then cut off and thirty-nine lashes on the bare back.[43]

Apprised of these penalties for perjury, Harry changed his confession. He implicated a white man, Nelson Newcomb, as the "main actor in the business."[44] Surprised by Harry's new information, "the Court the Bar and the Jury began interrogatorys," and Harry retreated to his first version of the crime. The jury then convicted Jim, and the court sentenced both slaves to hang on Saturday, May 31.[45]

Late in May, several inhabitants of Williamson

---

[43]Law of North Carolina, 1741, ch. 25, in Haywood, and Cobbs, Statute Laws, 1: 315.

[44]According to Harry, on the night of the crime, Newcomb "hailed" Jim, and they went into the Beard kitchen where Harry was asleep. Newcomb "kicked Harry to awaken him." The three men then went to the Beard house. Newcomb picked up an axe that was standing by the door and "told Harry that if he tried to get away he would knock his brains out." Newcomb, Jim, and Harry then went into the house where Newcomb "knocked Mr. Beard dead as he raised up."

Harry struck his mistress. He had been instructed to do so by Newcomb. Newcomb had told him that "if his mistress stirred," Harry must "knock" her down to keep her from knowing that Newcomb was present. It is not clear whether Harry struck Mrs. Beard with an axe or with a hickory stick that Newcomb had given him. It is also not clear just how Mr. Beard survived the blows that he apparently received.

Harry had been "very anxious" that Newcomb testify because he knew "some circumstances" which could show Harry's innocence. Harry's attorney "had Newcomb called but he did not appear." N.P.Perkins, Statement to Governor William Carroll, Harry's Case, Carroll Papers, TSA.

[45]Robert P. Curren to William Carroll, 13 June 1823; C.G. Olmstead to William Carroll, 13 June 1823; Joshua Farrington and Eli McGann to William Carroll, 10 June 1823; Stephen Childress to William Carroll, 11 June 1823; Transcript of Trial, ibid.

county, including two of the Justices who had presided on the trial, sent a petition for clemency for Harry to Governor William Carroll. They did not assert Harry's innocence. The petitioners based their request for pardon on Harry's "tender age," on the "uniform good character which he previously supported," and on the "probability that he would not of himself [have] conceived the design for an attempt to execute which he is now to suffer the penalties of the law." Furthermore, the petitioners described Harry as "unendowed even with that portion of understanding which generally marks the slave part of our population." He was "destitute, in some measure, of those attributes which designate us as intelligent beings," a person for whom the "boundaries between right and wrong are but faintly traced," a "legitimate object of executive mercy."[46] Governor Carroll did not pardon Harry, but he did grant him "respite" until the second Saturday in June.[47]

This reprieve saved Harry because Jim made an execution eve confession that corroborated Harry's implication

---

[46]Banks-Farrington Petition, ibid.

[47]Ibid. There was a counterpetition signed by sixty-two Williamson county inhabitants. They described Harry as "one of the most determined villians of his age the world ever produced, and . . . fit subject for the gallows." These petitioners asked Carroll not to extend mercy "to a villian who had not only been guilty of alarming society by the atrocity of his crime, but of using the greatest exertion to take the life of a master who raised him with almost unexampled care and tenderness." Petition of May 27, 1823, to Governor William Carroll, ibid.

of Nelson Newcomb. "Just at the moment" of his execution, Jim "persisted in declaring" that the white man had instigated the crime.[48] Prompted by Jim's confession, a number of Williamson county citizens began to reinvestigate the entire episode. They discovered that on the afternoon before the attempted murder Newcomb and Robert Beard had argued over the ownership of two stray sheep and that Newcomb could provide no alibi for the evening of the crime.[49]

Finally, the Williamson county jailer and some friends of Newcomb set up a confrontation between Newcomb and Harry, a confrontation that Newcomb's friends hoped would demonstrate his innocence. "Repeatedly exhorted, standing as he did between two worlds, to tell the truth, the whole truth and nothing but the truth," Harry persisted in his implication of Newcomb. "Reminded of the awful situation in which he was placed," Harry then was asked "to look Newcomb in the face and to answer as in the presence of his god, did he assist in the perpetration of the crime?" Harry "looked Newcomb steadily in the face and said 'he did.'"[50]

---

[48]Harry, uninformed of his reprieve from Governor Carroll and therefore "in momentary expectation of being swung up," also declared these facts to be accurate. Confession of Jim and Harry, ibid.

[49] N.P. Perkins' Statement to Governor William Carroll, ibid.

[50]William Peebles and Eli McGans, Statement to Governor William Carroll, ibid.

This new investigation seemed particularly damning to Newcomb. As one group of Williamson county citizens wrote Governor Carroll: "as to Newcomb, if innocent, we sincerely wish he may make it appear so; but we must confess that from the facts before us, we are far from being convinced of his innocence . . . the facts . . . all tend to fasten conviction upon him.[51]

This new information sparked a second round of petitions and correspondence to Governor Carroll to save Harry. The most noteworthy petition was signed by the three Justices of the Peace and seven of the twelve jurors who had sat on Harry's trial.[52] This time, Governor Carroll pardoned Harry "on condition that he should be immediately taken out of the state."[53]

---

[51]Petition to Governor William Carroll, 14 June 1823, ibid. There were those who still supported Harry's guilt. See Hudson Dawson to William Carroll, 11 June 1823, and James G. Jones to William Carroll, 9 June 1823, ibid.

[52]One singular missive to Governor Carroll was a statement by C.G. Olmstead, the prosecuting attorney, informing the governor that he refused to sign earlier petitions because he believed Harry guilty of both the attempted murder and perjury, but Jim's gallows admissions, N.P. Perkins' information about Harry's desire to have Newcomb at his original trial, and Beard's trouble with Newcomb combined to convince Olmstead to appeal on Harry's behalf. C.G. Olmstead to William Carroll, 13 June 1823; Petition to Governor William Carroll, 5 June 1823, ibid.

Also see, Robert P. Curren to William Carroll, 13 June 1823; William Manning to William Carroll, 13 June 1823; Robert Paine to William Carroll, 13 June 1823; N.P. Perkins, Statement to Governor William Carroll; and Petition to Governor William Carroll, 14 June 1823, ibid.

[53]William Carroll to Major Daniel Graham, 14 June 1823, ibid.

Harry's eventual pardon to the contrary notwithstanding, as late as 1823, the special slave court still contained few barriers against injustice. In Harry's and Jim's case, concerned whites seemed motivated less by fear than by desire to punish and to make an example of wayward slaves, but the demands of social control overcame any reluctance to convict on the basis of a dubious confession. A post-trial investigation eventually implicated another person as the instigator of the crime. This discovery did not establish Jim's and Harry's innocence, and Jim was hanged. Harry, clearly viewed as less culpable by those who knew the circumstances, was banished from the state. The white man who allegedly instigated the crime, however, never came to trial.[54]

The action of the slave courts in these two cases offers poignant support for Bertram Wyatt-Brown's observation that antebellum southerners tended to view the criminal law as a "means of carrying out communal wishes rather than as a set of abstract principles of justice." In such a view, "the law was honored" so long as it "represented the retributive will of society, exacting

---

[54]It is not clear why Jim did not receive executive clemency. Older and more alert than Harry, he may have been regarded more as a principal actor in the crime. Furthermore, he had a "bad reputation" in the neighborhood. Of course, blacks could not testify against whites. Apparently, without Jim's and Harry's statements, there was insufficient evidence to bring Newcomb to trial.

physical punishments commensurate with the emotional needs of the locality."

Wyatt-Brown also points to the "sometimes . . . intolerable" tension in the southern mind between law as a "vent to communal anger" and law as "struggling toward principles of equity."[55] In Tennessee, this tension was resolved in the direction of equity. To the credit of antebellum Tennesseans, the slave courts did not survive.

As early as 1815, the General Assembly began to modify the slave court as received from colonial North Carolina. The earliest slave courts were seven-man tribunals comprised of three JPs and four slaveholders. In 1815, the legislature increased the number of slaveholders from four to nine, enlarging the membership of the court to twelve.[56] Four years later, the legislature again altered the slave court by eliminating the JPs' voice in determining the verdict. The three Justices were now only to preside over trials. The General Assembly also increased the number of slave-holders on the trial to twelve. The twelve men would "serve as a jury" and render the verdict.[57]

The General Assembly also modified slave court procedure for sentencing a convicted slave. Under the

---

[55]Bertram Wyatt-Brown, "The Ideal Typology and Antebellum Southern History: A Testing of a New Approach," Societas 5 (Winter 1975): 27-28.

[56]Law of Tennessee, 1815, ch. 18.

[57]Law of Tennessee, 1819, ch. 35.

"colonial" law, the court had great latitude in sentencing. A slave convicted of a crime could be sentenced "as the nature of the crime or offense" required. As Ernest James Clark has observed, "this broad grant of power not only made the slave court the court of trial, but in large measure allowed the court to legislate in each case, determining at its discretion what punishment was proper for the offense committed."[58] In 1815, the legislature removed some of the slave courts' discretionary power over punishment. The lawmakers directed that when the statute "already prescribed a specific punishment" for a crime, the court should "cause such punishment, and none other to be inflicted." The legislature also required unanimity for imposition of the death penalty. Only a majority of the court was necessary to decide the punishment in other cases. In 1819, when the twelve-man jury was introduced in the slave court, the legislature gave the power of sentencing exclusively to the JPs who presided over the trial.[59]

Each modification seemed to increase the protection of slave defendants, but none of them changed the essential Crime Control nature of the slave tribunal. However, in 1825, the General Assembly moved significantly toward the Due Process Model for slaves accused of capital crimes by

---

[58]Law of North Carolina, 1741, ch. 23, in Haywood, Public Acts, p. 54; Clark, "Aspects of the North Carolina Slave Code, 1715-1860," p. 151.

[59]Laws of Tennessee, 1815, ch. 18; 1819, ch. 35.

removing the slave courts' exclusive jurisdiction over such offenses. In this instance, a Tennessee Supreme Court ruling was the decisive influence in the legislature's action.

In May 1825, in White county, a slave, Bob, was arrested for the murder of a white woman and her child. Bob was convicted by a slave court. Nothing in Tennessee law allowed a slave conviction to be appealed to a higher court, but Bob's owner carried the case to the White county circuit court.[60] The circuit court refused to hear the appeal. Bob's owner then appealed to the Supreme Court, and, in August, that body ordered that Bob's case be heard on appeal by the circuit court.[61]

---

[60]This was not the first attempt to appeal a slave court decision. For example, in Williamson county, in 1822, Allen, a slave owned by Pleasant Russell, was condemned by a slave court. An appeal was made to the circuit court. That court granted a _certiorari_ but later dismissed it and ordered the slave court to carry out its sentence. In _Bob_ (1825), Jacob Peck wrote that he knew of "two instances" where a circuit court had "controlled the convictions" of slaves by a slave court. Williamson County, County Court, _Minutes_, vol. 8, p. 224; Circuit Court, _Minutes_, August 1822, p. 67; February 1823, p. 113; _Bob, a Slave v. The State_, 10 Tenn. 163-64 (1826).

[61]_Bob, a Slave, v. The State_ is reported in 10 Tenn. 155 (1820-30) as being decided in Sparta, Tennessee, in August 1826. However, in _The State of Tennessee v. Richard Waterhouse_ 8 Tenn. 275-76 (1827), Justice Catron explained that Bob's case actually came before the Supreme Court twice; first in August 1825 and again in August 1826. In 1825, the issue was the right of appeal from the slave court to the circuit court. In 1826, the issue was Bob's reindictment at common law and his being placed in double jeopardy. Catron wrote that the 1826 decision "is not reported." It seems clear then that the decision reported as the 1826 decision was actually the decision rendered a year earlier in August 1825. This is an important distinction when the legislative reaction to _Bob_ is considered.

The Supreme Court clearly had gone beyond the provisions of state statutes, but the legislature did not oppose this judicial activism. It promptly placed its stamp of approval on the Court's action by providing that a conviction before a special slave court could be appealed to the regular circuit court, "in like manner as in cases of the conviction of white persons for similar offense." This same statute also provided slave defendants access to the Tennessee Supreme Court "as in prosecutions against free white persons."[62] This 1825 law meant that although in their original trials slaves were subject to the Crime Control slave courts, upon appeal slaves could be brought within the jurisdiction of the regular courts, the white man's courts, courts that provided Due Process protections for the rights and the life of defendants.

The new appeal procedure was not used frequently. In the records of the circuit courts of the counties in this study, only three appeals from a slave court were entered, two in Maury county and one in Shelby county. In two of these three appeals, the life of the accused slave was

---

[62]Law of Tennessee, 1825, ch. 24. This grant of appellate jurisdiction apparently was too broad. In 1831, Tennessee lawmakers narrowed the right to appeal a slave court conviction to those cases "where the punishment is death." In one class of capital cases, the legislature explicitly forbade an appeal. A slave was denied appeal "in any case of an actual rebellion or insurrection" where "proof" was made by an "overt act committed, by the preparation of arms and publicly assembling in numbers to carry the same in execution." Law of Tennessee, 1831, ch. 103.

saved. In Maury county in 1828, Jim, the slave of Garrard Greenfield, was convicted by a slave court of burglary. On appeal, the circuit court jury acquitted Jim of the capital offense but convicted him of larceny and sentenced him to thirty-nine lashes. The same general result occurred in the 1834 Shelby county murder trial of Sam. Convicted before the "justice court," on appeal Sam was acquitted of murder and convicted of manslaughter. He was sentenced to "be branded on the brawn of the left thumb with the letter 'M.'" In 1830, in Maury county, the slave Hardy was convicted of burglary by a slave court. On appeal, the circuit jury also convicted Hardy and sentenced him to hang. Hardy was not executed, however, for early the next year Governor Carroll pardoned him because "many citizens" of Maury county had "represented" to him that Hardy was a "fit object of executive clemency."[63]

---

[63] Maury County, Circuit Court, Minutes, June 1828, pp. 27,28; October 1830, pp. 361, 384-85, 429; Shelby County, Circuit Court, Minutes, December 1834, p. 325; June 1835, pp. 340-41; William Carroll to the Sheriff of Maury County, 28 February 1831, Letterbook, 1821-31, p. 76, Papers of Governor William Carroll, TSA.

There is one example of a white man appealing the verdict of a slave court. In Hickman county, John Hughlette accused Amos of the attempted murder of Hughlette's wife. The slave court acquitted Amos, and Hughlette appealed to the circuit court. The circuit jurors also acquitted Amos of the capital charge, but they did convict him of "committing the assault only by abusive language, within the distance of fifty or sixty yards" of Hughlette's residence. The judge sentenced Amos to "eight lashes on his bare back." "State v. Amos, a Slave," Case Files, Tennessee Supreme Court, Middle District, TSA.

In 1835, the legislature took the final step toward the Due Process Model for slaves and placed the slave accused of a capital crime, in one lawyers's words, "on the footing of a free man."[64] The General Assembly gave the regular circuit courts exclusive original jurisdiction over all trials of slaves for capital offenses. The circuit courts thereafter retained this jurisdiction during the antebellum period.

It is difficult to assess the motivation behind the elimination of the slave courts' jurisdiction over capital crimes. It may be that the movement away from the slave courts was part of a broader movement to reduce the criminal jurisdiction of the county courts and to transfer their authority to more professional tribunals. For many years, those same Justices of the Peace who had jurisdiction over slave crimes also had jurisdiction over all other crimes up to and including petit larceny.[65] Many of the JPs and slaveholders who sat in judgment on slaves may also have sat in judgment on their fellow white citizens. It is probably not coincidental that about the same time the General Assembly gave the circuit courts exclusive jurisdiction over slave capital crimes, it also directed that the circuit

---

[64] Prince, a Slave, v. The State, 26 Tenn. 11 (1846). Law of Tennessee, 1835, ch. 19.

[65] Law of North Caroline, 1777 (November), ch. 2, in Scott, Laws, 1: 184-85; Laws of Tennessee (Territorial Assembly), 1794, ch. 1, in Haywood, Public Acts, pp. 192-93; Laws of Tennessee, 1809, ch. 126; 1811, ch. 72.

courts were to exercise "exclusive jurisdiction" over all crimes committed by free men, except those for which the punishment was a fine of $50 of less.[66]

Andrew Fede has developed a theoretical framework regarding legal change in slave law which can be applied to the movement away from the slave courts. Fede asserts that legal change of this sort occurred as the master class recalculated its hierarchy of interests. In the colonial and early antebellum years, concerns of slave control dominated concerns for the master's economic interest--hence, the slave courts with their Crime Control method of operation. However, as we have seen, slave courts did not do well in preserving slave property. Therefore, as the plantation regime matured and as slave prices rose, the slaveholders turned to the formal delays of procedural due process to insure that their chattel would not be easily taken from them by the hangman's noose.[67]

---

[66]The 1829 penal code had removed the county courts' jurisdiction over petit larceny. Laws of Tennessee, 1835, ch. 5; 1829, ch. 23. Also see, Law of Tennessee, 1835, ch. 6; Tennessee, Constitution, art. 5, sec. 11 (1796); Law of Tennessee, 1848, ch. 55; Meigs and Cooper, The Code of Tennessee, p. 891.

[67]Fede has explored his ideas fully only in connection with crimes involving white violence against slaves, but he clearly intends them to apply to the the trend toward protection of the trial rights of slave defendants. Fede, "Legitimized Violent Slave Abuse," pp. 93-150; "Toward a Solution of the Slave Law Dilemma: a Critique of Tushnet's 'The American Law of Slavery,'" Law and History Review, 2 (Fall 1984): 314.

Without a doubt, such pecuniary considerations were present in Tennessee, as in any slave state, but among legal professionals, at least, concern for the trial rights of slave defendants also played an important part in the demise of the Tennessee slave courts. Two incidents illustrate this concern. The first was the 1806 Williamson county murder trial of Harriett.[68] Thomas Hart Benton was clearly unhappy with the way the eleven-year-old slave girl had been tried, indignant that his client had been convicted and condemned to hang on evidence that would have been inadmissable in the trial of of a free man. Harriet's death sentence was an injustice that stemmed from a blatant violation of the canons of the law.

In 1809, Williamson county elected Thomas Hart Benton to the Tennessee state senate.[69] As one of his first senatorial acts, Benton offered a resolution to investigate "what alteration is necessary to be made in the present mode of trying slaves, when the lives of the said slaves may be affected." This was one of the earliest

---

[68]See above, pp. 127-32.

[69]There was at least one other slave tried for murder and convicted in Williamson county between the time Benton was admitted to the bar and his election to the state senate. A female slave, Molly, was sentenced to hang "for the wilful murder of her child." Like Harriet, Molly was eventually saved from the hangman by executive clemency. There is no evidence that Benton was involved in Molly's trial, but it is highly likely that he was aware of it. Williamson County, Circuit Court, _Minutes_, vol. 1, pp. 253-54, 276; Diary of John Sevier, in Heiskell, _Andrew Jackson_, 2: 589.

efforts in the Tennessee legislature to secure reconsideration of the method by which slaves were tried.[70]

The second incident involved the 1825 Supreme Court decision in Bob.[71] Here, as noted previously, the Court opened up the regular court system to slaves convicted of capital crimes. The Justices' explanation of this truly significant step was that since the slave was a human being, the "rules of law" demanded that means be available to "rescue" a bondsman "condemned to death by a wrongful sentence."[72]

---

[70] Tennessee, Legislature, Senate, Journal, 8th Gen. Ass., 1st sess., 1809, p. 11. One other clue to Benton's intentions is that later in his life he incorrectly believed himself to have been the author of "a humane law, giving to slaves the same full benefit of jury trial which was the right of white men under the same accusation." William Nisbet Chambers, Old Bullion Benton: Senator from the New West (New York: Little, Brown and Company, 1956), p. 33.

[71] For a detailed examination of this case, see above, pp. 142-43, and below, pp. 158-63.

[72] Bob, a Slave, v. The State, 10 Tenn. 158-59, 165 (1826). Fede rejects judicial recognition of slave humanity as playing any meaningful role in the development of this area of slave law. Instead, he gives primacy to the pecuniary interest of the master, asserting that "it is logical that masters and lawmakers came to believe that the state owed slave owners greater procedural safeguards--'due process,' if you will--before they were deprived of rights in such valuable property." But, what Fede seems unwilling to accept is that, even if the other parts of his theory are accurate, concern for slave humanity could still be regarded as a significant element of slave law. In order for the judiciary to provide increased legal protection of slave property, policymakers might choose to rely upon judicial recognition of the humanity of the slave and upon granting bondsmen most of the trial rights attendant to that humanity.

The elimination of the slave courts' jurisdiction over capital crimes did not curtail their activities. It was not until 1854 that they were completely eradicated. Between 1825 and 1854, they continued to exercise jurisdiction over non-capital crimes that seemed to demand punishment greater than forty lashes; that is, crimes beyond the jurisdiction of a single Justice of the Peace but not within the jurisdiction of the circuit court. For example, in Lincoln county in 1852, the circuit jury acquitted a slave accused of attempted rape. The judge refused to release the defendant because "from the evidence of witnesses examined upon the trial," he thought the slave guilty of assault and battery "of too aggravated a character to be tried by a single Justice of the Peace." The judge ordered the slave to jail to await trial before a special slave court.[73]

In the final analysis, then, the point of departure makes little difference. On the one hand, if judges recognized slave humanity and accorded bondsmen human trial rights, that doctrine protected the economic interests of slaveowners. On the other, if judges decided that the economic interest of slaveowners demanded more legal protection, that protection could be afforded best by giving slaves the trial rights already accorded to "real people." Either way, the end result was the same: the humanity of the slave was recognized and the judicial protection and trial rights of bondsmen were significantly broadened. Fede, "Toward a Solution of the Slave Law Dilemma," pp. 317-18.

[73]Lincoln County, Circuit Court, Minutes, March 1852, pp. 382, 386. For a similar case involving a slave accused of assault with intent to murder, see Shelby County, Circuit Court, Minutes, January 1851, pp. 315-16, 384, 410, 412; September 1853, p. 67.

Manslaughter seems to have been the offense which most often called these special slave courts into session. In Davidson county in September 1837, a circuit court jury acquitted a female slave of the murder of a white infant. After she was acquitted, the circuit judge, "on motion of the attorney general," ordered her "to answer the charge of manslaughter before a special court of magistrates, this court having no jurisdiction to pronounce judgment in a case of manslaughter committed by a slave."[74] In Shelby county, the circuit jury acquitted one slave of the stabbing death of another, but declared that it believed the slave guilty of manslaughter. The judge then ordered him tried before a special slave court.[75] Finally, in November 1852, a Gibson county jury refused to convict a slave of the murder of a white man. The judge ordered the slave to remain in jail to be tried for manslaughter by a slave court.[76]

The continued operation of the slave courts, even for a limited range of crimes, must have troubled lawmakers, In 1854, the legislature abolished them. In the same statute, the legislators expressly gave the circuit court

---

[74] Davidson County, Circuit Court, Minutes, September 1837, pp. 259, 262.

[75] Shelby County, Circuit Court, Minutes, September 1852, pp. 256, 276-77.

[76] Gibson County, Circuit Court, Minutes, November 1852, p. 502. The killing actually took place in Dyer county. The trial was held in the Gibson county circuit court by a change of venue. Ibid., p. 498.

"as ample jurisdiction in the trial of a slave or slaves charged with manslaughter, as it now has in the trial of offenses committed by slaves punishable with death."[77]

Although the thrust of legislation was to treat slaves on trial similarly to free men, lawmakers, in considering slaves accused of insurrection, twice departed from this trend. Between 1825 and 1831, the circuit court had exercised appellate jurisdiction over the special slave courts. In 1831, the legislature expressly forbade appeals to the circuit court except in capital crimes and also forbade appeal "in any case of an actual rebellion or insurrection, and proof made of overt act committed, by the preparation of arms and publicly assembling in numbers to carry the same in execution." Presumably Tennessee lawmakers wanted to insure that punishment would be swift and sure in instances of "actual" rebellion.[78]

The second piece of legislation dealing with slave insurrection was enacted in March 1858, during the aftermath of the Panic of 1856. White fright in 1856-57 had produced a deadly outbreak of whippings, shootings, and lynching.[79]

---

[77]Law of Tennessee, 1854, ch. 88.

[78]Law of Tennessee, 1831, ch. 103.

[79]Harvey Wish, "The Slave Insurrection Panic of 1856," The Journal of Southern History 5 (May 1939): Charles B. Dew, "Black Ironworkers and the Slave Insurrection Panic of 1856," The Journal of Southern History 41 (August 1975): 326, 337; Nashville Daily Gazette, 7 December, 9 December, 21 December 1856.

The Tennessee Supreme Court publicly condemned this lawlessness.[80] The legislature, according to Charles B. Dew, "moved to prevent a recurrence of vigilante action in any future insurrectionary panics by providing for the rapid channeling of white hysteria into the regular court system.[81] When "five creditable persons" certified in writing to a circuit court judge that any blacks were involved in "an insurrectionary movement," the judge immediaately was "to open court" and to proceed to trial of those blacks. If there was no attorney general present to prosecute for the state, the judge was to appoint one <u>pro tem</u>. Otherwise, the special sesion of the court was to operate "regularly." The legislature specifically directed that alleged offenders had to be indicted by a grand jury and tried before a twelve-man petit jury. Thus, in insurrectionary situations, frightened whites demanding speedy trials would not have to go outside the law.[82]

In summary, then, the Tennessee legislture allowed the slave courts to try intermediate crimes like manslaughter until 1854, but, by 1836, for capital crimes, Tennessee had abandoned the Crime Control slave court and brought slaves fully within the same criminal justice system that applied to free men. That system was modified somewhat

---

[80] <u>Kirkwood v. Miller</u>, 37 Tenn. 455 (1858).

[81] Dew, "Black Iron Workers," p. 338.

[82] Law of Tennessee, 1858, ch. 86.

in times of fear over the presumed threat of servile insurrection, but even then the state attempted to conduct regular, if speedy, trials. Insofar as the statutes were concerned, then, much of the due process that applied to free men would apply to slaves as well. The next two chapters will examine how that legislation was carried out by the Supreme Court and the trial courts.

CHAPTER VI

THE SLAVE DEFENDANT: THE SUPREME COURT 1825-1860

By the end of 1835, legislative enactments had placed the slave accused of a capital crime "on the footing of a free man." However, the effect and meaning of those statutes depended upon their implementation in the courts. A study of that implementation must begin with the Supreme Court. Using its power to review the actions of the trial courts, the Supreme Court decisively influenced the treatment of slave defendants in the lower tribunals. The treatment of slaves in the trial courts cannot be understood apart from the guidelines set for those courts by the Supreme Court in exercising its appellate jurisdiction.

Before analyzing the Supreme Court's rulings, one must examine the capital crimes for which slaves were liable. As in other southern states, Tennessee slaves were subject to more capital crimes than were whites.[1] In 1819, in its first statutory enactment on the subject, the General Assembly designated five crimes as capital for

---

[1]Cobb, An Inquiry into the Law of Negro Slavery, p. 266; Stampp, The Peculiar Institution, pp. 210-211.

slaves: murder, arson, burglary, rape, and robbery.[2]

Lawmakers added to this list until, by 1858, the number had grown to thirteen. The first expansion came in 1831. In that year of Nat Turner, the Tennessee legislature allowed courts to inflict the death penalty for "conspiracy to rebel."[3] Attempted rape of a white female was added to the roster of capital crimes for slaves in 1833, attempted murder two years later.[4]

The next addition came in 1842 when Tennessee lawmakers extended the statutory definition of attempted rape to "include all and every white female" and expressly made attempted rape of a white female a capital offense for slaves.[5] This law was passed in response to a Robertson county case then working its way through the judicial system. In September 1841, a slave named Sydney was indicted for the attempted rape of a six-year-old white girl. Sydney's attorney had successfully challenged the indictment, and the State had appealed the case to the

---

[2]Law of Tennessee, 1819, ch. 32. Whites were subject to only two capital crimes, murder in the first degree and accessory before the fact to murder in the first degree. Law of Tennessee, 1829, ch. 23.

[3]The death sentence was not mandatory but was "discretionary with the court trying the case." Law of Tennessee, 1831, ch. 103.

[4]Law of Tennessee, 1833, ch. 75; Law of Tennessee, 1835, ch. 19.

[5]Law of Tennessee, 1842, ch. 193.

February term of the Supreme Court.[6] The statute defining attempted rape was passed on February 5, 1842. It appears to have been a legislative attempt to instruct the Supreme Court how to rule on the point of contention in Sydney's case, i.e. whether the definition of rape included a female under ten years of age. The Court refused to apply the legislation to Sydney's case because he had been charged before its passage and ruled further that Sydney could not be indicted for his offense because his victim was a child under ten.[7]

The 1842 legislation prompted by Sydney's case related only to attempted rape. In was not until 1852 that Tennessee lawmakers made rape of a white child under ten years old a capital crime for a slave defendant. The legislature again acted in response to the refusal of the Supreme Court to go beyond the letter of the law to convict a slave. In The State v. Dan Cherry (1851), the defendant was convicted in December 1851 in the Davidson County Criminal Court of the rape of "a white female child under the age of ten." The judge of the Criminal Court had upheld the defendant's motion in arrest of judgment and the State appealed. The question on appeal was whether there was "any law in this state that makes the carnal knowledge and abuse of a child under ten years punishable by death?" The

---

[6] Robertson County, Circuit Court, Minutes, October 1841, pp. 319-20; February 1842, p. 345.

[7] Sydney v. The State, 22 Tenn. 466 (1842).

Supreme Court concluded that there was not. The 1829 penal code set the sentence for the crime, when committed by whites, at ten to twenty-one years in the penitentiary.[8] Cherry, however, could not be sentenced under the 1829 penal code because his indictment "only alleges that the prisoner is a negro" and "the presumption in this state is that he is a slave."[9] The Court also pointed out that there was not statute that made the offense a capital crime for a slave; therefore the Criminal Court judge was correct in arresting the judgment in Cherry's case. In this instance, the Court openly cited the "singular omission of the legislature on the subject" and observed that the necessary statute "will doubtless be promptly supplied by the General Assembly."[10]

During the 1850s, lawmakers added other offenses to the list of capital crimes for slaves. The legislature made accessory before the fact to murder in the first degree a capital crime for slaves. In an interesting twist, this crime was a hanging offense for whites long before it brought the death penalty for slaves.[11]

---

[8]Law of Tennessee, 1829, ch. 23.

[9]Since the attorney general chose not to reindict Cherry as a free black, Cherry probably was a slave. See Davidson County, Criminal Court, Minutes, Book D, April 1852, p. 257. Also see, Nashville Daily Gazette, 10 December 1851.

[10]The State v. Dan Cherry, 31 Tenn. 136-39 (1851); Law of Tennessee, 1852, ch. 174.

[11]Law of Tennessee, 1850, ch. 114; Law of Tennessee, 1829, ch. 23.

Subsequently, the legislature made poisoning "with intent to kill" a capital offense.[12] Still later, the legislature gave the courts discretion to pass the death sentence in cases where a slave "wilfully or maliciously" burned or attempted to burn buildings or boats "whereby the life or limb of any person shall be endangered or destroyed, or with the intent to endanger or destroy human life or limb."[13] Finally, in 1860, the legislature made it a capital offense for slaves to "endanger the safe running" of railroad locomotives and cars.[14]

As noted previously, Tennessee shifted from a Crime Control Model to a Due Process Model of criminal justice for slaves accused of these capital crimes. The Tennessee Supreme Court played a pivotal role in this transition. In its first reported criminal case involving a slave defendant, the Court broadened the trial rights and protections of slave defendants well beyond that required by statute. In that instance, the Court held that slaves were entitled to the same judicial protection accorded free defendants. Because of its importance, this case merits close examination.

On May 25, 1825, a White county slave named Bob was arrested and charged with murder. Six days later,

---

[12] Law of Tennessee, 1852, ch. 174.

[13] Law of Tennessee, 1858, ch. 18.

[14] Law of Tennessee, 1860, ch. 118.

Bob was tried for the crime by a special slave court, convicted, and sentenced him to hang. Nothing in Tennessee law provided for the appeal of a slave court conviction to a higher court. Nevertheless, Bob's owner petitioned the White county circuit court for a writ of certiorari, asking that the proceedings against his bondsman be brought into the circuit court. The circuit judge refused to issue the certiorari, and Bob's owner appealed to the Supreme Court.[15]

The Supreme Court heard Bob's case in August 1825. By a three to one vote, the Court reversed the circuit judge's decision and ordered him to issue the writ sought by Bob's owner.[16] John Haywood and Jacob Peck wrote opinions for the majority, and John Catron wrote in dissent.

Although Judge Peck carefully excused the magistrates who presided over the slave trials from any "voluntary abuse of power,"[17] neither he nor the other judges believed Bob's guilt established by the evidence. Even Catron remarked that "in the course of a life of some considerable experience in criminal prosecutions, I never have known any person convicted of a crime upon evidence so slight."[18] The central question, then, was not Bob's

---

[15] Bob, a slave, v. The State, 10 Tenn. 155-57 (1826).

[16] Ibid., pp. 159, 162.

[17] Ibid., p. 162.

[18] Ibid., p. 171.

guilt, but whether, in Judge Peck's words, the "peculiar jurisdiction for the trial of slaves" was "above control," whether a slave defendant had a remedy when he received an "unjust and illegal" sentence.[19]

Judge Haywood did not believe the law unable "to obviate an evil so distressing to humanity." Would it be said, he asked,

> . . . that a human being shall be condemned to death by wrongful sentence, and that there is no power residing in the law to rescue him from it? Does the law delight in cruelty? Will it inflict punishment where it is not deserved? Will it give no power to avoid the unjust sentence? Then where is the justice of the law, and where is its boasted humanity? And for what good end and purpose is it, that the arm of the law should be lengthened to strike the fatal blow, but made too short to save an unfortunate victim who is unjustly doomed to suffer? It is enough to ask the question, and every heart will respond that it should not be so.

In order "to vindicate the title of the law to the esteem and reverence of mankind," Haywood declared that the law had "made ample provision, and given a plain and easy mode" to save the slave from an unjust sentence. That "plain and easy mode" was a writ of <u>certiorari</u> issued by a circuit court judge.[20]

Judge Peck was forced to admit that in the legislation on slave trials "no appeal is given to any other tribunal in express words,"[21] but he, like Haywood, did

---

[19]Ibid., pp. 162, 163.

[20]Ibid., pp. 158-59.

[21]Ibid., p. 162.

not consider himself limited to the wording of those statutes which dealt only with the trials of slaves. Indeed, in a remarkable assertion, Peck insisted that "color, rank, or situation can make no difference; even the slave has such rights as the statutes of the country have afforded him." In other words, those legislative enactments which prescribed correct judicial proceedings for free men should be read so as to include slaves unless slaves expressly were excepted. If the circuit courts governed such "light and trivial matters" as laying out roads, levying taxes, and regulating the poor, they were "bound to interfere" in a case like Bob's, a case that threatened the property of a citizen and the life of a human being.[22]

Both Peck and Haywood acknowledged that granting a writ of <u>certiorari</u> was up to the discretion of the circuit judge. Peck, however, insisted that "discretion must not be arbitrary; discretion depends upon the rules of law, and should be so exercised that the administration of law should be uniform and alike to all."[23] Haywood agreed that the judge's discretion was "not an arbitrary one, to do as he pleases; but to discover by right rule of law what is right, and so do that."[24] In Bob's case, Peck said, a

---

[22]Ibid., p. 163, 164.

[23]Ibid., p. 165.

[24]Ibid., pp. 160-61.

"legal discretion" had been "illegally exercised,"[25] and, if the circuit judge had committed an error by refusing to grant the certiorari to Bob's owner, such "unrighteous discretion" could be "purified" by the Supreme Court reversing the circuit judge's refusal to grant the writ, thus forcing the circuit court to hear the case.[26]

Judge John Catron disagreed with his colleagues, but even his dissent underscores the broad view that the Tennessee Supreme Court took concerning the trial rights of slaves. Catron dissented on narrow grounds. Essentially, he argued that a circuit judge who refused to grant a certiorari could not be reversed.[27] However, it is significant that Catron agreed with his colleagues that the circuit judge had the right to issue a certiorari where the defendant was a slave and considered it a "matter of regret" that the writ had not been granted in Bob's particular case.[28]

Subsequent developments in this case suggest that the opinions in Bob should not be read as evidence of undue solicitude for slaves. The case established the general right of appellate review, but it did not exonerate

---

[25]Ibid., p. 165.

[26]Ibid., p. 161.

[27]Ibid., pp. 160, 166-69.

[28]Catron even went to considerable pains to outline some grounds "worthy of consideration" upon which the circuit judge could grant the writ. Ibid., pp. 169-71.

the particular defendant. After Bob's successful appeal, the White county circuit court quashed his slave court conviction. He then was "indicted at common law" and tried in the circuit court. He was again convicted, and he again appealed to the Supreme Court. This time the Court reversed the circuit court because Bob's conviction "upon the common law indictment" was not "warranted by our statutes."[29] However, the Court did not release Bob, but ordered him "to be again put upon his trial, before the justices who first submitted his cause to the jury which disagreed."[30]

We do not know what finally happened to Bob, but, regardless, in his case, the Tennessee Court clearly indicated that unless expressly directed to do otherwise by the state legislature, it would read the laws governing criminal trials as applicable to slaves as well as to whites. The Court never retreated from this initial stance, nor did the legislature ever seek to force it to do so.

Later courts even viewed the protections afforded slave defendants as rights guaranteed by the Tennessee Constitution. In 1851, a slave convicted of felonious assault appealed his conviction on the grounds that during jury deliberations the jurors had heard testimony from one

---

[29] Presumably, Bob should have been indicted under the 1819 statute that outlined the capital crimes for slaves.

[30] The State of Tennessee v. Richard Waterhouse, 8 Tenn. 275-77 (1827)

of its own number about a material matter. The Court reversed the conviction because, as Judge McKinney wrote, "among other rights absolutely secured by Constitution to the accused, in all prosecutions is the right 'to meet the witnesses face to face.'" Without that rule, "trial by jury," McKinney said, "would too often be perverted to purposes of the grossest injustice and oppression."[31] Similarly, in an 1857 case, basic constitutional protections led the court to overturn a slave's conviction for rape. Here, the Court did not believe the evidence supported the verdict. In reversing the lower court, Judge Harris wrote that is was

> . . . the imperative duty of the court to see as far as it is practicable, that the accused shall have a fair trial by an impartial jury. This right, so essential to the preservation of the life and liberty of the accused, is secured by the Constitution of our own state.

The provision, Harris insisted, "is not unmeaning--was not placed in our Bill of Rights without motive, and can not be disregarded by the courts."[32]

Statistically, the record of the Tennessee Supreme Court in slave cases reinforces the observation that these defendants received even-handed treatment at the appellate level. Thirty-three reported cases involving slave

---

[31] Sam v. The State, 31 Tenn. 63-64 (1851).

[32] Major v. The State, 36 Tenn. 353, 357 (1857). Also see, Henry, a Slave, v. The State, 23 Tenn. 262 (1842); Alfred and Anthony v. The State, 32 Tenn. 418 (1853).

defendants were appealed to the Tennessee Supreme Court. In twenty-three of the cases, the Supreme Court sustained the cause of the slave defendant.

In ten cases, the Supreme Court decided against a slave defendant and upheld a sentence of hanging. Only in those cases where a slave had been convicted of murdering his owner did the Supreme Court decide against the slave more frequently than for him. In that category, four of the five cases went against the slave defendant. In the eight appeals involving slaves accused of murder when the victim was white but not the owner of the slave, only one decision went against the slave. A single case of murder of a black man and a case of attempted murder of a white went against the slave defendant.[33]

The result of the appeals process in slave cases compares favorably with the result of appeals in cases of whites accused of murder, the only offense for which the Court held the lives of whites, as well as slave defendants, in its hands (see Table 9). Indeed, the Supreme Court actually reversed a larger percentage of slave

---

[33]The twenty-three reversals involved twenty slaves. Successful appeal was not tantamount to acquittal. After each reversal, the trial court had to consider the case again. I have found the outcome of seventeen of the twenty-three reversals. Two were acquitted and six released without a retrial. There were two mistrials, and seven slaves were convicted again. In terms of the twenty individual slaves, the final outcome is known in thirteen cases. Three of those resulted in acquittal and seven in release. There were three convictions.

appeals (70 percent) than it did appeals of whites convicted on capital charges (53 percent).

In reversing trial court convictions of slave defendants, the Supreme Court did not hesitate to insist upon a careful interpretation of the law. Cases involving rape or attempted rape are particularly illustrative of this point. In the cases of Sydney (1842) and Dan Cherry (1851), the Supreme Court refused to uphold convictions because the victims were under ten years of age. In two other instances, Grandison (1841) and Henry (1842), the Court overturned convictions because the victim was not clearly designated in the indictment as a white woman. By statute, attempted rape by a slave was a crime only when the victim was white.[34]

One of the most fascinating of such cases decided by the Tennessee Court dealt with the 1852 conviction of Wyatt for the attempted rape of Mrs. Catherine Francis Evans. Wyatt had broken into the Evans home and had approached the bed where Mr. and Mrs. Evans were sleeping. When Wyatt put his hand upon Mrs. Evans, "she gave the alarm," and Wyatt fled. The circuit judge had charged the jury that if they believed that Wyatt had "attempted, either by force, or by fraudulently inducing the prosecutor's wife to believe that it was her husband, and thereby to have carnal knowledge of

---

[34]Grandison, a slave, v. The State, 21 Tenn. 473 (1841); Henry, A Slave, v. The State, 23 Tenn. 263 (1842); also see, Kit v. The State, 30 Tenn. 117-18.

her, that then they ought to find him guilty."

Speaking for the Court, Justice Caruthers acknowledged that "in the black catalogue of crime there is none which shocks all men as the one under consideration; none should be more severely punished." Caruthers also agreed that the "moral turpitude of the crime would be as great, when perpetrated by fraud and deception, as by force." However, Caruthers insisted, "we cannot permit even a slave to be punished without the full benefit of the law as it is, either under the influence of popular feeling, or our own abhorrence of his acts."

Tennessee statutes clearly defined the crime.[35] "Actual force" was an "essential element" of the offense." In the circuit judge's charge, "the idea of force, as one ingredient of the offence . . . is entirely discarded in the instruction to the jury, and was well calculated to mislead them." Caruthers would not comment on Wyatt's guilt or innocence, but he insisted that "if he has forfeited his life, let it be legally taken, and the law will be thereby honored and public justice sustained." As Caruthers wrote, "the question with us should ever be, not what the offence deserves, nor what our feelings and individual opinions would dictate, but 'What Sayeth the law.'"[36]

---

[35]Law of Tennessee, 1829, ch. 23.

[36]Wyatt, a slave, v. The State, 32 Tenn. 281-84 (1852).

Caruthers' eloquent insistence upon the impartiality of the law in slave cases underscores the central tendency of the Tennessee Supreme Court. This tendency, however, did not hold in every instance. As already discussed, in one important area, the law of homicide when slaves killed whites, the Court shaped the law to fit slave defendants because to have done otherwise would have threatened the principal relationship of the Peculiar Institution.

The Court might not allow the rules of homicide to undermine the due subordination of slaves, but where that was not at issue the Court unhesitatingly applied such rules on behalf of a slave defendant. Consider, for example, Ann v. the State. Ann was a young slave, about fifteen years old. She was owned by Nicholas Marr, who employed her as a nurse for his five-year-old daughter, Mary. Ann had held this job only a few days when a slave named Tom asked her "to meet him out at night." Tom finally persuaded Ann to give Mary Marr a dose of laudanum so that she would sleep until Ann returned from her rendezvous. Ann gave her charge an overdose, killing the child.[37]

Ann was convicted of murder. In his instructions to the jury, circuit judge Thomas Maney had charged that if Ann drugged the Marr child "by force" the act "would amount to a battery, and she would be responsible in law for

---

[37] Ann v. The State, 20 Tenn. 111-12 (1850).

the natural effects of the laudanum, although they may have been more serious than she designed or expected." Maney also instructed that if the slave had been ordered by her owner not to give anything to the child and "if she, without authority wilfully administered laudanum . . . intending thereby to produce unnecessary sleep, and, contrary to her expectation, it cause death, she would be guilty of murder."[38]

The Supreme Court would have none of this. Justice McKinney wrote the decision reversing the lower court conviction. By the common law, McKinney pointed out, to be murder a homicide "must be with malice." If there was no "mischievous intention . . . and the act was done heedlessly and incautiously, it will be manslaughter only." According to McKinney, the "tenderest of mothers" might give laudanum to an infant "incautiously, in order to be enabled to attend to some pressing call of her household affairs." A "gay and thoughtless matron" might do the same thing "in order to have opportunity to attend the theater or ballroom." If the infant died in these cases, McKinney doubted that any one would contend that either mother was guilty of murder or manslaughter. If Ann's purpose was simply to put the child to sleep in order to carry out her "illicit intercourse" with Tom, "this," McKinney said, "however, culpable in morals, would not involve her in the

---

[38]Ibid., p. 112.

guilt of murder." The "gross heedlessness and incautiousness" of her actions "might constitute her offence manslaughter, but certainly nothing more." As for the act being murder because Ann had given the drug against her master's order, McKinney wrote, "this is not the law." To so hold would put

> . . . disobedience to the master's order on the same footing with a violation of a command or prohibition of the law. This is a great mistake. Such violation of the master's order is not an 'unlawful act' . . . . It is no offence against the law of the land, nor is it cognizable by any tribunal created by law.[39]

One of the hallmarks of the Due Process Model of criminal justice is a high regard for procedural formality. The Tennessee Supreme Court extended that benefit to slave defendants. The Court did not hesitate to reverse a slave's conviction when a procedural error had been made in the trial.[40] Such was the case with Mahala, a Robertson county slave indicted for murder. At her trial, the jury reported that it could not agree and, with one full day left in the session of the court, the judge declared a mistrial. At the next term of court, Mahala was tried again and convicted. She appealed to the Supreme Court on the grounds that the action of the judge on the first trial had

---

[39] Ibid., pp. 114-16.

[40] Judith K. Schafer's study of the Louisiana Supreme Court shows that bench to have taken a very different stance. Schafer, "The Long Arm of the Law: Slave Criminals and the Supreme Court in Antebellum Louisiana, 1803-1862," Unpublished Paper, Read at the Southern Historical Association Convention, November 1984.

constituted an acquittal. Justice Turley wrote the opinion of the Supreme Court. He admitted that the circuit judge had the power to discharge a jury which could not reach a verdict, but, Turley ruled, unless "prevented by a physical impossibility" the jury should be kept together until court adjourns. Mahala's jury had been discharged twenty-four hours before adjournment. This was an "improper exercise" of the power of the court, and Mahala went free.[41]

The Supreme Court also overturned slave convictions because of imperfections in the record of the trial in the lower courts. In 1846, the Court reversed the conviction of a slave for murder merely because the record did not show that the circuit court was held at the courthouse "where, by law, it is required to be holden."[42] In 1841, the Court overturned Grandison's conviction for attempted rape because the record of the lower court conviction was "wholly defective." The caption failed to state where court was held or that a grand jury "of good and lawful men" had returned the indictment. Justice Nathan Green wrote,

> . . . to presume that the court was holden at McMinnville, and a grand jury was regularly empannelled, is going farther than any case has ever gone; and farther than we can go, consistent with that regularity and strictness which is required in criminal proceedings.[43]

---

[41] Mahala v. the State, 18 Tenn. 404-406 (1837).

[42] Bob, a slave, v. The State, 26 Tenn. 102-103 (1846).

[43] Grandison, a slave, v. The State, 21 Tenn. 247 (1841).

The Court also insisted that the record of a slave trial show that the indictment was found on a true bill by the grand jury. In an unreported decision in 1839, Green gave a new trial to Grandison because the trial record was silent on this point. Green cited Chappel v. the State, a case involving a white defendant, where the Court had established that such information was essential. In a subsequent case, Blevins v. the State, the Court criticized Chappel as going "to the very verge of the law." Nevertheless, said Green, "it is recognized *as the law*, and he would not deny a slave the full benefit of that law.[44] It was not until 1842 that the Supreme Court in a reported opinion insisted upon the "true bill" entry in a slave case. In reversing a Stewart county slave's conviction for attempted rape, Judge Green again cited Chappel and Blevins, declaring that he still would adhere to the necessity of that entry "as the settled law of the court."[45]

The choosing of jury members was a major source of procedural error in criminal trials.[46] In 1850, Justice

---

[44]The emphasis is Green's. Opinion of Nathan Green in "State v. Grandison (slave)," Case Files, Tennessee Supreme Court, Middle District, TSA.

[45]Henry, a slave, v. The State, 23 Tenn. 261 (1842).

[46]Flanigan, "The Criminal Law of Slavery," pp. 111-13; Nash, "Negro Rights," pp. 426-30.

McKinney wrote that "in the present state of our law, in respect to trials in criminal cases, difficulties of a most perplexing and delicate nature not unfrequently arise in the selection of jurors."[47]

One of these "perplexing and delicate" difficulties was the requirement that trials be held in the county where the crime was committed. This requirement often made it difficult to find jurymen who had not formed some opinion on the case. By the time this issue arose in a slave case, the Tennessee Court had already developed its position in cases involving white defendants. The Court held that if a prospective juror had "heard the circumstances" of a case and had formed an opinion that person "ought to be rejected." However, if a juror had formed an opinion merely "upon rumor," he need not be rejected.[48] In 1842, the Court extended this principle to cases involving slave defendants and did not deviate from it thereafter.[49]

The Court reversed slave convictions because of irregularities in the make-up or behavior of juries. In 1859, the Court overturned the Memphis Criminal Court conviction of Isaac for the murder of a white man.

---

[47] Moses v. The State, 28 Tenn. 304 (1850).

[48] M'Cowan v. The State, 17 Tenn. 141-42, 145 (1836).

[49] Henry, a slave, v. The State, 23 Tenn. 261-62 (1842); Moses v. The State, 28 Tenn. 305 (1850); Alfred and Anthony v. The State, 32 Tenn. 415-18 (1858); Major v. the State, 36 Tenn. 353-54 (1857).

One of the jurors had refused to take the "usual oath" because of "conscientious scruples in regard to capital punishment." The criminal court judge had discharged and jailed the juror. After a night in jail, the juror was ready to take his seat in the jury box. The judge accepted him over the objections of both Isaac and the prosecuting atttorney. The Supreme Court admitted that the juror was properly discharged but ruled that "the court had no power to recall him and force him upon the prisoner, or even upon the State."[50]

In 1851, a Shelby county slave named Wesley was convicted of the murder of his master. It took three days to select a jury. After each of the first two days, the jurors who had been selected were permitted to disperse. This was done with the consent of both the prisoner and the prosecuting attorney. On appeal, the question before the Supreme Court was whether such separation was grounds for a new trial. The Court ruled that it was. The Court had already faced the issue of the separation of the jury in two capital cases involving whites and ruled in both that such separation was cause for a new trial.[51] Justice Green admitted that a distinction could be made between a separation before the jury had been sworn and one after

---

[50]<u>Isaac (a slave) v. The State</u>, 39 Tenn. 290-91 (1859).

[51]<u>McLain v. The State</u>, 18 Tenn. 178-81 (1837); <u>Hines v. The State</u>, 27 Tenn. 478-80 (1848).

it had been sworn. Green pointed out, however, that no such distinction had been made either by the law or by the courts in Tennessee, and, he thought, "none exists in reason." According to Green, "the mischief which may result" would be the same in either case.[52] Green also ruled that the circuit judge could not take the consent of the defendant as ground to dispense with the requirement that the jury be sequestered.[53]

In other instances, the Supreme Court overturned convictions of slaves, in whole or in part, because of the way in which the juries actually reached a verdict. In November 1850, an Anderson county slave was convicted for felonious assault on a white man. A point of dispute at the trial was whether the crime was committed in Anderson county or in Roane county. While the jury was deliberating, the matter was discussed, one jurors reporting certain facts about the boundary between the two counties. Justice McKinney delivered the Court's opinion and ruled that the juror's comments invalidated the verdict. McKinney ruled that no verdict could be made upon the "private knowledge" of jurymen but only upon such evidence as was produced in open court by sworn witnesses.[54]

---

[52] Wesley v. The State, 30 Tenn. 345-46 (1851).

[53] Ibid., p. 346.

[54] Sam v. The State, 31 Tenn. 61-64 (1851).

In Jim, a slave, v. The State (1843), the defendant was convicted of the murder of another slave. In this case, the jury had to resolve two difficult points in order to reach its verdict. First, two witnesses, slaves named Beck and Nancy, had testified that before the murder happened they heard the accused talking in a cabin other than the one in which the homicide actually took place and that after the crime occurred one of them had gone into that "other" cabin and had seen Jim still there. Of course, this testimony made it difficult to place the accused at the scene of the crime at time of the killing and thus pointed to his innocence. In order to assess this evidence, the jurors shut themselves in the jury room, sent the constable outside, talked in loud voices, and then asked the constable if he could hear them. The constable replied that he could not; the jurors then disregarded the testimony of Beck and Nancy. Second, Jim's shoes were about half an inch longer than the tracks found leaving the scene of the crime. The jurors measured the tracks made by one of their number while walking and then while running. The tracks made while running were shorter; therefore, the jury concluded that Jim could have made the shorter tracks while running from the scene of the crime.

The Supreme Court would have none of the jury's unscientific efforts to test testimony and evidence.

As Justice McKinney wrote,

> We can not permit verdicts which have been obtained like this, upon uncertain and dangerous experiments, instead of a calm, deliberate and philosophical examination of the proof, to stand where the lives of individuals are at stake.[55]

The admission or non-admission of testimony was also vital to procedural due process, and the Tennessee Court reversed convictions of slaves because of the admission of improper testimony. For example, the Court would not permit the improper admission of the testimony of a dying victim. In cases involving white defendants, the court adhered to the traditional rule that for dying declarations to be admitted "it must appear that the deceased, at the time of making such declarations, was conscious of his danger, such consciousness being equivalent to the sanction of an oath."[56]

There was one slave case in which this issue was relevant. When Nelson was tried in Hardin county for the stabbing death of David Sellars, the circuit judge had admitted into evidence statements made by Sellars about an hour before he died. In these statements, Sellars said that Nelson had attempted to kill him "two or three times before." The prosecution relied upon this testimony to

---

[55] _Jim, a slave, v. The State_, 23 Tenn. 279-82 (1843).

[56] _Anthony v. The State_, 19 Tenn. 276 (1838). Also see, _Smith v. the State_, 28 Tenn. 7-9 (1848); _Logan v. The State_, 28 Tenn. 11-12 (1848); and _Willis S. Brakefield v. the State_, 33 Tenn. 150-51.

prove that the stabbing was done maliciously and that Nelson was guilty of murder, rather than manslaughter. The Supreme Court threw out Sellars' testimony because shortly before making the statments he had said that he "was not badly wounded, and was not going to die."[57]

As Nash has observed, "perhaps no protection is more vital to a fair trial than the exclusion of coerced confessions."[58] Even in the antebellum era, the admission of any confession was a sensitive matter and strict guidelines obtained. As Judge Haywood wrote in 1823,

> Evidence of confession, though admissible, is yet received with great distrust, and under the superintendence of very solicitous apprehensions for the wrong it may do. The admissibility is made to depend on its being free from all suspicion of having been obtained by any threats of severity or promise of favor, and of every influence, even the minutest, having been exercised over the mind of the person in order to induce a disclosure.[59]

In two cases involving slave defendants, the admission of a confession was passed on by the Supreme Court. The first of these was <u>Ann v. the State</u>, in which the young defendant, acting as a nurse, had killed her master's daughter by an overdose of laudanum. After the child's death, Ann was confined in the slave quarters with "chains around her body and neck." She was interviewed

---

[57] <u>Nelson, a slave, v. The State</u>, 26 Tenn. 445-46 (1847).

[58] Nash, "Negro Rights," p. 447.

[59] <u>State v. Elizabeth Fields and Webber</u>, 7 Tenn. 148 (1823).

by two overseers who told her that "she had better . . . tell the truth--it would be better for her." Ann admitted to these men that she had administered the laudanum, and her statement was used as evidence at the trial. Upon appeal, Justice McKinney ruled Ann's confession inadmissible.

> This is a question which admits of no discussion. All the authorities concur, that a confession, to be admissible as evidence, must have been freely and voluntarily made, and not under the influences of promises, or threats. As to what is such a promise or threat, as will exclude a confession, it is laid down, that saying to a prisoner it will be worse for him if he does not confess; or, that it will be better for him if he does, is sufficient to exclude the confession.

McKinney would not "indulge in speculation" about the "probable influence" of a promise or threat in a specific case:

> Certinly not in the case of a timid girl, of tender age, ignorant and illiterate, a slave in chains, whose life had been threatened by her master, and against whom the hand of every one, even those of her own color and condition seems to have been raised.[60]

In the second case, two slaves, Alfred and Anthony, were convicted in February 1853 in Weakley county for the murder of their master. In this case, Justice Caruthers ruled the slaves' confession "legal evidence" because the confessions were made to a justice of the peace during the preliminary examination. According to Caruthers, the magistrate had done his "duty" by informing the prisoners that what they said might be used against them and that

---

[60] Ann v. The State, 30 Tenn. 113-14 (1850).

they were not bound to incriminate themselves. Therefore, Carthers ruled that the confessions were "free and voluntary rather than coerced, and therefore admissible.[61]

One other case dealing with the improper admission of testimony illustrates the protection that the Tennessee Supreme Court provided slave defendants. This case involved the question of whether a master could testify on behalf of his own slave. The Smith county circuit judge had rejected the master's testimony on the "ground of his incompetency from pecuniary interest." The Supreme Court reversed the conviction. Using analogy, Justice Reese pointed out that a father could testify for a minor son and a master for an apprentice even though each might have a valuable interest in the individual on trial. In some cases, furthermore, the master might be the only person cognizant of the guilt or innocence of the slave. Finally, said Reese, "humanity forbids" that society should tell a master he could not testify in favor of his slave. "On the grounds of public policy, of common humanity, of absolute necessity, the master must be held to be competent as a witness for or against the slave"; the master-slave relationship must be treated so that "the guilty should not escape punishment, or the innocent be made to suffer."[62]

---

[61]Alfred and Anthony v. The State, 32 Tenn. 419-21 (1853).

[62]Elijah, a slave, v. The State, 20 Tenn. 100-101 (1831).

Just as the Tennessee Supreme Court reversed trial court convictions of slaves because of procedural irregularities, so it granted slaves new trials because the evidence did not support their conviction. In capital cases involving white defendants, the Supreme Court had established its willingness to conduct an independent review of the evidence and to reverse trial court convictions when "not satisfied with the verdict." As Justice Turley explained in 1849,

> We will weigh the evidence, and, if it preponderate against the verdict, grant a new trial; and we do this out of the great regard in which the law holds life and liberty, declaring as it does, that in every instance where either the one or the other is sought to be assailed by a criminal prosecution, the guilt of the prisoner charged shall be established beyond a reasonable doubt.[63]

In ten capital cases involving white defendants, the Court heard appeals based on the alleged insufficiency of the evidence, reversing three convictions.[64] There were also ten slave cases appealed upon grounds that the evidence did not support the verdict. In <u>Henry v. the State</u>, a case involving attempted rape in Stewart county, the Court felt "scarcely authorized" to give a new trial upon the evidence. However, the Court did reverse the

---

[63]<u>Leake v. the State</u>, 28 Tenn. 93-99 (1849).

[64]<u>Grainger v. the State</u>, 13 Tenn. 377-80 (1830); <u>Allen v. the State</u>, 13 Tenn. 373-75 (1830); <u>Jesse Mitchell v. The State of Tennessee</u>, 13 Tenn. 279-92 (1833).

conviction upon other grounds.[65] In the other nine cases, the Court upheld the circuit court verdict five times and overturned the lower court verdict four times. The Court, then, reversed in about the same proportion of cases involving slaves as it did in cases involving whites.

In one of the slave cases, Moses v. the State, the Court faced the question of whether upon the facts a slave had committed murder or manslaughter. In that case, previously noted, the Court detailed the evidence and decided that Moses had indeed killed his master with malice aforethought.[66] In each of the other four cases where the Court upheld the lower court conviction, the evidence of guilt was circumstantial. In capital cases with white defendants, the Supreme Court had already developed its rules for convicting a defendant upon circumstantial evidence. In Kirby v. The State (1842), the defendant's conviction depended "altogether upon circumstantial evidence." Speaking for the Court, Justice Green wrote the Supreme Court opinion in which he detailed the "train of circumstances" and concluded Kirby's "innocence utterly inconsistent with these circumstances, and unopposed by a single fact inconsistent with his guilt."[67]

---

[65] Henry, a slave, v. The State, 23 Tenn. 263-64 (1852).

[66] See above, pp. 75-78.

[67] Kirby v. The State, 22 Tenn. 290 (1842); also see, Carroll v. The State, 22 Tenn. 305 (1842).

In the four slave cases, the Supreme Court seemingly followed the rule established in Kirby. In each opinion, the Court detailed the evidence upon which it had reached its decision. In fact, in a footnote to two 1844 cases, the court reporter wrote that the cases were "deemed worthy of preservation, as illustrating the principles of circumstantial evidence, and exhibiting the state of facts on which the Supreme Court have felt themselves bound to affirm convictions in cases of capital felony." In one case, the defendant, Jim, had been convicted of the murder of another slave. In the other, Bill had been convicted of assault with intent to commit a rape.[68]

Of the four slave cases which the Supreme Court did reverse "upon the facts," three involved attempted rape and the fourth the murder of another slave. Two appeals involved a single defendant.[69] In one of the most intriguing cases in the annals of antebellum Tennessee jurisprudence, a slave named Major was accused of the attempted rape of a sixteen-year-old white girl named Myra Looper. Major was originally put on trial in Scott county, then

---

[68] Jim, a slave, v. The State, 24 Tenn. 137 (1844); Bill, a slave, v. the State, 24 Tenn. 145-53 (1844). In the other two cases, a Henry county slave named Gilbert was convicted of the murder of his master and a Williamson county slave named Henry was convicted of the murder of two white men who probably were strangers to him. Gilbert v. The State, 26 Tenn. 430-37 (1847); Henry v. the State, 30 Tenn. 155-60 (1850).

[69] The other two cases were Peter v. the State, 24 Tenn. 428-32 (1844) and Nelson v. The State, 32 Tenn. 169-87 (1852).

because no impartial jury could be empaneled, the case was transferred to Morgan county and finally to Fentress county, where Major was tried and convicted. The case was then appealed to the Supreme Court. The Court rejected the technical errors but called for a new trial upon "the merits of the case." The Court was "not content to affirm the conviction" because the record of the proof was "brief, imperfect, and in some respects obscure." The Court was particularly concerned that the identify of the person who had committed the assault had not been proved. The assailant was "greatly disguised," his head "all bundled up with rags." The tracks at the scene of the crime had been made by "broad-toed shoes," and, although Major had worn a pair of broad-toed shoes "a few months before," he was barefoot at sunset on the day of the crime.[70]

In 1857, Major's case was again before the Supreme Court, this time on appeal following conviction at the re-trial. Justice Harris delivered the opinion of the Court. He again rejected the technical grounds for dismissal and considered the case on the "sufficiency of the proof to support the verdict." Harris began by stating that much of the evidence

> . . . will strike the candid, unprejudiced mind with some force as being somewhat incompatible with our views and impressions of human nature and human action and well calculated to excite doubt and distrust of the accuracy of the statements made by the main witness for the prosecution.

---

[70]<u>Major v. The State</u>, 34 Tenn. 8-12 (1854).

Harris catalogued parts of the testimony that he considered "a little strange." He then demonstrated the contradictory nature of the testimony against the prisoner. The Court, Harris said, would not permit a verdict involving capital punishment to stand upon such evidence. He observed that "this case strongly admonished us of the necessity of a watchful vigilance and an unyielding firmness on the part of the judicial officers to see that the invaluable right of a fair trial by an impartial jury" should not be disregarded.[71]

Judge Harris' remarks provide a fitting conclusion to this chapter. With the exception of cases involving slaves who killed whites while resisting punishment, in its appellate jurisdiction the Supreme Court of Tennessee insisted that slave defendants be treated according to the same Due Process Model that applied to free men and accorded slave defendants whatever fairness and impartiality that model afforded.

---

[71] Major v. The State, 36 Tenn. 347-57 (1857).

CHAPTER VII

THE SLAVE DEFENDANT: CAPITAL CRIMES IN THE CIRCUIT AND CRIMINAL COURTS, 1825-1860

The Tennessee Supreme Court's regard for the trial rights of slaves penetrated the judicial structure; its rulings translated into due process for slaves in their original trials. After 1835, Tennessee required that slaves accused of capital crimes be tried in the same courts as free men.[1] Daniel Flanigan has suggested that "where the regularly established courts had jurisdiction over slave crimes," slaves"were more likely to benefit from the entire procedural system that protected whites." Flanigan's suggestion accurately describes the situation in Tennessee.[2]

In the criminal process in Tennessee, an individual accused of a serious crime was entitled to a preliminary examination, a procedure popularly known as the "committal

---

[1]Between 1825 and 1835, the criminal and circuit courts had appellate jurisdiction in such cases, and those trials are included in the statistical data for this chapter.

[2]Flanigan, "Criminal Procedure," p. 553.

trial" or the "committing court."[3] In this procedure, one or more justices of the peace conducted an "examination of witnesses, both on behalf of the state and the prisoner," to determine if the accused should be held for trial.[4] Slaves accused of capital crimes were accorded the benefit of this preliminary examination. Some "committing trials" of slaves lasted for days with the magistrates questioning many witnesses.[5]

The statute required that at the preliminary examination, the magistrate "immediately inform" the accused of "his right to the aid of counsel in every stage of the proceedings" and "allow the defendant a reasonable time to send for counsel, and, if necessary . . . adjourn the examination for that purpose."[6] The precise impact of this statute on the "committing trials" of slaves is uncertain. Some slaves did have counsel at this stage, but others did not.[7]

---

[3]John Hallum, The Diary of an Old Lawyer: Scenes Behind the Curtain (Nashville: Southwestern Publishing House, 1895), p. 39.

[4]Law of North Carolina, 1715, ch. 16, in Scott, Laws, 1: 13, Law of Tennessee, 1817, ch. 100; Meigs and Cooper, The Code of Tennessee, pp. 887, 891, 894.

[5]Greene County, Circuit Court, Minutes, February 1841, pp. 47-48; June 1843, p. 565; January 1853, pp. 26-28; June 1857, p. 571; June 1859, pp. 615-16.

[6]Meigs and Cooper, The Code of Tennessee, p. 899.

[7]Nashville Republican Banner, 7 September 1858; 10 January 1859; Nashville Daily Gazette, 16 September 1858.

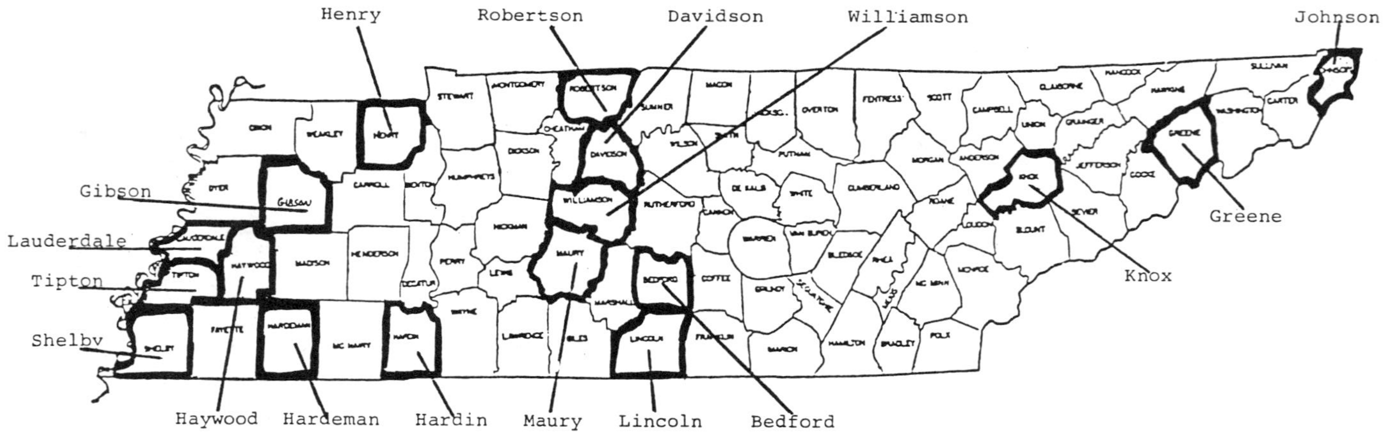

Map 3. Map of Tennessee, 1860; circuit courts surveyed.

The "committing court" usually bound a slave over to the grand jury, but not always. In Putnam county, in 1856, a slave was "arrested on suspicion" of the murder of a local storeowner. The slave "underwent an examination before the magistrate . . . but no evidence was elicited to implicate him, and he was discharged from custody." That December, a Nashville slave was arrested on suspicion of arson but was "subsequently discharged." Finally, in Maury county, a slave named Burrell was taken and tried before Henry A. Miller for a felony and "said negro slave was on trial before said justice discharged."[8]

Slaves bound over to the grand jury could be released on bond. Tennessee law provided that "in all cases of proceedings against slaves," bail could be given "in the same manner as bail is given in prosecutions against free white persons." This provision was qualified in two ways: first, in capital cases, slaves could not be bailed "when proof [was] evident or the presumption great"; second, bail for slaves was set at "double the amount of the value of the accused slave."[9]

---

[8] Nashville Daily Gazette, 12 March 1856; Nashville Republican Banner, 2 December 1856; Maury County, Circuit Court, Minutes, January 1858, pp. 629-30; Garrett Scrapbook, TSLmd.

[9] Law of Tennessee, 1825, ch. 24; Meigs and Cooper, The Code of Tennessee, p. 511. Presumably, the double bail provision was to guarantee that the master would present the slave for trial. Tennessee never enacted a law to compensate a master for a slave executed for a crime. An executed slave, then, would be a total

Even with these restrictions, some slaves were freed on bond after the committing court had decided to turn their cases over to the grand jury. In Nashville, in January 1860, a slave named Ellen was accused of attempted poisoning. The examining magistrate decided that she should be held for trial and set her bail at $3,000, "which was given by the master of the girl."[10]

A slave not discharged by the "committal court" was bound over to the grand jury. Tennessee law expressly provided that no slave accused of a capital crime could be tried "unless an indictment or presentment is first found by the grand jury."[11]

Occasionally, a case might not make it from the committing court to the grand jury. In December 1860, the Davidson county criminal court granted a writ of _habeas corpus_ and released the slave Florence prior to grand jury action because she was of "such tender years and age that she is incapable of the commission of a crime."[12]

---

financial loss. If bail were set at the actual value of the slave, the owner might prefer, out of humane instincts perhaps, to sell the slave out of state rather than to see his chattel executed. The double provision, however, increased the owner's potential loss if the accused slave was not presented for trial. The owner would lose not only the slave but the dollar value of the slave as well.

[10] _Nashville Daily Gazette_, 21 January 1860; _Nashville Republican Banner_, 21 January 1860. Also see, _Nashville Republican Banner_, 17 September 1858.

[11] Law of Tennessee, 1835, ch. 19.

[12] Davidson County, Criminal Court, _Minutes_, April 1860, p. 79.

Another circumstance could prevent grand jury action. A grand jury could act only upon a bill of indictment filed by the attorney general of the circuit court. However, prosecution in antebellum Tennessee was a function of the private citizen. Ordinarily, an attorney general would not send a bill of indictment to the grand jury unless it was signed by some private individual as prosecutor, and, from time to time, slaves were released from custody because no person was willing to prosecute. In 1849, in Henry county, with "no prosecutor appearing," the circuit court released Jim, a slave accused of attempted murder.[13]

However, when there was no prosecutor, the judge could order the attorney general to file a bill of indictment "ex officio." For example, in September 1836, in Henry county, the judge ordered that a bill of indictment be preferred "without any prosecutor marked thereon" against Jacob, a slave accused of attempted murder.[14]

The attorney general could also send a bill of indictment to the grand jury based on the inquest of a coroner's jury. In Bedford county in 1857, the "return of the verdict of the jury of inquest by Moses Marshall

---

[13]Henry County, Circuit Court, _Minutes_, January 1849, p. 466. For other cases with a similar result, see ibid., January 1851, p. 9; Hardeman County, Circuit Court, _Minutes_, October 25, 1848, n.p.; Maury County, Circuit Court, _Minutes_, January 1860, p. 587.

[14]Henry County, Circuit Court, _Minutes_, September 1836, pp. 162, 163.

coroner" served as the basis for the indictment of the slave Dick for the murder of his master. In Williamson county, in 1854, the grand jury returned a bill of indictment against Jack for the murder of another slave. The bill of indictment had been "filed upon an inquisition of murder by coronor's jury."[15]

Because of the secrecy of grand jury proceedings, not much is known about their activities in cases regarding slaves. The evidence that does exist contains little to indicate that grand juries treated slave defendants differently than white defendants. Witnesses, both black and white, slave and free, were called to testify.[16]

---

[15]Bedford County, Circuit Court, Minutes, August 1857, pp. 57-59; Williamson County, Circuit Court, Minutes, March 1854, p. 37. Also see, Haywood County, Circuit Court, Minutes, September 1859, p. 121.

[16]Students of slavery consistently have condemned statutory prohibitions of slave testimony against white offenders, but little has been written about slave testimony when blacks were defendants. William Goodell, The American Slave Code (n.p.: The American & Foreign Anti-Slavery Society, 1853; reprint ed., New York: Negro Universities Press, 1968), pp. 300-304; Stampp, The Peculiar Institution, p. 222; Genovese, Roll, Jordan, Roll, pp. 32, 38.

Tennessee statutes in this regard were contradictory. According to a 1794 territorial statute, slaves could testify only "against" other black men. With this law still on the books, the legislature in 1815 directed that slave courts could hear any slave testimony they wished, for or against a slave, so long as it was supported by "pregnant circumstances." In 1836, however, the Supreme Court ruled that the 1794 statute controlled and that slaves could not testify on behalf of black defendants, slave or free. The legislature quickly annulled this Supreme Court decision by directing that "all negroes" could be competent witnesses "for each other." This added significantly to the protection

Indictments were framed with care, and the grand juries did not always indict. Enough returns of "Not a True Bill" have survived to demonstrate that grand juries did not automatically indict slave defendants. In the counties surveyed, grand juries refused to indict sixteen (10 percent) of the one hundred and sixty slaves accused of capital offenses.

It is uncertain whether slaves were represented by counsel before the grand jury. However, once indicted, slaves clearly were entitled to an attorney. In 1835, when the General Assembly gave the regular courts exclusive jurisdiction over the trial of slaves for capital crimes, the lawmakers guaranteed this right to slaves, directing that when a master did not employ counsel in his slave's defense, "the court shall assign him counsel."[17]

The assignment of counsel in such cases took place at the arraignment, the next step in the trial process following grand jury indictment. The need to assign counsel to slave defendants did not arise frequently. Only

---

afforded slave defendants. Law of Tennessee, 1794, ch. 1, in Haywood and Cobbs, The Statute Laws, 1: 377; Law of Tennessee, 1815, ch. 138; Jones v. the State, 19 Tenn. 120 (1838); Law of Tennessee, 1839, ch. 41; Meigs and Cooper, The Code of Tennessee, p. 687.

[17]Law of Tennessee, 1835, ch. 19; Meigs and Cooper, The Code of Tennessee, p. 511. An 1821 Tennessee law directed that "every person" accused of a crime was entitled to an attorney and if "unable to employ counsel . . . to have counsel appointed by the court." There is evidence that the courts applied this law to slaves even before 1835. Law of Tennessee, 1821, ch. 22.

thirteen of the one hundred and sixty slaves in this study had court-appointed counsel. In such cases, the court usually assigned more than one attorney to defend a slave. In fact, in only two cases was a single attorney assigned to the defense.[18]

Court-appointed attorneys seem to have been of high caliber. Many were or would become men of prominence in the state. Capable court-appointed attorneys to the contrary notwithstanding, only one of the thirteen slaves so defended was acquitted.[19] The other twelve were convicted and sentenced to death. Of those twelve, one was granted a new trial but was not retried, and was re-leased.[20] Another had her conviction overturned by the Supreme Court and was not retried.[21] Of thirteen

---

[18]Williamson County, Circuit Court, Minutes, November 1849, pp. 90-92; Henry County, Circuit Court, Minutes, September 1836, pp. 162-64.

[19]Williamson County, Circuit Court, Minutes, March 1850, p. 128.

James P. Thomas recalled that, on the whole, "the Negro was ably defended by the best legal Talent." Schweninger, ed., From Tennessee Slave to St. Louis Entrepreneur, p. 58.

[20]Henry County, Circuit Court, Minutes, September 1836, pp. 171, 172-73.

[21]Williamson County, Circuit Court, Minutes, March 1850, pp. 154-55; March 1851, p. 238. For the other cases involving court-appointed attorneys, see Davidson County, Criminal Court, Minutes, June 1842, pp. 43, 44, 45, 46, 63; Henry County, Circuit Court, Minutes, September 1845, p. 269, 272; March 1846, pp. 297, 300, 302, 305; May 1846, p. 314; September 1846, pp. 336, 337, 338, 347; Lincoln County, Circuit Court, Minutes, November 1859, pp. 97-98, 107; March 1860, p. 143; July 1860, pp.

individuals defended by court-appointed counsel, then, only three escaped the gallows. Given this record and the professional standing of court-appointed attorneys, it is at least a reasonable speculation that such lawyers might have been forced to take likely "losing" cases.

At the arraignment, slave defendants, like free defendants, were allowed to answer the charges against them. Packer has suggested that in a "successful" Crime Control criminal justice system, defendants would enter pleas of guilty.[22] In Tennessee, this was not the case for slaves accused of capital crimes. Only two of the slaves in this study pleaded guilty upon their arraignment.

At the slave's arraignment, his attorney could file a motion for a continuance. When requested, continuances were routinely granted. In the courts under study, only once was a motion for a continuance denied, and that case had already been delayed one term by an earlier request for a continuance which had been granted.[23]

191, 220; Williamson County, Circuit Court, Minutes, July 1842, p. 31; March 1843, pp. 459, 470, 498; July 1843, pp. 539-40; March 1850, pp. 115, 129; November 1850, pp. 194, 199, 208, 215; Maury County, Circuit Court, Minutes, January 1837, pp. 397, 406, 414; Gibson County, Circuit Court, Minutes, July 1842, pp. 403-404; November 1842, p. 426; Greene County, Circuit Court, Minutes, February 1843, pp. 482-85, 496-97, 503, 505; October 1852, pp. 624-25, 637, 647, 653, 660-61.

[22] Packer, The Limits of the Criminal Sanction, pp. 162-63.

[23] Hardin County, Circuit Court, Minutes, January 1846, pp. 330-31; May 1846, p. 353.

Although continuances were possible, a slave's case was likely to be dealt with quickly (see Table 10). Ninety-nine of the one hundred and sixty slaves in this study had some decision made the first term their cases appeared in the minutes. Fifty-five of the slaves had their cases heard by the petit jury the same term that the grand jury returned its indictment. Only forty-three had their cases heard by a petit jury at a term later than the one in which the grand jury returned its indictment. Slaves seem to have had little to fear from a speedy trial. Only fifteen percent of those slaves whose cases were disposed of in the first possible term were convicted while thirty-one percent of those tried at a later term were judged guilty.

Jury selection is, of course, central to the fairness of criminal trials. As one scholar has observed, "the right to challenge jurors is necessary to give meaning to the right of trial by jury."[24] Tennessee slaves accused

---

[24]Clark, "Aspects of the North Carolina Slave Code," p. 151.

The Tennessee legislature had difficulty settling on the proper make-up of the jury in a slave trial. Originally, jurors had to be slaveholders. Tennessee lawmakers eliminated this requirement in 1815 and then reinstated it in 1819. In 1825, the legislature relaxed the requirement somewhat by allowing nonslaveholders to serve as jurors if not challenged by either the prosecution or the defense, and, in 1835, when the legislature gave the circuit courts exclusive original jurisdiction over capital trials of slaves, it directed that "all persons who would be competent jurors to serve on the trial of a free a person, shall be competent jurors on the trial of any slave or slaves." This remained unchanged throughout the remainder of the antebellum era. Law of North Carolina, 1741, ch. 24, in Haywood, Public Acts, p. 54; Law of

of capital crimes fared well in this regard. The 1825 legislation that gave the circuit courts appellate jurisdiction over the slave courts provided that the owner of a slave on trial for his life "shall have the right to challenge preemptorily as many jurors as a free white person is allowed to challenge in similar cases."[25] Presumably, the owner of a slave faced no restrictions on challenges for cause; The Code of 1858 provided that the owner of a slave "may challenge for cause, in the same manner as a free white person charged with a like offense."[26]

The evidence suggests that courts allowed attorneys to use these challenges in good measure in protecting their slave clients. For example, in the 1859 Memphis trial of two slaves for the murder of a white man, it took five days to empanel the jury.[27] In the 1849 Sumner county trial of Moses for the murder of his master, the court exhausted three panels of veniremen on the first day of jury

---

Tennessee, 1815, ch. 138; Law of Tennessee, 1819, ch. 32; Law of Tennessee, 1825, ch. 25; Law of Tennessee, 1831, ch. 103; Law of Tennessee, 1835, ch. 19; Meigs and Cooper, The Code of Tennessee, p. 510.

[25]Law of Tennessee, 1825, ch. 24.

[26]Meigs and Cooper, The Code of Tennessee, p. 511.

[27]City of Memphis, Criminal Court, Minutes, February 1859, pp. 90-97. Also see, ibid., December 1860, pp. 489-500; Williamson County, Circuit Court, Minutes, July 1858, pp. 79, 87; Hardin County, Circuit Court, Minutes, May 1846, p. 349; Lincoln County, Circuit Court, Minutes, July 1860, pp. 191, 195, 196; Maury County, Circuit Court, Minutes, May 1856, pp. 239, 241.

selection, two on the second, and five on the third, and two more on the fourth before a jury could be chosen.[28] In the Dyer county trial of a slave, Ned, for the murder of Bartley Ridings, the court exhausted "three panels consisting of forty men each" without selecting a jury. The judge decided that "there was no possibile chance to get a fair and impartial trial" and granted Ned a change of venue to Gibson county.[29]

Tennessee law provided that in all criminal trials, the judge could order the site of the trial changed to another county when an impartial jury could not be selected in the county where the crime was committed or when "undue excitement" against the defendant meant that "a fair trial could not probably be had."[30] As Ned's case demonstrated, slaves were allowed the benefit of this provision but changes of venue in slave cases were not common. Only seven of the one hundred and sixty slaves in this study had their trials moved to another county. The results in these

---

[28] "State v. Moses," Manuscript Transcript, pp. 3-4, Case Files, Middle District, Tennessee Supreme Court, TSA. Also for the same result in other trials, see "Major alias Nig v. State of Tennessee" (1857), Manuscript Transcript, pp. 42-43, ibid.; "State v. Major alias Nig" (1854), Manuscript Transcript, pp. 7-8, ibid.; "The State of Tennessee v. Bob and Jacob Slaves," Manuscript Transcript, ibid.

[29] Gibson County, Circuit Court, Minutes, November 1852, pp. 496, 497.

[30] Laws of Tennessee, 1825, ch. 68; 1825, ch. 78; 1827, ch. 30; Meigs and Cooper, The Code of Tennessee, p. 921.

cases were mixed. Of five whose final disposition is known, only one produced an outright acquittal. Two slaves accused of murder were acquitted of the capital charge but were convicted of manslaughter, and two slaves were convicted and executed.[31]

When a slave's case finally did go to the jury, as in the trials of free men, a number of results might occur. The jury might not be able to reach a verdict which would necessitate the judge's declaring a mistrial. The evidence suggests that a mistrial was almost tantamount to an acquittal. Only five of the fourteen cases producing mistrials were tried a second time. Three of the retrials resulted in acquittals, and one resulted in another mistrial.[32] In only one case for which the outcome is known was a slave who experienced a mistrial tried again and convicted of the original capital charge.[33]

---

[31]Two were switched from Shelby county to Fayette county where the records are not extant, and the results are therefore unknown. Shelby County, Circuit Court, Minutes, September 1851, pp. 388-89; January 1860, p. 259; Hardin County, Circuit Court, Minutes, January 1848, pp. 458-59; Perry County, Circuit Court, Minutes, September 1850, p. 422; Gibson County, Circuit Court, Minutes, August 1859, pp. 47-58; Weakley County, Circuit Court, Minutes, October 1859, pp. 460, 464, 465; Gibson County, Circuit Court, Minutes, October 1852, pp. 497-98.

[32]Maury County, Circuit Court, Minutes, September 1850, pp. 559-60; May 1851, pp. 28, 40-41; Lauderdale County, Circuit Court, Minutes, October 1850, p. 291; Haywood County, Circuit Court, Minutes, November 1850,p. 451.

[33]This was a case, in Hardeman county, of one slave killing another. Hardeman County, Circuit Court, Minutes, March 1, March 3, June 27, June 30, 1854, n.p.;

From the point of view of a defendant the happiest verdict a jury could reach was one of acquittal. However the defendant might be acquitted of the capital charge and held for trial on a lesser offense.[34] In Lincoln county in 1852, the slave Adam was acquitted of attempted rape but held for trial on a charge of aggravated assault and battery.[35] In Davidson county in 1837, the jury acquitted Charlotte of the murder of "an infant," but the court ordered her held "to answer to a charge of manslaughter.[36]

After 1854, the statutes allowed the circuit or criminal court jury to acquit a slave charged with murder

---

The outcome is unknown in two Shelby county mistrials: Manuel, charged with the murder of a white man, William Lewis; and Peter, charged with the murder of David Skanklin "a free man of color." Shelby County, Circuit Court, <u>Minutes</u>, May 1859, pp. 8-9, 100-101; September 1859, pp. 132, 134, 222; Janury 1860, p. 259; City of Memphis, Criminal Court, <u>Minutes</u>, February 1861, pp. 750-51; October 1861, p. 651.

One slave, Angelina in Robertson county, was retried on non-capital charges. See below, pp. 208-209.

[34]The same thing could occur after a grand jury failed to indict. In 1851, in Davidson county, the grand jury failed to return an indictment against a slave charged with an unspecified felony. The court then ordered the slave "handed over to a magistrate to be proceeded with according to law." Davidson County, Criminal Court, <u>Minutes</u>, April 1851, p. 104.

[35]Lincoln County, Circuit Court, <u>Minutes</u>, July 1851, pp. 300, 307; November 1851, pp. 343, 344, 347, 353; March 1852, p. 386.

[36]Davidson County, Circuit Court, <u>Minutes</u>, September 1837, p. 267. The same result occurred in the 1852 Gibson county trial of Ned, accused of murdering Bartley Ridings with a weeding hoe. Gibson County, Circuit Court, <u>Minutes</u>, November 1852, pp. 494-99, 502.

of the capital offense and convict him of manslaughter. Eight murder trials ended in such a verdict. The resulting sentences varied, but they tended to be harsh, whether the victim was white or black. Two slaves received one hundred lashes for the killing of other slaves.[37] Another bondsman was sentenced to receive one hundred lashes, to spend ten days in jail, and then to receive another one hundred lashes.[38] In Tipton county in 1856, Tom was convicted of the axe slaying of a fellow slave and sentenced to two hundred and fifty lashes "to be inflicted from time to time" over the course of a week.[39] The worst sentence in manslaughter cases were handed down when the victim was white. In Davidson county in 1860, Jim had gotten into a fight with a fellow black man. He had lashed out at the man with a saw, missed, and fatally struck Julia, the daughter of Jim's white employer.[40] Tried for murder, Jim was convicted of manslaughter and sentenced by the jury

---

[37]Davidson County, Criminal Court, Minutes, April 1861, pp. 370, 381, 385; Williamson County, Circuit Court, Minutes, November 1860, pp. 348, 378, 383; Nashville Daily Gazette, 10 April 1861; Nashville Republican Banner, 11 August 1860, 10 April 1861.

[38]This slave, Bob, was convicted in Bedford county of beating another slave to death. Bedford County, Circuit Court, Minutes, August 1859 (vol. 1858-59), pp. 631-32; (vol. 1859-60), pp. 31-32, 34, 37, 99.

[39]Tipton County, Circuit Court, Minutes, September 1855, pp. 700-701; January 1856, p. 721.

[40]It is clear that Jim was a slave. Apparently, he was hired to the victim's father.

to three hundred and fifty lashes. With perhaps unintended irony, the jury instructed that the lashes "be administered so as not to jeopardize life or health." The judge, however, left it to the "discretion of the sheriff as to the number of lashes to be applied at any one time."[41]

The most brutal non-capital sentences came in two trials for attempted murder in Shelby county. In each case, the slave was acquitted of the capital offense but convicted of a lesser offense; aggravated assault in one instance and malicious stabbing in the other. Squire, convicted in September 1861 of aggravated assault, was sentenced to ten days in jail and "thirty-nine lashes on each of those days." The judge ordered that the punishment be omitted on the "intermediate sabbath" and be given "in moderation." Sam, convicted of the malicious stabbing of William Reddit in January 1860, received an even more frightful sentence. He was sentenced to ten days in the county jail "and each morning of the ten days that he receive one hundred lashes on his naked hide with a leather strap and each morning of the ten days that he stand in the stocks one hour."[42] The only exception to this

---

[41]Davidson County, Criminal Court, Minutes, December 1860, p. 226; August 1861, pp. 452, 456, 458; Nashville Republican Banner, 8 November 1860; Nashville Daily Gazette, 11 September 1861.

[42]Shelby County, Circuit Court, Minutes, January 1861, p. 30; September 1861, pp. 66-67; January 1860, pp. 262-63, 263-64, 310-311.

pattern of harsh sentences in manslaughter convictions was that handed down to Spencer in Memphis in 1859. Convicted of manslaughter in the shooting death of a white man, Gideon Brown, Spencer was sentenced to be "confined in the pillory for the period of one hour" and to forty lashes "on the bare back."[43]

Of course, the petit jury might convict the slave outright, an outcome that condemned the defendant to execution. However, this result was not unalterable. Even when a jury convicted a slave of a capital crime, the Tennessee criminal process provided obstacles which could impede or even prevent his progress to the gallows. The trial judge, for example, might sustain a motion for a new trial. This did not happen frequently, but it did occur. In 1836, in Henry county, Jacob was convicted of attempted murder. The circuit judge "set aside the verdict," and Jacob was never tried again.[44] In Williamson county in 1837, Frank was convicted of the attempted rape of Prudence Young. Although the _Nashville Daily Gazette_ reported that the "evidence of his guilt is said to be conclusive," the

---

[43]Spencer's light sentence may have resulted from his having been tried with another slave, Isaac, who was convicted of the murder and eventually was sentenced to hang. City of Memphis, Criminal Court, _Minutes_, October 1858, pp. 505-507, 736; February 1859, pp. 190, 120-21.

[44]The attorney general entered a _nolle prosequi_ in the case. Henry County, Circuit Court, _Minutes_, September 1836, pp. 162, 163, 164, 171, 172-73; January 1839, p. 376.

circuit judge granted him a new trial. On his retrial, Frank was convicted again and sentenced to hang.[45]

Appeals to the Supreme Court constituted the most frequent obstacle to execution thrown up after conviction for a capital crime. In the counties under study, appeals were made following twenty-four of the forty convictions (see Table 11). The results of these appeals were mixed. In fourteen instances, the trial court convictions were overturned. In eight cases, lower court convictions were upheld and the defendants went to the gallows.[46]

Of course, an overturned conviction did not conclude a case. It still had to be acted on by the lower court. After the fourteen successful appeals, only four slaves were again tried and convicted. Three of those cases were appealed a second time, but the outcome of those appeals is unknown. Only one slave of the fourteen was acquitted on retrial. However, six slaves were released rather than tried again. One slave was retried and convicted of a lesser non-capital offense. Taken together, over one-half of the fourteen slaves whose convictions were successfully appealed had the process work in their favor; seven were released and eight escaped the hangman.

---

[45] Williamson County, Circuit Court, Minutes, July 1857, pp. 500-501; November 1856, pp. 512, 520, 524; July 1858, pp. 89, 91; Nashville Daily Gazette, 9 August 1857, 23 July, 25 July 1858.

[46] The outcome in two cases is unknown.

In the final analysis, the appeal process was only moderately successful in terms of saving lives. The twenty-four appeals involved twenty-one slaves. The appeals process saved eight slaves from execution, while only delaying the march of nine others to the gallows.[47]

For forty-six of the one hundred and sixty slaves in this study, a jury verdict was not the final disposition of the case. A case might never reach the jury. Some defendants escaped or died before coming to trial,[48] but more commonly the attorney general, with the court's permission, refused to proceed with the case.[49]

---

[47] The outcome is unknown in four cases.

[48] For example, in Maury county in 1861, Tom, accused of the attempted rape of Hannah Roberts, died of "jail fever" before he could be brought to trial, and the court ordered that "this suit abate." Maury County, Circuit Court, Minutes, January 1861, p. 202; May 1861, pp. 367, 395; Nashville Daily Gazette, 19 February 1861.

In Robertson county, the grand jury indicted John on a charge of rape. He was released on bail. He defaulted and the attorney general was forced to dismiss the case. In December 1860, in Davidson county, Henry was accused of the murder of another slave, Ephraim. He also was released on bail and never came to trial. In 1864, his case was stricken from the docket. Robertson County, Circuit Court, Minutes, February 1848, pp. 338, 348-49; February 1850, p. 383; Davidson County, Criminal Court, Minutes, December 1860, pp. 234-35, 251; April 1861, p. 435; August 1861, p. 505; December 1861, pp. 565, 599; April 1862, p. 59; April 1864, pp. 379-80. Also see, Maury County, Circuit Court, Minutes, May 1837, p. 497; September 1838, p. 188.

[49] With the "assent" of the court, the attorney general would enter a nolle prosequi in the case. Some such entries merely indicated that the attorney general was unhappy with the way the indictment was framed. In these instances, new bills of indictment were presented immediately and the defendants went to trial. Shelby

The attorney general might choose not to prosecute because he had decided that the slave had not committed a capital offense and therefore that the circuit court had no jurisdiction. In Gibson county in 1855, for example, John arrested for burglary, but the court, "being satisfied from the statement of the attorney general" that John "has not been guilty of burglary," ordered that he "be handed over to a Justice of the Peace . . . to be tried for larceny."[50] The attorney general might not want to go to trial because he thought the evidence insufficient to convict. This seems to have occurred in the case of Ellen, a slave accused in Davidson county of having served "poisoned coffee." During Ellen's committal trial, the Nashville Daily Gazette reported that the evidence against her "was not of a very positive character."[51] One case appears to have involved a plea bargain. In 1859, in Davidson county,

---

County, Circuit Court, Minutes, May 1850, pp. 441-42, 476, 478-79; September 1853, pp. 75-76, 78; Williamson County, Circuit Court, Minutes, July 1842, pp. 29, 30-31; Bedford County, Circuit Court, Minutes, August 1855, pp. 516, 526-27; April 1856, p. 156.

[50] Gibson County, Circuit Court, Minutes, November 1853, p. 16. For other examples of this same type of action, see Davidson County, Circuit Court, Minutes, September 1837, p. 250; Bedford County, Circuit Court, Minutes, December 1859, p. 229; Hardeman County, Circuit Court, Minutes, June 28, 1853, n.p.; Maury County, Circuit Court, Minutes, January 1858, pp. 602, 619; Robertson County, Circuit Court, Minutes, February 1860, pp. 493, 575.

[51] Davidson County, Criminal Court, Minutes, April 1860, p. 27; December 1860, p. 269; Nashville Daily Gazette, 17 January, 21 January 1860.

Comfort Eakin was arrested for infanticide while her mother, Mary Eakin, was charged as an accessory. The attorney general refused to prosecute the mother, and Comfort pleaded guilty to manslaughter. She received five lashes.[52]

Finally, the attorney general might refuse to go to trial because the accused slave had already been dealt with in an extra-judicial fashion. In 1858, in Greene county, three slaves, Andy, Tom, and Joe, were accused of a "felony." The slaves, "by consent of their masters," were "after the trial before the Justice severaly [sic] whipped." The prosecutor "suggested" to the court that he did "not desire further to prosecute," and the court, believing "that the ends of justice have been substantially reached," dismissed the slaves.[53] It may never be known how many times _nolle prosequi_ disguised a reality like that of the Gallatin slave who was "whipped and cleared" for the murder of another black.[54]

Even after a case went to trial, there were many points at which the attorney general might stop the proceedings by refusing to prosecute further. For example, in Knox county in 1842, a slave, Pleasant, was indicted three times for the burglary of three separate houses. Pleasant

---

[52]Davidson County, Criminal Court, _Minutes_, December 1859, pp. 480-81; August 1860, p. 102; _Nashville Daily Gazette_, 26 September 1859.

[53]Greene County, Circuit Court, _Minutes_, June 1858, p. 193.

[54]_Nashville Daily Gazette_, 13 March 1860.

was acquitted twice by different juries and the attorney general decided not to take the third indictment to trial.[55] An attorney general also might be reluctant to retry a slave after a mistrial. Thus, in Davidson county in 1853, the jury failed to agree on a verdict in the trial of Henry for attempted rape. During the next term, the attorney general dismissed the case. In Haywood county in 1859, the circuit jury could not agree on a verdict in the trial of Beddy for the murder of her child. The case was continued for a number of terms after the mistrial and was finally dismissed. In Robertson county, Angelina was tried twice for attempted murder. Both times the jury failed to agree and mistrials were declared. The attorney general refused to prosecute a third time. However, Angelina was not released. In an extraordinary procedure, "all the parties" agreed that she "should be further punished." To "avoid the trouble and expense of assigning her to another tribunal for that purpose," the "parties" submitted her to the circuit judge for punishment. He sentenced her to receive "on her bare skin one hundred lashes or blows . . . publically at the Court house." The punishment was "to be inflicted with a paddle or some instrument other than a cowskin, so as not to break or lacerate the person." Ten "lashes or blows" were to be inflicted each day, "unless

---

[55] Knox County, Circuit Court, Minutes, February 1842, pp. 196-97; June 1842, pp. 282-84, 304, 311, 313-14; October 1842, pp. 464, 471.

said Angelina shall elect to receive more or less per day." Angelina was allowed to give bond "that she make her appearance every day to receive her lashes."[56]

An attorney general might not want to risk another trial if the judge sustained a motion for a new trial after the original conviction. For example, in the 1836 Henry county conviction of Jacob for attempted murder, the judge sustained a motion for a new trial, but the attorney general was "unwilling to prosecute further." The grand jury reindicted Jacob, whereupon the attorney general refused to prosecute on that indictment, as well.[57]

Finally, the attorney general might not be willing to try a case again after it had been successfully appealed to the Supreme Court. In Franklin county in 1853, Tom was indicted for the murder of a white woman. Two mistrials occurred before Tom secured a change of venue to Lincoln county. In Lincoln county, Tom was convicted and sentenced to hang. He appealed to the Supreme Court. The decision is not reported, but the lower court conviction must have been overturned because the next year the attorney general

---

[56]Davidson County, Criminal Court, Minutes, December 1852, p. 343; April 1853, p. 385; August 1853, p. 583. Haywood County, Circuit Court, Minutes, September 1859, pp. 121, 289, 304; September 1860, p. 423; February 1861, p. 479; May 1861, p. 490; Robertson County, Circuit Court, Minutes, February 1853, pp. 318-19, 335-36; October 1853, pp. 392, 405; February 1854, pp. 430, 441; June 1854, p. 464.

[57]Henry County, Circuit Court, Minutes, September 1836, pp. 162, 163, 171, 172-73; January 1849, p. 376.

said that he wished to proceed "no further against the defendant." The case was "dismissed," and Tom was ordered "discharged from custody" and delivered to his owner.[58]

In the seventeen counties included in this study, during the years 1825-1861, there were one hundred and ninety-eight prosecutions against one hundred and sixty slaves.[59]

Only forty (20 percent) of these prosecutions ended in conviction on the capital charge (see Table 13). Another eighteen (9 percent) ended in conviction for a

---

[58] Lincoln County, Circuit Court, Minutes, November 1854, pp. 199-200; March 1856, pp. 106, 126, 144, 153-54; March 1857, p. 337.

The same result occurred in two Williamson county cases and one in Shelby county. Peter was convicted in November 1844 for the attempted rape of Minerva Skelly. His appeal to the Supreme Court was successful and the attorney general refused to prosecute further. In 1851, the Williamson county attorney general refused to put Ann back on trial for the death of her owner's daughter after her earlier conviction had been overturned by the Supreme Court. In Shelby county in June 1856, Ruben was convicted of the murder of another slave. He appealed successfully and the case was "nollied" in the June term 1860. Williamson County, Circuit Court, Minutes, July 1844, pp. 404-405, 416; November 1844, pp. 444, 446, 455; March 1845, p. 487; November 1849, pp. 90-92; March 1850, pp. 126, 128, 154-55; March 1851, p. 238. Peter v. The State, 24 Tenn. 432 (1844); Ann v. the State, 30 Tenn. 116 (1850). City of Memphis, Criminal Court, Minutes, October 1856, pp. 477-78; June 1857, pp. 256, 263, 401; June 1860, p. 125.

[59] A prosecution is defined as an opportunity to proceed to trial. It takes into account multiple trials of a single individual. When there was more than one indivdual included within an indictment, each was counted separately.

Forty-five percent of the slaves were tried for murder, seventeen percent for attempted murder, thirteen percent for burglary, ten percent for rape or attempted rape, and eight percent for arson (see Table 12).

non-capital offense.[60] Therefore, only fifty-eight of the one hundred and ninety-eight prosecutions (29 percent) produced any kind of conviction whatsoever. Sixty-eight (34 percent) of the prosecutions ended in acquittal of the capital charge, either by the grand jury or the petit jury, and fifty-five (28 percent) ended in acquittal of all charges. Sixty-five (33 percent) of the capital prosecutions were dismissed and fourteen (7 percent) ended in a mistrial.

Because of multiple indictments, multiple trials and multiple defendants, these statistics for prosecution should be refined. Perhaps a better analysis is the final outcome of each case for the individual slave involved (see Table 14). Of the one hundred and sixty slaves, only twenty-two (14 per-cent) went to the gallows. Eighteen more (11 percent) were either convicted or held for trial for lesser offenses. This means that one hundred and nine (68 percent) of the slaves eventually were released.[61]

---

[60]The verdict is known in only twelve of the cases, but in each the slave was convicted. It is a safe assumption that the outcome was the same in the other six cases.

[61]There is little support here for Bertram Wyatt-Brown when he, citing a Tennessee example, asserts that in slave trials the "outcome was foreordained . . . as one would expect . . . slaves were usually . . . hanged." In fact, we do not even know what finally happened to the defendant, Elijah, in Wyatt-Brown's example. Elijah was twice convicted of attempted murder of a white man in Smith county. Both convictions were overturned by the Supreme Court. The circuit judge then declared that "a fair and impartial trial [for Elijah] cannot be had" in Smith county

These statistics reveal some regional variation in the treatment of slave defendants. By far, the highest rate of acquittal and the lowest rate of convictions were registered in East Tennessee. Conversely, the lowest rate of acquittal and the highest rate of conviction were recorded in West Tennessee. The rates in Middle Tennessee tended toward those in the West.

The murder cases also show revealing variation when the outcomes are analyzed by race of the victims (see Table 15). When the murder victim was white, the rate of conviction and the rate of conviction on the capital charge was higher. On the other hand, less than one-half of the prosecutions against slaves for killing whites ended in a conviction of murder and the rate of acquittal was about the same whether the victim was black or white. It should also be noted that all of the victims of the twenty-seven slaves accused of attempted murder were white, and that in those cases, only two bondsmen were convicted on the capital charge and two for a lesser offense. Nine slaves were acquitted, and fourteen were dismissed before coming to trial.

---

and transferred the case to to Dekalb county, for which, sadly, there are no extant antebellum circuit court records. _Elijah, a Slave, v. The State_, 20 Tenn. 99 (1839); _Elijah, a Slave, v. The State_, 21 Tenn. 476 (1841); Smith County, Circuit Court, _Minutes_, April 1942, p. 26; Wyatt-Brown, _Southern Honor_, p. 389. Other scholars have reached different conclusions. See Edward L. Ayers, _Vengeance and Justice: Crime and Punishment in the 19th-Century American South_ (New York and Oxford: Oxford University Press, 1984), p. 134.

In capital trials, it made a difference if the white victim was the master of the accused slave. Eight slaves were tried for the murder or attempted murder of their masters. Two were acquitted, and six were convicted and sentenced to hang (see Table 16). Slaves accused of murder or attempted murder of whites who were not their owners fared much better. Twenty-eight slaves were charged with killing whites other than their masters; six were convicted of murder and two of manslaughter. Twenty-six slaves were accused of attempted murder of whites not their owners. Two were convicted on the capital charge and two for a lesser offense. (See Table 17.)

Comparing the data for prosecutions against slaves with the same data for prosecutions against whites for murder in the first degree, the only capital offense for whites, one is struck by the similarities. (Tables 18 & 19) The rate of acquittal by grand and petit juries is nearly the same for slaves (28 percent) and whites (31 percent). Slave prosecutions were dismissed at a somewhat higher rate, thirty percent as opposed to twenty-one percent for whites. The gross conviction rate only slightly favored whites, twenty-eight percent of white prosecutions ending in conviction compared with twenty-nine percent of those involving slaves. A capital prosecution against a slave, then, was not much more likely to complete the Due Process "obstacle course" than a similar prosecution against a white man.

A significant difference does emerge, however, from an analysis of conviction rates. (See Table 20). Petit juries rendered verdicts in 257 white murder trials and in ninety-two trials of slaves for capital crimes. Overall, juries acquitted slaves of the capital offense more often than they convicted them. Still, they did so at a much lower rate than for white offenders. Fifty-nine percent of slaves were acquitted of the capital charge compared with eighty-nine percent of white offenders.

When convictions for lesser offenses are taken into account, the racial difference between acquittal rates narrows (see Table 21). Juries acquitted forty-one percent of slave offenders and forty-nine percent of white offenders. However, petit juries seldom convicted a white man of the capital charge. Only twenty-one percent of such convictions resulted in a sentence of death. In the other cases, whites were convicted of lesser grades of homicide for which a term in the penitentiary was the punishment.

In slave cases, seventy-seven percent of the convictions were for the hanging offense. However, it should be pointed out that a jury did face different alternatives when a slave stood accused of murder. As Justice Nathan Green wrote in 1850, "there is no second degree of murder, as to slaves."[62] and, until 1854, the circuit and

---

[62] Nelson v. The State, 28 Tenn. 353 (1850).

criminal courts did not exercise jurisdiction over manslaughter. Once given the opportunity to convict slaves of lesser offenses, juries did demonstrate some willingness to do so. For example, after 1854, seven of fifteen slaves convicted of felonious homicide were found guilty of the non-capital charge of manslaughter.

Regional differences in the behavior of the petit juries in slave cases were pronounced. Eighty-two percent of East Tennessee slaves on trial for their lives were acquitted, compared with only forty-nine percent of those in West Tennessee. In terms of all charges, the acquittal rate in West Tennessee dropped even further, from forty-nine percent to thirty percent. There is no such decline in East Tennessee. Without further study, little more can be done than note such differences and the difficulty of explaining them. Still, it is possible to speculate that the smaller percentage of slaves in the East Tennessee population reduced the pressure on the petit juries to treat slave and free defendants differently. However, one must be careful to avoid statements of relative "fairness" to slaves among the grand divisions. For example, in the extreme, every slave acquitted may have been innocent and every slave convicted, guilty. If that was the case, East Tennessee would have had a much higher percentage of innocent bondsmen going on trial for their lives.

In conclusion, the evidence presented in this chapter suggests that Tennesseans did extend the benefits of the Due Process Model to slave defendants and that the measure of the fairness that scholars have found in the South's appellate courts was also present in the Tennessee trial courts. Two qualifications are in order. First, although in none of the state's three grand divisions was the prosecution of a slave more likely to proceed to trial than the prosecution of a white man, petit juries did seem more willing to return a verdict of guilty when a slave was in the dock. Second, regional variations must be taken into account. Relative to those in the other grand divisions, slave defendants in West Tennessee did not fare well. Still, in absolute terms, West Tennessee slaves did not do badly. Of the sixty-one West Tennessee bondsmen on trial for their lives, only ten were executed and seven punished. Thirty-six were released, including sixteen acquitted outright by either a grand or petit jury.

On the whole, then, we can accept as valid the words of circuit judge Abraham Caruthers in his charge to the jury in the 1839 trial of Grandison, a slave accused of attempted rape. Although the defendant "is a slave," Caruthers instructed, "he is entitled . . . to the same deliberate and impartial trial that the most important free man in this country would be were he on trial."[63]

---

[63]"State v. Grandison (Slave)," Case Files, Middle District, Tennessee Supreme Court, TSA. For similar charges in other cases, see "State v. Major alias Nig [1854]," "Henry a slave v. Tennessee [1850]," "State v. Howell," and "Elijah, a slave, v. the State," ibid.

CHAPTER VIII

THE FREE BLACK DEFENDANT

In the trial of a slave, judicial concern for the human rights of the defendant coincided with concern for the property rights of the defendant's master, anything less than careful due process constituting unjust destruction of the owner's chattel. Such a direct economic interest was less likely to be present in the trial of a free black. Yet, even more so than with slaves, Tennessee courts treated free black defendants in a fashion essentially similar to the way they treated whites.

As James Merton England has observed, "the exact legal status of the Free Negro seems never to have been fully determined in ante-bellum Tennessee."[1] In defining crimes for which free blacks were liable, whites treated them like slaves in some instances and like whites in others. Free blacks also were liable to laws written especially for them, a "web of constraint" that Roger Raymond Van Dyke has called the "free Negro code."[2]

---

[1]England, "The Free Negro in Tennessee," p. 160.

[2]Van Dyke, "The Free Negro in Tennessee," p. 59; Berlin, Slaves Without Masters, pp. 316-40.

Free Negroes had to register with the county court and faced restrictions on their travel. A free black travelling out of the county where he resided, "without any lawful business; or . . . loitering about without any occupation" without his certificate of registration was liable to be arrested.[3] An 1833 law forbade free blacks to travel on stage coaches or steam boats without certification of freedom.[4]

Free blacks also faced occupational restrictions. None could "keep any grocery or tippling house or booth, or stall, for the purpose of vending spirituous liquors or groceries" or "engage in the business of peddling or bartering." In order "to guard against accidents on railroads," the legislature forbade free blacks from becoming railroad engineers.[5]

Other legislation regulated contact between free blacks and slaves. A free black could not marry or live with a slave "without the owner's consent, attested by two Justices of the Peace," nor "harbor or entertain" a slave without the owner's consent. Of course, free blacks were forbidden to be present at "any unlawful meeting" of

---

[3]Law of Tennessee, 18Ø6, ch. 2; Meigs and Cooper, The Code of Tennessee, pp. 523-25.

[4]Law of Tennessee, 1833, ch. 3.

[5]Law of Tennessee, 1835, ch. 57; 1856, ch. 72; 1858, ch. 44; Meigs and Cooper, The Code of Tennessee, pp. 275, 525.

bondsmen.[6]

In Tennessee, as elsewhere in the South, many free blacks resided in urban areas, and city officials enacted special ordinances "to regulate and restrain" free blacks within city limits.[7] As in the countryside, free blacks residing in cities had to register with local officials and receive a certificate of that registration. Free blacks without such certificates who could not "establish their freedom by testimony of credible witnesses" might be "deemed to be slaves" and treated as runaways.[8] Various municipal ordinances were designed to eliminate free black vagrancy, prohibit unauthorized and unsupervised assemblies, restrict movement, establish curfews, and limit contact with slaves.[9]

The punishment for violation of city ordinances varied. Nashville's free blacks were subject only to a

---

[6] Law of North Carolina, 1729, ch. 5, in Scott, _Laws_, 1: 40-42; Law of Tennessee, 1806, ch. 32; Meigs and Cooper, _The Code of Tennessee_, p. 525.

[7] Berlin, _Slaves Without Masters_, p. 175; Leonard P. Curry, _The Free Black in Urban America, 1800-1850: The Shadow of the Dream_ (Chicago and London: The University of Chicago Press, 1981), pp. 81-95. Smith and Lea, _Laws of Nashville_, pp. 44, 49, 123-24; Dupree, _Ordinances of Memphis_, pp. 50, 122.

[8] Dupree, _Ordinances of Memphis_, pp. 122-24; Smith and Lea, _Laws of Nashville_, pp. 124-25.

[9] Smith and Lea, _Laws of Nashville_, pp. 86, 124; Dupree, _Ordinances of Memphis_, pp. 124, 153; Van Dyke, "The Free Negro in Tennessee," pp. 66-68; _Memphis Daily Appeal_, 11 December, 14 December 1856.

fine for most offenses, municipal ordinances usually distinguishing between free and slave offenders in prescribing punishments.[10] In Memphis, on the other hand, many ordinances lumped free and slave blacks together as liable to receive "such corporal punishment at the workhouse as the [court] may determine." However, free blacks, like slaves, could escape the lash by paying the fine attached to the offense. Memphis ordinances stated that if a specific punishment was not designated, free blacks, like whites, would be subject to fine.[11]

In regard to general misdemeanors, early state statutes tended to lump slaves and free blacks together as subject to the lash or other corporal punishment, disdinguishing merely between the punishment due white violators and that due "if a negro."[12] However, as the lash fell into disuse for whites, it was also discontinued for free blacks. Later misdemeanor statutes only set separate punishments for slave and free defendants.[13] With enactment of the 1858 criminal code, only two crimes

---

[10] Smith and Lea, Laws of Nashville, pp. 87, 124, 155-56.

[11] Dupree, Ordinances of Memphis, pp. 74-75, 109, 124-26, 144, 184-85.

[12] Law of North Carolina, 1741, ch. 8; 1777, ch. 25, in Haywood, Public Acts, pp. 35-36, 103; Law of Tennessee, 1809, ch. 5.

[13] For example, see Law of Tennessee, 1838, ch. 114.

carried lashes as the punishment for free blacks, furnishing a slave with a pass and perjury. All other non-capital crimes were punished by fine and/or imprisonment.[14]

Tennessee made no special provisions for the trial of free blacks. The criminal process that applied to whites accused of a particular offense applied to free blacks similarly accused. Violations of municipal ordinances, for example, were tried according to a Crime Control Model. Like whites, free blacks who transgressed against city codes were tried by a single magistrate. In Nashville, some free blacks were tried by the City Justice, but more often they faced the Recorder.[15] Nashville newspaper reports support James Merton England's observation that free blacks "were frequent offenders" and that some free blacks "were among the most turbulent element of the local population."[16]

Consider the career of Joe Sumner, a hack driver and a "free and easy man of color."[17] In January 1855,

---

[14]Another offense, burning woods, did carry a sentence of thirty-nine lashes if the free black could not pay the fine. Meigs and Cooper, The Code of Tennessee, p. 358. A free black who could not pay the fine also could be hired out "to the person who will take him for the shortest time and pay the fine and all the costs." Ibid., pp. 525-26.

[15]Nashville Daily Gazette, 28 September, 6 December 1854; 27 February, 28 February, 3 March, 24 March, 7 July 1858.

[16]England, "The Free Negro in Davidson County," p. 98; Van Dyke, "The Free Negro in Tennessee," pp. 125-16.

[17]Nashville Daily Gazette, 7 October 1856.

Sumner was fined fifty dollars for assaulting Nancy Walker, a white woman. He could not pay and went to jail.[18] In November of the same year, the Recorder fined Sumner three dollars for driving his hack "faster than a moderate gait across the public square." The following January, he was fined twenty-five dollars for disorderly conduct. He could not pay this fine and once again "was induced to retire to the quietude of the Work House."[19] That October, Sumner was back before the Recorder for two instances of disorderly conduct. One charge was brought by a white woman who complained that Sumner "broke open the door of her house, and by force of arms, and with malice aforethought, and with violence divested her of fifty cents in silver." In the second case, a "dark skinned damsel" accused Sumner of returning to the same house and threatening "to demolish her caput with a bludgeon." Sumner was fined twenty dollars in the first case and five dollars in the second.[20]

During 1857, Sumner faced the Recorder at least three times. In August, he was fined fifty dollars for throwing rocks at a white women; in November, he was fined

---

[18]Walker herself was fined ten dollars for "renting a house to nymphs of the pave." Nashville Republican Banner, 28 January 1855; Nashville Daily Gazette, 28 January 1855.

[19]Nashville Daily Gazette, 3 November 1855; 24 June 1856.

[20]Nashville Republican Banner, 7 October 1856; Nashville Daily Gazette, 7 October 1856.

three dollars and fifty cents for being "out after hours without his passports," and, in December, the Recorder fined him thirteen dollars and fifty cents for making another assault on Nancy Walker.[21] Finally, in 1858, Sumner was fined twenty-five dollars when he "gave free scope to his imagination and his tongue and abused some . . . woman." He went to the workhouse to pay off this fine. Two days later, he was taken out "long enough to prove that he was interested in a contraband business in wet groceries" managed by Nancy Walker. Sumner was fined twenty-four dollars and fifty cents for this offense and sent back to the workhouse to pay it "in pulverizing limestone." In May, Sumner was fined twenty-three dollars for disorderly conduct, a fine which he also had to "liquidate in minerological investigation."[22]

Joe Sumner was a "turbulent" character, but he never was sentenced to be whipped. When unable to pay, he was sent to the workhouse. He did receive some large fines, but not all of them were set at the statutory maximum.[23]

From newspaper reports of Nashville police court

---

[21] Nashville Republican Banner, 13 August, 12 November, 4 December 1857.

[22] Ibid., 28 January, 30 January, 18 May 1858.

[23] Gabriel Scott was another free black "whose phiz has become quite familiar in police circles." Nashville Daily Gazette, 10 September, 1 October 1856; Nashville Republican Banner, 10 September, 1 October 1856; 1 December 1857.

activity, the largest cause of arrests of free blacks was disorderly behavior.[24] The second greatest cause was being found "without any papers" or "without a certificate."[25] Smaller numbers of free blacks were tried for other offenses, such as traffic violations, gambling, and entertaining slaves.[26]

---

[24] Nashville Daily Gazette, 3 August 1854; 6 June, 27 June, 17 August, 16 September, 22 September 1855; 16 July, 12 August, 14 August, 9 September, 12 September, 17 September 1856; 2 May, 3 May, 17 May 1857; 7 June, 25 July, 8 November, 1 December 1858; 1 September, 15 December 1860; Nashville Republican Banner, 13 May, 15 July, 14 August, 9 September, 12 September, 17 September, 4 November, 14 November 1856; 8 January, 28 January, 11 February, 12 February, 11 March, 29 March, 2 April, 26 April, 2 May, 3 May, 5 May, 17 May, 24 May, 26 May, 5 June, 6 June, 11 June, 1 July, 7 July, 16 July, 17 July, 30 July, 2 October, 10 October, 25 October, 29 October, 30 October, 3 November, 22 November, 1 December, 2 December, 12 December, 18 December, 23 December 1856; 16 January, 20 January, 24 January, 3 February, 12 February, 16 March, 8 April, 11 April, 27 May, 8 June, 15 June, 16 June, 18 June, 1 July, 3 July, 25 July, 8 October, 9 October, 19 October, 20 December, 30 December 1858; 28 January, 9 February, 2 March, 17 November, 12 December, 16 December 1860.

[25] Nashville Daily Gazette, 19 June 1858; 20 February 1861; Nashville Republican Banner, 17 August 1856; 21 February, 14 June 1857; 15 February, 24 February, 1 March, 3 March, 5 March, 17 March, 15 April, 6 June, 14 June, 30 June, 2 July, 25 October, 30 October, 4 November, 6 November, 11 November 1857; 10 January, 13 February, 9 March, 12 March, 31 March, 1 April, 4 April, 14 April, 25 May, 8 June, 19 June, 14 December 1858; 10 November 1859; 4 April, 23 May, 26 August, 20 November, 13 December 1860; 20 February 1861.

[26] Nashville Republican Banner, 17 January, 30 January, 16 February 1855; 26 November 1856; 6 February, 21 June, 22 September, 25 October, 18 December, 1857; 26 January, 19 March, 28 October 1858; 10 January, 16 February 1859; 1 February, 17 July, 13 December 1860; 26 May 1861; Nashville Daily Gazette, 30 August 1856, 17 July, 14 August, 12 December, 13 December 1860.

Most free blacks, but not all,[27] were convicted. Almost all of those convicted were sentenced to pay fines. Free blacks unable to pay fines were "sent down" to the workhouse. Ordinarily, a free black was not sentenced to lashes in lieu of paying the fine, but it did occur. In July, 1860, a free black named Adam Young was arrested and fined for selling liquor to slaves on the Sabbath, and "in default of payment thereof, he is to receive thirty lashes on the bare cuticle."[28] If newspaper reports were representative, such a sentence was rare.

Comparisons on the basis of dissimilar evidence must be made with care, but the practice in Nashville newspaper accounts of free black involvement with the Recorder's Court differs from that revealed in the dockets of the Recorder's Court of Memphis for roughly the same period. In thirty-nine of the final fifty-eight months of the antebellum period, two hundred and fifty-two free blacks were tried before the Memphis Recorder. One-half of Memphis free black offenses were violations of the free black code. The most frequent violation (43 percent) was living in the city contrary to ordinance or state law. Of the other offenses, unspecified misdemeanors ranked first, followed by disorderly behavior (see Table 22).

---

[27] Nashville Republican Banner, 6 February, 18 February, 14 June, 12 July, 22 July 1857.

[28] Ibid., 21 July 1860.

As in Nashville, a number of Memphis free blacks (50 or 20 percent) were acquitted. Their rate of acquittal actually was higher than the acquittal rate for both Memphis whites and Memphis slaves (see Table 23). No Memphis free blacks were sentenced to be whipped. Twenty-eight were ordered to leave the city. The others were fined. Of those fined, forty-four (22 percent) spent time in the workhouse, surprisingly a smaller percentage than white defendants.[29]

If accused of committing a misdemeanor under state criminal law, free blacks, like whites, but unlike slaves, were tried in the regular county, circuit, and criminal courts. When statutes required, free blacks did receive racially specific sentences. An 1852 law provided that free blacks who became "disorderly in their conduct" could be "hired out" by the county court for one to five years.[30] In 1857, the Maury county judge ordered Ellick Stuart "hired out to the highest bidder for twelve months" because of his disorderly conduct. That same year, in Gibson county, Richard, "a free man of color," was ordered to be hired "to the highest bidder" for three years.[31]

---

[29] City of Memphis, Recorder's Court, Docket Books, see above, p. 112.

[30] Law of Tennessee, 1852, ch. 160; Meigs and Cooper, The Code of Tennessee, pp. 523-24.

[31] Maury County, County Court, Minutes, October 1856, p. 598 (vol. 11), p. 2 (vol. 12); January 1856, p. 62; February 1857, p. 80; Gibson County, County Court, Minutes, April 1857, p. 420.

By statute, whites and blacks could not marry, but they did sometimes live together and were occasionally prosecuted for their cohabitation. Thus Francis, a free black woman, was indicted in Hamilton county because she "unlawfully, lewdly, openly, and publicly and notoriously did cohabit and have illicit sexual intercourse" with Edward F. Overdeen.[32] In 1837, in Greene county, the grand jury indicted Mary Bell, a white woman, and Abraham Bell, "a negro man," for "living together as man and wife." The attorney general refused to prosecute on this indictment, but he indicted Mary Bell alone for "living with a free negro man." She was acquitted by the jury.[33]

For most minor crimes, however, the statutes did not single out free blacks, and the treatment of free blacks accused of these offenses does not seem distinctive; they seem to have been accorded whatever trial rights the system afforded other free men.

Some courts even assigned counsel to free blacks accused of misdemeanors. For example, two free black women, Lucina and Caroline, were charged in Knox county with

---

[32]"The State vs. Francis, a Free Woman of Color [1854]," Case Files, Eastern Division, Tennessee Supreme Court, TSA. The state appealed the circuit judge's decision, but his action was upheld by the Supreme Court.

[33]Greene County, Circuit Court, Minutes, July 1837, pp. 85, 87, 92. Also see Greene County, Circuit Court, Minutes, February 1844, p. 670; January 1853, p. 22; February 1853, p. 85; February 1854, p. 301; October 1858, p. 313; February 1859, p. 438; October 1859, pp. 16, 18; Davidson County, Circuit Court, Minutes, January 1830, pp. 229, 253; May 1839, p. 400.

"keeping a bawdy house." They proved "unable to employ counsel," and the court assigned two lawyers to defend them The women pleaded guilty. They were fined fifty dollars and sentenced to thirty days in jail.[34] In Maury county, "Nancy (alias) free Nancy" was indicted for assault and baattery and trespass. The court assigned two attorneys as her counsel. She pleaded not guilty, but when the jury was empaneled she changed her plea to guilty and was sentenced to three months in the county jail.[35]

On the whole, Tennessee free blacks accused of misdemeanors do not seem to have been treated harshly. In Davidson county in 1816, "Seac, a mulatto," was tried twice for assault and battery. Acquitted by the jury on the first charge, he was convicted on the second and fined twelve dollars. That same term, two white men were tried for assault and battery; one was convicted and fined fifty-one dollars; the other pleaded guilty and was fined ten dollars.[36] In 1846, a Davidson Criminal Court jury acquitted William Sumner, "a free man of colour," of assault and battery.[37] Two years later, a jury in the court

---

[34] Knox County, Circuit Court, Minutes, June 1855, pp. 195, 218.

[35] Maury County, Circuit Court, Minutes, May 1842, p. 310.

[36] Davidson County, County Court, Minutes, October 1816, pp. 42, 43, 59.

[37] Ibid., Criminal Court, Minutes, October 1846, pp. 552, 560. Also see, Greene County, Circuit Court, Minutes, February 1858, p. 113; June 1858, pp. 189, 196.

convicted "Sol King alias Steel a free man of color" and sentenced him to a five dollar fine and ninety days in jail. James McGarr, a white man convicted of assault and battery later that same term, received a fine of five dollars and sixty days in jail.[38]

Alleged violations of the regular tippling laws frequently led to the prosecutions of free blacks. Again, the outcome of their cases varied, and their punishments did not seem to have been very different from those given to whites. In 1855, the Johnson county grand jury made three presentments against Peter Wilson, a free black, for tippling, but the attorney general refused to prosecute the cases.[39] In June 1852, the Knox county grand jury refused to indict Valentine Henderson, "a free man of color," for unlawfully retailing liquor. A year later, the grand jury did make two presentments against him for that offense. He was convicted and fined five dollars in each case. The same term, three white men either pleaded guilty or were convicted of the same offense. Each received the same fine as Henderson.[40] Two free blacks--Free Bill and William Cheatham--and a white man, Lewis Whitley, were indicted

---

[38] Davidson County, Criminal Court, Minutes, August 1848, p. 272; December 1858, pp. 306, 307.

[39] Johnson County, Circuit Court, Minutes, November 1854, p. 319; November 1855, p. 343, 360.

[40] Knox County, Circuit Court, Minutes, June 1852, p. 515; June 1853, p. 126; June 1854, pp. 361, 362, 374, 413-14, 418-19.

in Williamson county for unlawfully selling spirituous liquors. Free Bill and Cheatham pleaded guilty and received a one dollar fine. Whitley was convicted by the jury and fined five dollars.[41] In Gibson county, in 1852, the the grand jury returned two presentments against Jacob Hix, "a free man of colour," for tippling. Hicks pleaded guilty to both and was fined two dollars and fifty cents in each case. The next term, a white man, P.H. Kinney, pleaded guilty to two presentments of tippling and was fined one in each case. This might seem discriminatory except that on a later day in the same term, the reverse occurred. Ned Bass, "a free man of color," was fined one cent in each of two cases of tippling in which he had pleaded guilty, and John McDaniel, a white man, was twice fined two dollars and fifty cents in the same circumstances.[42]

In treating felonies and their punishment, the 1829 penal code did not exclude free blacks, therefore,

---

[41]Williamson County, Circuit Court, Minutes March 1848, p. 365; July 1848, pp. 388, 395; November 1848, p. 462. For examples of courts reaching similar results in trials of free blacks and whites for gaming, see ibid., March 1849, p. 493; November 1849, p. 55; Knox County, Circuit Court, Minutes, June 1849, p. 107; October 1849, p. 131.

[42]Gibson County, Circuit Court, Minutes, March 1852, pp. 410, 424; July 1852, pp. 431, 437-38; also see ibid., March 1856, p. 589; November 1856, p. 51; Greene County, Circuit Court, Minutes, June 1840, pp. 505, 506, 507, 511; June 1848, pp. 475, 587, 490-91; October 1852, p. 668; October 1853, pp. 249-50; June 1854, pp. 336-37, 345-47, 365; October 1854, pp. 53, 456-57, 460, 462; Maury County, Circuit Court, Minutes, May 1836, p. 216; January 1837, p. 384; March 1832, p. 70; Lincoln County, Circuit Court, Minutes, March 1851, p. 287; July 1851, p. 309.

for non-capital felonies, free blacks, like whites, were subject to imprisonment in the penitentiary.[43] However, where capital crimes were concerned, Tennessee statutes bear out England's observation that "especially after 1830 there was a tendency to identify the Free Negro with the slave in the matter of crimes."[44] In 1819, when the Tennessee legislature initially spelled out the five capital crimes for slaves, free blacks were not included.[45] After 1839, however, much of the legislation expanding the number of capital crimes for slaves also included free blacks, and in 1850, rape of a white female was made a capital offense for free blacks.[46] This trend culminated with the provision in the 1858 code that "all offenses made capital by this Code when committed by slaves, shall be capital when committed by free persons of color."[47]

No special courts were established for the felony trials of free blacks. Like whites, they were tried in the regular circuit and criminal courts, and their convictions

---

[43] Law of Tennessee, 1829, ch. 23.

[44] England, "The Free Negro in Tennessee," p. 193.

[45] Law of Tennessee, 1819, ch. 35.

[46] Law of Tennessee, 1833, ch. 75; 1850, ch. 114; 1852, ch. 174; 1860, ch. 118. The exceptions were attempted murder and burning property where life was endangered or with the intent to endanger life. Law of Tennessee, 1835, ch. 19; 1858, ch. 18.

[47] Meigs and Cooper, The Code of Tennessee, p. 524.

were subject to review by the Supreme Court.

In exercising its appellate jurisdiction, the Supreme Court upheld the racial discrimination contained in Tennessee law. For example, in 1838, the Court upheld a 1794 prohibiton against blacks testifying on behalf of each other in criminal trials, ruling that the statutes premitted blacks only to testify against one another. Although the Supreme Court admitted that "practice in Tennessee may have been . . . more liberal," it would abide by the 1794 statute; "as the law speaks, so it is our duty to speak."[48]

The Supreme Court, in The State v. Claiborne, also upheld the 1831 prohibition against free blacks immigrating into Tennessee. Jack Claiborne was a Kentucky free black indicted in Maury county for violating that 1831 law. Upon appeal, the case turned upon the constitutionality of the 1831 law itself, Claiborne arguing that it was "repugnant" to the provision of the United States Constitution that entitled citizens of each state "to all the privileges aand immunities of citizens in the several states." Justice Green wrote the opinion of the Supreme Court. Free blacks, Green wrote, "are not citizens." They "have always been a degraded race in the United States . . . an inferior caste in society . . . never in any of the States entitled to all the privileges

---

[48] Jones v. The State, 19 Tenn. 119-20 (1838).

and immunities of citizens." Therefore, free blacks were "not intended to be included when this word was used in the Constitution." The 1831 act excluding free blacks from other states, then, was constitutional, and Claiborne's indictment and conviction under that act was valid.[49]

The Supreme Court's support for discriminatory legislation notwithstanding, it protected the trial rights of free blacks. The Court heard eleven cases involving free black defendants and reversed the lower court conviction in seven instances.

Three cases illustrate the Supreme Court's protection of free blacks against arbitrary treatment. Holly v. the State, involved a fifteen-year-old Nashville free black who had killed another free black, Jack Burnett.[50] Burnett, about twenty-five years old, had interrputed a marbles game in which Holly and some other youngsters were engaged. When the boys resisted the intrusion, Burnett grabbed one of them, "slapped his face,

---

[49] The State v. Claiborne, 19 Tenn. 337-40 (1838). In his opinion, Green clearly anticipated certain aspects of Chief Justice Taney's opinion in the Dred Scott case. Vincent C. Hopkins, S.J., Dred Scott's Case (New York: Atheneum, 1971), p. 102; Don E. Fehrenhacher, The Dred Scott Case: Its Significance in American Law and Politics (New York: Oxford University Press, 1978), pp. 341-64.

[50] "State v. William Holly," Case Files, Middle District, Tennessee Supreme Court, TSA. (Hereafter cited as "Holly" Transcript, 1849.) Also see Young v. the State, 30 Tenn. 139-40 (1850) and George Lee v. The State, 41 Tenn. 43-46 (1860).

stove him to the ground, got astraddle of him and was beating him." At this point, "Bill" Holly threw a rock at Burnett, striking him on the forehead, and giving him a mortal wound.[51] Holly was tried in the Davidson County Criminal Court, convicted of second degree murder, and sentenced to ten years in the state penitentiary.[52] Justice Turley wrote the opinion of the Supreme Court that overturned the lower court conviction. He indicated that the High Court was "much astonished at the verdict," one that "cannot be permitted." Malice was "requisite" for the killing to be murder, and there clearly had been none in this case. For Holly to be held guilty of murder and punished as a murderer, Turley wrote, "would be cruelty and not justice."[53]

The second case was Wiley v. the State, involving a Maury county free black convicted of "enticing a slave to leave his master's service." In Wesley (1851), a capital case involving a slave defendant, the Supreme Court had ruled that the circuit judge could not take the consent of the defendant as grounds to dispense with

---

[51] "Holly" Transcript, 1849, pp. 5-8.

[52] Ibid., p. 5; Davidson County, Criminal Court, Minutes, October 1849, pp. 383, 420, 421-22.

[53] Holly v. The State, 28 Tenn. 96-97 (1849). Upon retrial, Holly was convicted of manslaughter and sentenced to three years in the penitentiary. He appealed this conviction, but the Supreme Court upheld the lower court. Davidson County, Criminal Court, Minutes, December 1850, pp. 82, 92, 96; "William Holly v. State," Case Files, Middle District, Tennessee Supreme Court, TSA, pp. 8-9.

the requirement that the jury be sequentered.[54] The same issue was before the Court in Wiley. Justice A.W.O. Totten, speaking for the Court, asserted that in a felony prosecution, a jury could not be separated without the consent of the defendant, and that consent must be given "in the free and unembarrassed exercise of his judgment and discretion." However, Totten did not believe it was ever possible to make the decision in such a fashion. He concluded that the Court would not "suppose that a prisoner's mind is free and unembarrassed" and did not think that "the responsibility of a refusal should be imposed upon him." Thus, the Court extended to all felony trials a ruling that had originally be applied only in a capital case.[55]

In the final case, Winfield, a free black, was jailed and fined for violating a Memphis curfew that prohibited all blacks from being "out" after ten o'clock at night. Winfield sued to have his ten dollar fine refunded. In its decision, the Supreme Court showed no concern whatsoever for the real or supposed "dangers" of free movement of blacks at night. It upheld Winfield, voiding the curfew ordinance as "high-handed and oppressive, and enacted . . . without any authority." The Court described it as "an attempt to impair the liberty of a free person

---

[54] Wesley v. the State, 30 Tenn. 345-46 (1851).

[55] Wiley v. The State, 31 Tenn. 210-211 (1851).

unnecessarily to restrain him from the exercise of his lawful pursuits, and to make an innocent act a crime."[56] In terms of the judicial protection afforded a black defendant against arbitrary treatment, this decision, aaccording to Daniel Flanigan, was "the most remarkable" of the antebellum period.[57]

At the trial court level, as well, free blacks benefited from due process procedures designed to protect defendants from unjust conviction. Free blacks, for example, were entitled to a preliminary examination by a "committing court." In Nashville, a free black, Tom Daniels, was accused of the shooting death of a white man, John Lyons. Daniels was defended at his "committing trial" by a trio of attorneys, including a former governor of the state. Three magistrates presided. The trial was a "protracted" affair, extending over three days. One of the points in dispute was the deposition of the dead man. By a two-to-one vote, the magistrates ruled it inadmissible "upon the grounds that it was not a dying declaration." Finally, "after reviewing all the testimony, which was conflicting," the magistrates decided "that if Daniels did shoot Lyons, Daniels was justifiable; but, from the amount of conflicting

---

[56]<u>Mayor, Etc., of Memphis v. Winfield</u>, 27 Tenn. 565-67 (1848).

[57]Flanigan, "The Criminal Law of Slavery," p. 207; Nash, "Negro Rights," p. 408. Winfield actually won this case in the lower courts. It was the Memphis authorities who appealed the case.

testimony, we are doubtful that Daniels did shoot Lyons." The attorney for the state could only ask, "Then you discharge him?" The Court answered, "We do."[58]

As Daniels' experience demonstrates, free blacks were not automatically bound over for trial by the committing court.[59] However, if that preliminary examination did go against the defendant, free blacks benefited from all subsequent aspects of the procedural system that applied to whites. Free blacks had to be indicted by a grand jury. They were entitled to bail and to have an attorney appointed if they could not afford one.[60] They had the right to all appropriate

---

[58] Nashville Republican Banner, 28 May, 23 June, 25 June, 26 June 1859.

[59] For other examples of committing courts releasing free black defendants, see Maury County, Circuit Court, Minutes, January 1858, pp. 629-30; Scrapbook of Slavery Materials, Garrett Collection, TSLmd; Nashville Republican Banner, 2 June 1859; 21 March, 27 March 1861; Nashville Daily Gazette, 21 March, 28 March, 29 March 1861;

[60] In the counties under study, six free black defendants had court-appointed counsel. Three of these defendants were convicted, two were acquitted, and one was discharged by the attorney general after a mistrial. Knox County, Circuit Court, Minutes, February 1844, pp. 218, 240; June 1844, p. 299; October 1844, p. 381; June 1845, pp. 481, 490, 496; Greene County, Circuit Court, Minutes, October 1848, pp. 529-30, 533, 545, 557; Williamson County, Circuit Court, Minutes, July 1856, pp. 367, 376, 377; Davidson County, Criminal Court, Minutes, April 1858, pp. 322, 325, 330-31; ibid., Circuit Court, Minutes, September 1840, pp. 522, 544.

For examples of free blacks being released on bail, see Davidson County, Circuit Court, Minutes, November 1819, pp. 259, 261; City of Memphis, Criminal Court, Minutes, October 1857, p. 599; July 1858, p. 401.

pre-trial and post-conviction motions.[61] Their cases were subject to dismissal by the prosecuting attorney, and they enjoyed the right to appeal to the Supreme Court. As we will see, an examination of free black cases in the counties under study indicates that these procedural formalities influenced the substantive outcome in free black trials much the same as they did in the trials of whites.

In the counties surveyed for this study, there were one hundred and fifty prosecutions against one hundred and thirty free blacks (see Table 24). The majority of these cases (103, 69 percent) occurred in Knox, Davidson, and Shelby counties, which contained large urban centers. In the following discussion, comparisons will be made between these cases and those involving whites in the same counties.[62]

Thirty-four (23 percent) of the total prosecutions against free blacks were for violations of the 1831 statute prohibiting immigration into Tennessee, an offense for which whites obviously were not liable (see Table 24). Most of the other offenses were crimes against property. Free

---

[61] For example, free blacks were granted continuances, changes of venue, and new trials. See Memphis, Criminal Court, *Minutes*, November 1857, p. 60; Bedford County, Circuit Court, *Minutes*, August 1857, p. 35; December 1857, p. 221; Davidson County, Criminal Court, *Minutes*, August 1857, pp. 40-41, 51, 170; Knox County, Circuit Court, *Minutes*, February 1860, p. 639.

[62] The tables, however, contain data for free black cases in all the counties under study. The number of free black cases in each of the rural counties was so small that detailed percentage comparisons with white cases would reveal very little.

blacks were prosecuted more frequently than whites for such offenses, especially larceny. However, the majority of crimes charged to both whites and free blacks were against property. Most of the prosecutions against both whites and free blacks for crimes against persons involved felonious assault or homicide (see Table 25).

The statistical data with regard to free black prosecution for rape requires some explanation. The percentage figure represents six prosecutions against three individuals. In December 1851, a Davidson County Criminal Court jury convicted Dan Cherry upon a badly drawn indictment accusing him of the rape or attempted rape of Adelia J. Hughlett. The Criminal Court judge arrested the judgment, and the attorney general appealed that decision. The Supreme Court upheld the lower court judge, and the attorney general refused to bring Cherry to trial a second time.[63] Nine years later, the Davidson grand jury indicted Lewis Brown for the attempted rape of Virginia McDaniel. Rather than bring Brown to trial, the attorney general dismissed the felony charge in the indictment, and Brown pled guilty to a charge of assault and battery. The Court fined him twenty-five dollars.[64] Finally, in Knox

[63] Davidson County, Criminal Court, Minutes, August 1851, pp. 170, 203; December 1851, pp. 221-22, 249, 257; Nashville Daily Gazette, 10 December 1851.

[64] Davidson County, Criminal Court, Minutes, December 1860, pp. 231, 255, 256; Nashville Daily Gazette, 15 November 1860.

county, in 1859, the Grand Jury indicted a free black named Elihu for the attempted rape of Charity C. Barry. After two mistrials, the circuit judge shifted the venue of Elihu's trial to Blount county where he was acquitted.[65]

There were two instances of free blacks being tried for insurrection. In Davidson county in 1843, the criminal court grand jury indicted Celia Cocral, a free black woman, because "in the presence and hearing of divers slaves and free Negroes," she used "the following language . . . 'Liberty or blood. You have no right to us you did steal us,'" as well as "various other expressions calculated to produce insubordination, insurrection, and rebellion." With perhaps unintended irony, the case was tried upon a "plea of insanity," the jury deciding that Celia Cocral was indeed "insane and further that it would endanger the peace of the community to set her at liberty." The court sentenced her to be taken "to the Lunatic Hospital there to be kept as other lunatics."[66] The second case occurred in Shelby county in 1856. Morris, "a free man of color," was indicted in the Memphis Criminal Court for attempting to "excite" two slaves "to insubordination, insurrection, and

---

[65]Knox County, Circuit Court, Minutes, June 1859, pp. 297-98, 315, 317-18, 339; October 1859, pp. 516-17, 528; February 1860, p. 639; Blount County, Circuit Court, Minutes, May 1860, p. 407. Since Blount county was not one of the counties under study, Elihu's acquittal is not recorded on the tables for this chapter.

[66]Davidson County, Criminal Court, Minutes December 1843, pp. 367-68.

rebellion" by "discourse and conversation" and by the "delivery" of "knives and pistols and other deadly weapons." On the defendant's affidavit, the case was continued for a term, and when Morris did go to trial, he was acquitted.[67]

In crimes of violence of which blacks were accused and where the race of the victim is known, eighteen of the victims were white and fifteen were black, either slave or free. In cases where the victim was white, the free black defendant was acquitted by either the grand or petit jury in twenty-eight percent of the prosecutions; only twenty-two percent of the prosecutions ended in conviction. By comparison, when the victim was black, there were no acquittals, and sixty percent of the prosecutions ended in conviction (see Table 26). Free black defendants, then, actually seemed to be able to mount a more successful defense when the victim of the crime was white than when the victim was black.

Overall, juries convicted free blacks in felony cases only slightly more frequently than they did whites, thirty-nine percent to thirty-three percent (see Table 27). Petit and grand juries also released a slightly larger percentage of white defendants, thirty percent compared with twenty-two percent of free blacks. All together, then, sixty-seven percent of the felony

---

[67]City of Memphis, Criminal Court, Minutes, November 1856, pp. 434-35, 438; April 1857, p. 122.

prosecutions against whites failed to produce a conviction, but the same result occurred in sixty-one percent of the felony prosecutions against free blacks.[68] In only thirty-six percent of the cases was an individual free black ultimately convicted. (see Table 28).

The trial disposition statistics should be refined in one regard, by shifting out the single felony for which whites were not liable, violation of the 1831 prohibition against free blacks entering the state.[69]

As has been shown, the Supreme Court upheld free black exclusionary legislation in Claiborne. Regardless of the Supreme Court's action in that case, free black convictions under the statute were rare. If fact, in the counties under study, Claiborne's appears to have been the only such verdict. In these counties there were thirty-four prosecutions involving thirty-two individuals charged with violating the 1831 immigration restriction. In two cases, the grand jury refused to indict the individuals charged.[70] Of those individuals indicted, only nine went to trial, and, except for Jack Claiborne, all

---

[68]In the "rural" counties, only sixteen of the forty-seven prosecutions (34%) ended in conviction. Eleven (23%) ended in verdicts of acquittal, and in seventeen cases (36%), the attorney general entered a nolle prosequi. There were three cases in which the final disposition is unknown.

[69]Law of Tennessee, 1831, ch. 102.

[70]Shelby County, Circuit Court, Minutes, January 1842, p. 628.

were eventually acquitted.[71] In most instances, the case never went before the petit jury, the attorney general refusing to prosecute.[72]

If these cases are removed from consideration and free black and white cases are compared, the picture for the free black worsens (see Table 29). Fewer than one-half of the prosecutions ended in conviction, but the conviction rate for free blacks was much higher than for whites. Even if over one-half of the free blacks escaped conviction for common felonies, Tennessee's Due Process "obstacle course" was more effective in safeguarding white defendants.

---

[71] Knox County, Circuit Court, Enrollment Docket, February 1843, pp. 352-53; Minutes, October 1841, p. 73; October 1842, pp. 497, 503; February 1843, p. 2; Greene County, Circuit Court, Minutes, October 1839, p. 403; October 1840, p. 29; February 1841, p. 44; Robertson County, Circuit Court, Minutes, June 1842, p. 370; Bedford County, Circuit Court, Minutes, April 1857, p. 596; August 1857, pp. 111, 116-17; Davidson County, Circuit Court, Minutes, January 1839, p. 264; Henry County, Circuit Court, Minutes, May 1849, p. 491; May 1850, p. 563.

[80] Shelby County, Circuit Court, Minutes, December 1832, p. 188; August 1833, p. 205; Memphis, Criminal Court, Minutes, June 1856, p. 41; October 1847, pp. 358-59; Bedford County, Circuit Court, Minutes, April 1854, p. 155; August 1854, p. 209; Davidson County, Circuit Court, Minutes, January 1839, p. 269; Robertson County, Circuit Court, Minutes, June 1841, p. 309; June 1842, p. 369; February 1843, p. 428; Greene County, Circuit Court, Minutes, October 1839, p. 403; June 1841, p. 117; March 1841, p. 92; Johnson County, Circuit Court, Minutes, March 1838, p. 86.

In other cases, the defendants never came to trial; they simply defaulted. Greene County, Circuit Court, Minutes, February 1861, p. 445; Bedford County, Circuit Court, Minutes, April 1857, p. 596; December 1858, p. 330; Davidson County, Circuit Court, Minutes, August 1841, p. 391; September 1841, p. 538; January 1842, p. 70; Shelby County, Circuit Court, Minutes, June 1831, p. 264.

In those cases that did come to trial, petit juries were tougher on free black defendants than on whites (see Table 30). Juries convicted sixty-two percent of the free black defendants and fifty-four percent of the whites. Again, if prosecutions for violation of the 1831 immigration restriction are removed, the picture worsens for free blacks, the conviction rate increasing to sixty-six percent (see Table 31).

No free black defendant in the counties under study was ever sentenced to hang; none was sentenced to life imprisonment, and, after the Tennessee legislature eliminated whipping in its penal code reform, none was ever sentenced to the lash. The stiffest sentence meted out to free black defendants went to John Ransom in 1835 and Cato Catauley in 1858. Both Ransom and Catauley were convicted of second degree murder and sentenced to twenty and twenty-one years respectively. Ransom had killed a slave; Catauley a white man.[73]

An analysis of the sentencing pattern in the Davidson county Criminal Court by race underscores the similarity of the treatment of free blacks and whites (see Table 32). In the Davidson Criminal Court, during 1842-1861, the mean sentence length for free blacks was 4.5 years,

---

[81] Davidson County, Circuit Court, Minutes, May 1835, pp. 253-56; Criminal Court, Minutes, April 1858, pp. 322, 325, 330-31, 474.

higher than for whites, 3.8 years. However, the median sentence for both blacks and whites was the same, three years. The modal sentence for both whites and free blacks was three years. Sentences of five or fewer years made up eighty-five percent of the sentences of convicted whites, but five-year or shorter terms made up seventy-six percent of the sentences handed to free blacks.

This data does lend some support the negative assessments of criminal justice for free blacks as propounded by Ira Berlin and Lenoard Curry.[74] On the other hand, it also challenges Berlin's assertion that "free negroes rarely received justice" at the hands of an all-white judicial system. Elsewhere, as Berlin argues, the whipping post may have been the "negro's exclusive preserve," but, in Tennessee, it was not the preserve of free Negroes. It was rare for Tennessee whites to be whipped; it was equally rare for Tennessee free blacks to be lashed. Only mean sentence length suggests "greater severity" in felony punishments for free blacks, and, given the frequency distribution of sentences, there is little reason to hold, as Berlin and Curry do, that free blacks "could expect stiffer sentences." Certainly, the free blacks were not "punished like slaves," a point that one former

---

[74]Berlin, <u>Slaves Without Masters</u>, pp. 96, 317, 334-35; Curry, <u>The Free Black in Urban America</u>, pp. 114, 116, 119.

Tennessee bondsman recalled:

> Now if you was a free nigger and did something you didn't have no business doing, you was sent to the penitentiary like anybody else; that was the difference; the slaves never went to the penitentiary for nothin' they did.[75]

By most accounts, free blacks in antebellum Tennessee were a detested and denigrated people. Certainly, little concern for property rights animated the judicial system in its approach to them as criminal defendants. Yet, as in the cases of slaves accused of capital crimes, their trials were handled fundamentally the same as those of whites, and, in absolute terms, they received a measure of due process that was striking.

---

[75] George P. Rawick, ed., The American Slave: A Composite Autobiography, vol. 18: Unwritten History of Slavery (Westport, CT: Greenwood Publishing Company, 1974), p. 225. James Thomas also made this observation. Schweninger, ed., From Tennessee Slave to St. Louis Entrepreneur, p. 62.

CONCLUSIONS

This study has explored the treatment of slaves and free blacks in the courts of Tennessee. The inquiry has demonstrated the importance of the statutes and appellate court opinion. With one glaring exception, the punishment of masters and other whites for unlawful violence against bondsmen, the law of slavery as written in the code books and Supreme Court reports was reflected in the law as practiced in the trial courts, the men who implemented the laws acting in harmony with those who made and interpreted them.

As a point of departure, the Tennessee judicial system accepted the humanity of the slave, recognizing it as integral to slaves as property. At all levels, Tennessee courts also took cognizance of a limited range of human rights accorded to bondsmen. Under specifically defined circumstances, the slave had a right to liberty. When conferred by the master, that liberty became a "substantive" thing protected on its own merits, even in contradiction of legislative efforts, first, to regulate and, then, to retard the growth of the free Negro class. Further, the slave had a right to be protected against unlawful physical violence. Because of the concern of lawmakers and jurists that the power of whites over slaves not be weakened, this right was even more narrowly construed. The Supreme Court held the sanctity of the slave's person subordinate to his duty to submit to proper punishment. The Court refused to spell out the limits of proper punishment but clearly regarded those limits as broad and would not easily permit the slave to claim self-defense as justification for resistance. In regard to the punishment of whites for violence against slaves, the statutes provided for it in a narrow range of circumstances, which the Supreme Court broadened by its decisions on the matter. However, a significant disparity existed between the law in the statutes and appellate court opinions and that provided by the lower courts. The county, circuit, and criminal courts seldom actually convicted whites for killing or assaulting slaves.

Insofar as judicial recognition of human rights was concerned, slaves came closest to equality with whites in criminal trials, especially those for capital offenses after 1835. It can be argued that in this area the protection of property was the paramount consideration of legislators and jurists.[1] There can be no doubt that strengthening due process for slave defendants also strengthened property rights for slave owners, a connection that Tennessee policymakers definitely understood and fostered. Still, I do not believe them disingenuous; the language of the statutes and Supreme Court opinion simply does not support

---

[1] Andrew Fede does this especially well. See above, pp. 84, 148-49.

the view that concern for property excluded all others or even that it was primary. The content of statutes and Supreme Court decisions clearly indicate that policymakers sought to protect the human rights of slave defendants. That this position also protected property rights may have eased its acceptance but it does not seem to have been what animated policymakers. It might also be argued that the Supreme Court opinions were rhetorical flourishes designed to refute abolitionist criticism of the Peculiar Institution. This simply does not square with the facts. Far from being rhetorical, Supreme Court opinions resulted in overturned convictions, a concrete insistence on Due Process treatment of slaves on trial for their lives, and, as suggested previously, Supreme Court doctrine generally was implemented in the trial courts. Furthermore, neither concern for property nor the desire to counter the attack of abolitionists can fully explain the Due Process treatment extended by the trial courts to free black defendants in felony cases.

In explaining the Due Process treatment afforded slave defendants, the "legislative mandate of equality" is crucial, for where that mandate did not exist--e.g., South Carolina and Virginia--slaves remained subject to Crime Control mechanisms with their scant regard for defendants' rights.[2] There is no legislative history of slavery for

---

[2]Flanigan, "The Criminal Law of Slavery," pp. 105-106. Also see, Schafer, "The Long Arm of the Law."

any state; as a consequence, it is uncertain what motivated lawmakers in Tennessee, and other southern states for that matter, to bring (or not to bring) slaves accused of capital crimes within the regular Due Process criminal system. There are indications, however, in Tennessee, at least, that the movement was part of a more general reform of the legal system and that lawmakers responded to concerns of legal professionals. It seems clear that judicial recognition of the trial rights of slaves preceded and perhaps stimulated that of the General Assembly.[3]

One important aspect of the explanation for the Due Process treatment of slave defendants, then, seems to rest within the legal profession. In part, it was ideological. As Mark Tushnet has written, antebellum southern jurists "largely accepted the moral framework of Western law," in which "procedural fairness in general was an important element."[4] Another part of the explanation, particularly for the behavior of the lower courts, is best understood, perhaps, in sociological terms, in terms of role theory.[5]

---

[3]See above, pp. 183-88.

[4]Mark Tushnet, "Approaches to the Study of the Law of Slavery," Civil War History 25 (December 1979): 333; Tushnet, "The American Law of Slavery, 1810-1860: A Study in the Persistence of Legal Autonomy," Law and Society 10 (Fall 1975): 121, 125.

[5]Nash also has found role theory useful, but in a somewhat different way, distinguishing between the behavior towards blacks called for by the role of "judge," as opposed to the role of "editor" or "legislator." Nash, "A More Equitable Past," pp. 236-38; Nash, "Negro Rights," pp. 494-500.

A textbook definition of role is a set of behavioral expectations associated with a particular position within a given social group.[6] The roles played by mid-nineteenth century lawyers, judges, and grand and petit jurors emerged from a legal tradition extending to the Plantagenets and beyond. These roles developed with little regard to the racism or chattel bondage of the antebellum South. Such firmly rooted behavioral expectations might prove difficult to change simply because the personal characteristics of the prisoner in the dock changed.[7]

By analogy, the courtroom trial of a slave, or a free black can be viewed as a drama. It was far easier to

---

[6]Robert A. Nisbet, The Social Bond: An ntroduction to the Study of Society (New York: Alfred A. Knopf, 1970), pp. 148-221; Peter Berger, Invitation to Sociology: A Humanistic Perspective (New York: Doubleday Company, Inc., 1963), pp. 93-100, 135-36.

[7]Certainly, such ideological and sociological considerations operated across the South. Why they produced different results in different states is an important question yet unanswered.

I have oversimplified this discussion for purposes of emphasis. Antebellum lawyers, judges, and jurors played many roles, some of which called for contradictory behavior, i.e., caused "role confict." For example, if an individual was both circuit judge and slaveowner, he might not always resolve the inherent conflict between those two roles in favor of the behavioral expectations of his occupation. Certainly, the resolution would depend upon time, place, and circumstance. A single role might call for contradictory behavior. A circuit judge was both the guardian of private property and the protector of the trial rights of defendants. The two sets of behavioral expectations contained within the single role of judge could pull in opposing directions. This "role strain" might not always be resolved in favor of the slave defendant. This, too, would depend upon time, place, and circumstance.

allow the slave, or free black, to play the normal part of the accused rather than rewrite the entire script to fit the pecularities of the defendant. In the intimacy of the courtroom, to treat a slave or free black defendant differently from a white defendant would put judicial actors too much at odds with themselves; it would put too much distance between "ideal roles" and actual role performance. The psychosociological and ideological costs of distinguishing slave or free black from white defendants would simply be too great, especially when Due Process posed no particular threat to the Peculiar Institution or to the subordinantion of all blacks, free as well as slave.

The audience to which judges and attorneys played was not the outside community so much as it was other judges and lawyers.[8] The legal profession was their "significant other," evaluating role performance against historically derived "ideal roles." Grand and petit jurors may have played more to the community from which they were recruited as their "significant other," but the officers of the court exerted a countervailing pressure by instructing them on how to play their roles, how those roles had always been played, and why there was no reason for playing them differently just because a slave or free black was on trial. Even if

---

[8]For an excellent analysis of this legal community in Tennessee, see Daniel H. Calhoun, "Branding Iron and Retrospect: Lawyers in the Cumberland River Country," in Calhoun, ed., Professional Lives in America: Structure and Aspirations (Cambridge: Harvard University Press, 1965), pp. 59-87, 206-209.

the community complained, participants in the courtroom drama could adopt the classic position of "role distance," explaining that the role itself demanded that they perform in a particular fashion, even against their personally held class and racial beliefs. In summary, against a background of recognition of the common humanity of all men, slave and free, when the law and slavery interacted in a criminal courtroom, the institutionalized behavorial demands of the legal order prevailed, modifying the system of bondage to the benefit of the individual slave, with the understanding that those institutionalized behavioral demands challenged neither slavery nor white supremacy.[9]

In a different light, this book has been a case study of the practical outcome, in one setting, of what Edmund Morgan has called the "central paradox" of American history, the simultaneous but contradictory development of chattel slavery and American "devotion" to liberty and equality.[10] This heritage of liberty and equality is what Louis Hartz has called the American "liberal tradition."[11]

---

[9] Wyatt-Brown, Southern Honor, p. 393; Finkleman, Imperfect Union, p. 182; Ayers, Vengeance and Justice, p. 32; Charles S. Sydnor, "The Southerner and the Laws," Journal of Southern History 6 (February 1940): 8.

[10] Edmund S. Morgan, "Slavery and Freedom: The American Paradox," The Journal of American History 59 (June 1972): 5-6.

[11] Louis Hartz, The Liberal Tradition in America: An Interpretation of American Political Thought Since the Revolution (New York: Harcourt, Brace & World, Inc., 1955), pp. 153, 154, 166, 167, 180.

In their dealings with slaves and free blacks, the Tennessee courts clearly support Hartz's contention that southerners were deeply immeresed in that tradition, with its recognition of human rights.[12] As Tennessee jurists singled out humanity as the hallmark of slave property, they also accepted the general principal that a slave had rights of which the judicial system would take cognizance. As Nash has observed, this "linkage" with the American liberal tradition was "genuine," but it was flawed.[13] The notions of natural rights, of liberty and equality, if carried to their logical conclusion, would threaten the very existence of the Peculiar Institution. However, in their courtrooms, Tennesseans would not, could not, follow this logic to that conclusion. Only in a narrow range of circumstances did Tennesseans grant their slaves a right to be treated equally with free men. Beyond those circumstances, slaves were property, pure and simple, and had no rights at all. Devoted to liberal ideas in the abstract, Tennesseans extended only so much freedom and equality to individual slaves as could safely be done without endangering slavery itself. This was their accommodation to the American paradox.

---

[12]Ibid.; also see, Charles Grier Sellers, Jr., "The Travail of Slavery," in The Southerner as American (Chapel Hill: University of North Carolina Press, 1960), pp. 40-41, 48-49, 51, 56-57; Duncan J. McLeod, Slavery Race and the American Revolution (London and New York: Cambridge University Press, 1974), pp. 119-21.

[13]Nash, "Reason of Slavery," p. 179.

APPENDIX

TABLE 1

1860 POPULATION OF COUNTIES STUDIED

	Total Population	Slaves No.	Slaves %	Free Blacks No.	Free Blacks %
East Tennessee					
Greene	19,004	1,297	6.8	222	1.2
Johnson	5,018	233	4.6	28	.6
Knox	22,813	2,370	10.4	423	1.8
Middle Tennessee					
Bedford	21,584	6,744	31.2	52	.2
Davidson	47,055	14,790	31.4	1,209	2.6
Lincoln	22,828	6,847	30.0	55	.2
Maury	32,498	14,654	45.1	143	.4
Montgomery	20,895	9,554	45.7	106	.5
Robertson	15,265	4,861	31.8	29	.2
Williamson	23,827	12,367	51.9	45	.2
West Tennessee					
Fayette	24,327	15,473	63.6	28	.1
Gibson	21,777	6,141	28.2	91	.4
Hardeman	17,769	7,236	40.7	28	.2
Hardin	11,214	1,623	14.5	37	.3
Haywood	19,232	11,026	57.3	41	.2
Henry	19,133	5,530	28.9	11	.1
Lauderdale	7,559	2,854	37.8	21	.3
Shelby	48,092	16,953	35.2	276	.6
Tipton	10,705	5,288	49.2	9	.1

Source: *Population of the United States in 1860; . . . the Eighth Census*, pp. 459-67.

TABLE 2

MANUMISSION PETITIONS
(NUMBER OF PETITIONS AND NUMBER OF SLAVES)

	1801-31		1832-41		1842-49		1850-60	
	P	S	P	S	P	S	P	S
East Tennessee	31	39	18	44	24	39	8	28
Greene	10	17	9	26	10	16	5	23
Knox	21	22	9	18	14	23	2	4
Johnson	0	0	0	0	0	0	1	1
Middle Tennessee	86	152	17	56	31	36	26	42
Davidson	52	93	12	40	9	11	15	24
Lincoln	4	4	0	0	7	7	1	1
Montgomery	5	9	3	3	8	8	2	3
Maury	8	13	0	0	12	15	0	0
Robertson	7	12	1	3	3	3	5	17
Williamson	10	21	1	10	8	18	3	5
West Tennessee	1	1	3	3	10	12	21	41
Fayette	0	0	0	0	0	0	0	0
Gibson	0	0	1	1	0	0	0	0
Haywood	1	1	0	0	0	0	0	0
Henry	0	0	0	0	1	1	0	0
Shelby	0	0	2	2	9	11	21	41
Total	118	192	38	103	65	87	55	111

TABLE 3

MANUMISSION PETITIONS
(ANNUAL RATE)

	1802-31	1832-41	1842-49	1850-60
East Tennessee	1.0	1.8	3.0	.7
Greene	.3	.9	1.2	.5
Knox	.7	.9	1.7	.2
Johnson	0	0	0	.1
Middle Tennessee	2.9	1.7	3.9	2.4
Davidson	1.7	1.2	1.1	1.4
Lincoln	.1	0	.9	.1
Maury	.3	0	1.5	0
Montgomery	.2	.3	1.0	.2
Robertson	.2	.1	.4	.5
Williamson	.3	.1	1.0	.3
West Tennessee	.03	.3	1.3	1.9
Fayette	0	0	0	0
Gibson	0	.1	0	0
Haywood	.03	0	0	0
Henry	0	0	.1	0
Shelby	0	.2	1.1	1.9
Total	3.9	3.8	8.1	5.0

TABLE 4

OUTCOME OF TOTAL FELONY PROSECUTIONS OF WHITES FOR CRIMES AGAINST SLAVES

	Murder		Felonious Assault		Rape		Total	
	No.	%	No.	%	No.	%	No.	%
No Bill	1	3	0	0	0	0	1	2
Acquitted	12	36	1	5	1	100	14	26
Mistrial	2	6	1	5	0	0	3	6
Nolle Prosequi	3	9	5	25	0	0	8	15
Convicted:								
Felony	3	9	5	25	0	0	8	15
Misdemeanor	0	0	5[a]	25	0	0	5	9
Other	12	36	3	15	0	0	15[b]	28
Total	33	(61)	20	(37)	1	(2)	54	--

[a]Two were convicted by the petit jury, three pled guilty after the felony charge was dismissed.

[b]This includes thirteen cases which were "stricken" because the defendant was "not found," one case abated by the death of the defendant, and one case where the result was not listed.

TABLE 5

OUTCOME (PER INDIVIDUAL) OF FELONY PROSECUTIONS OF WHITES FOR CRIMES AGAINST SLAVES

	Murder		Felonious Assault		Rape		Total	
	No.	%	No.	%	No.	%	No.	%
No Bill	1	3	0	0	0	0	1	2
Acquitted	12	39	1	7	1	100	14	30
Mistrial	1	3	1	7	0	0	2	4
Nolle Prosequi	2	6	1	7	0	0	3	6
Convicted:								
Felony	3	10	4	27	0	0	7	15
Misdemeanor	0	0	5	33	0	0	5	11
Other	12	39	3	20	0	0	15	32
Total	31	(66)	15	(32)	1	(2)	47	--

TABLE 6

OFFENSES TRIED IN THE MEMPHIS RECORDER'S COURT, 1856-1861

	Whites		Slaves	
	No.	%	No.	%
Disorderly Behavior	506	51	285	34
Misdemeanor	262	26	312	37
Vagrancy	58	6	--	--
Unlawful Retailing	56	6	5	1
Traffic Violations	37	4	79	9
Larceny[a]	--	--	46	5
Slave Code[b]	6	1	39	5
Gaming	--	--	30	4
Other[c]	75	7	38	5
Total	1,000[f]		834	

[a]Whites accused of larceny would be tried in the circuit or criminal court.

[b]For whites, this category includes selling to a slave, allowing a slave to act as free, entertaining a slave on Sunday, and letting a slave rent a house. For slaves, it includes hiring own time, acting as free, being out after curfew, living to oneself, harboring a runaway, living in the city contrary to ordinance.

[c]This category includes offenses such as operating a disorderly house, indecent exposure, carrying concealed weapons, shooting, creating a nuisance, resisting arrest, abusing animals, whipping one's wife, and "bathing in the corporation."

[d]This table compares actual slave offenses tried with a random sample of actual white offenses tried.

TABLE 7

SENTENCES IN MEMPHIS RECORDER'S COURT, 1856-1861

	Whites		Slaves	
	No.	%	No.	%
Not Guilty	148	15	103	12
Fined	852	85	217	26
Ordered to Leave	--	--	--	--
Work House[a]	354	42	15	2
Stripes	--	--	514	62
Total	1,000		834	

[a]These figures are not reflected in the totals because the individuals were also fined. They were sentenced to the work house only when they could not pay their fine.

TABLE 8

SENTENCES TO LASH, MEMPHIS RECORDER'S COURT, 1856-1861

Number of Stripes	Number Sentenced	Percent
5	4	1
10	28	5
15	21	4
18	1	1
20	64	12
25	126	25
30	14	3
39	256	50
Total	514	

TABLE 9

RESULTS OF APPEALS TO THE SUPREME COURT IN CAPITAL CASES

	Number		Sustained		Percent	
	Slave	White	Slave	White	Slave	White
Murder	18	36	12	19	67	53
Attempted Murder	4	--	3	--	75	--
Attempted Rape	10	--	7	--	70	--
Robbery	1	--	1	--	100	--
Total	33	36	23	19	70	53

TABLE 10

OUTCOME OF TRIALS
(BY TERM)

	First Term		Later Term	
	No.	%	No.	%
No Bill	16	16	0	0
Acquittal	34	34	17	28
Mistrial	6	6	7	11
Nolle Prosequi	28	28	16	26
Conviction	15	15	19	31
Other	0	0	2	3
Total	99		61	

TABLE 11

RESULTS OF SLAVE APPEALS TO THE
SUPREME COURT

	No.	%
Convictions	40	--
Convictions Appealed	24	60
Convictions Unheld on Appeal	8	33
Convictions Overturned on Appeal	14	58
Results of Appeal Unknown	2	8
Outcome of Retrial		
Acquitted or Released	7	50
Convicted of Non-Capital Offense	1	7
Convicted Outright	4	29
Unknown	2	14
Summary of Appeal Outcome by Individual (21)		
Acquitted or Released	7	33
Convicted of Non-Capital Offense	1	5
Executed	9	43
Unknown	4	19

TABLE 12

CAPITAL OFFENSES COMMITTED BY SLAVES

	East	Middle	West	Total	Percent
Murder	2	38	32	72	45
Attempted Murder[a]	7	8	13	28	17
Rape	--	3	1	4	3
Attempted Rape	2	10	--	12	7
Burglary	4	12	4	20	13
Arson	1	4	8	13	8
Other[b]	2	6	3	11	7
Total	18	81	61	160	

[a]Includes six cases of poisoning.

[b]Unspecified felonies and one case of malicious stabbing.

TABLE 13

RESULTS OF CAPITAL PROSECUTIONS AGAINST SLAVES

	By Number				By Percent			
	East	Middle	West	Total	East	Middle	West	Total
No Bills[a]	2	9	5	16	9	9	6	8
Acquittals[b]	9	27	16	52	43	27	21	26
Mistrial	--	10	4	14	--	10	5	7
Dismissed[c]	8	31	26	65	38	31	33	33
Convicted[d]	2	19	19	40	9	19	24	20
Other[e]	--	3	8	11	--	3	10	6
Total	21	99	78	198				

[a]This includes one slave (Middle Tennessee) held for trial for a lesser offense.

[b]Because they actually were acquitted of the capital charge, this includes those twelve slaves who were either convicted or held for trial on a lesser offense.

[c]This includes five slaves held for trial on a lesser offense.

[d]This includes the 1860 Shelby county conviction of Sam for malicious stabbing.

[e]This includes cases abated by death, stricken by default, changes of venue, and unknown outcomes.

TABLE 14

FINAL OUTCOME OF CAPITAL PROSECUTIONS AGAINST SLAVES

	By Number				By Percent			
	East	Middle	West	Total	East	Middle	West	Total
Executed[a]	2	10	10	22	11	12	16	14
Released	16	57	36	109	89	70	59	68
Convicted/ Non-capital Offense	--	11	7	18	--	14	11	11
Other	--	3	8	11	--	4	13	7
Total	18	81	61	160				

[a]On the belief that 1,000 lashes in ten days was tantamount to execution, this includes Sam's 1860 Shelby county conviction for malicious stabbing.

TABLE 15

FINAL OUTCOME OF SLAVE MURDER PROSECUTIONS BY RACE OF VICTIM

	Black		White		Unknown	
	No.	%	No.	%	No.	%
No Bill	2	8	1	3	1	8
Acquitted	5	21	9	26	4	31
Dismissed	5	21	5	14	4	31
Convicted Outright	2	8	12	34	2	15
Convicted Non-Capital Offense	5	21	2	6	2	15
Other	5[a]	21	6	17	-	--
Total	24[b]		35		13	

[a]This category includes mistrials, changes of venue, and cases where the outcome is unknown.

[b]Twenty-three of these were slaves. The single trial of a slave for the murder of a free black ended in a mistrial.

TABLE 16

FINAL OUTCOME OF PROSECUTIONS OF SLAVES
FOR MURDER OR ATTEMPTED MURDER
OF THEIR MASTERS

	Murder		Attempted Murder	
	No.	%	No.	%
Acquitted	1	14	1	100
Convicted	6	86	--	--
Total	7		1	

TABLE 17

FINAL OUTCOME OF PROSECUTIONS SLAVES
FOR MURDER OR ATTEMPTED MURDER
OF WHITES OTHER THAN
THEIR MASTERS

	Murder		Attempted Murder	
	No.	%	No.	%
No Bill	1	4	--	--
Acquitted	8	29	8	31
Dismissed	5	18	14	54
Convicted	6	21	2	8
Convicted:				
Manslaughter	2	7	2	8
Other	6[a]	21	--	--
Total	28		26	

[a] This category includes four changes of venue and two cases where the outcome is unknown.

TABLE 18

OUTCOME OF CAPITAL PROSECUTION:
COMPARISON OF SLAVE AND WHITE
(BY NUMBER)

	East		Middle		West		Total	
	White	Slave	White	Slave	White	Slave	White	Slave
No bill	4	2	13	8	6	5	23	15
Acquitted	12	9	63	20	51	11	126	40
Mistrial	--	--	8	10	12	4	20	14
Dismissed	7	8	43	28	53	24	102	60
Convicted	6	2	11	19	11	19	28	40
Convicted/ Non-capital Offense	13	--	50	11	40	7	103	18
Other	7	--	32	3	36	8	76	11
Total	49	21	220	99	209	78	478	198

TABLE 19

OUTCOME OF CAPITAL PROSECUTION:
COMPARISON OF SLAVE AND WHITE
(BY PERCENT)

	East		Middle		West		Total	
	White	Slave	White	Slave	White	Slave	White	Slave
No bill	8	9	6	8	3	6	5	8
Acquitted	24	43	29	20	24	14	26	20
Mistrial	--	--	4	10	6	5	4	7
Dismissed	14	38	19	28	25	31	21	30
Convicted	12	9	5	19	5	24	6	20
Convicted/ Non-capital Offense	26	--	23	11	19	9	22	9
Other	14	--	14	3	17	10	16	6

TABLE 20

OUTCOME OF TRIALS (VERDICT ON CAPITAL CHARGE) BY PERCENTAGE

	Acquitted		Convicted	
	Slave	White	Slave	White
East Tennessee	82	81	18	19
Middle Tennessee	59	91	41	9
West Tennessee	49	89	51	11
Total	59	89	41	11

TABLE 21

OUTCOME OF TRIALS (VERDICT ON ALL CHARGES) BY PERCENTAGE

	Acquitted		Convicted		Convicted/ Non-capital Offense	
	Slave	White	Slave	White	Slave	White
East Tennessee	82	39	18	19	--	42
Middle Tennessee	43	51	40	9	17	40
West Tennessee	30	50	51	11	19	39
Total	41	49	41	11	18	40

TABLE 22

OFFENSES TRIED IN THE MEMPHIS RECORDER'S COURT, 1856-1861

	White		Slave		Free Blacks	
	No.	%	No.	%	No.	%
Disorderly Behavior	506	51	285	34	53	21
Misdemeanor	262	26	312	37	55	22
Vagrancy	58	6	--	--	--	--
Unlawful Retailing	56	6	5	1	--	--
Traffic Violations	37	4	79	9	9	4
Larceny	--	--	46	5	--	--
Unlawful Residence	--	--	--	--	109[a]	43
Slave Code	6	1	39	5	18[b]	7
Gaming	--	--	30	4	3	1
Other	75	7	38	5	5[c]	2
Total	1,000[d]		834		252	

[a]Fifty-one of these cases actually had no offense listed, but when convicted the offenders were ordered to leave the city. This leaves little doubt as to the nature of the offense.

[b]This category includes not being registered, entertaining slaves, assaulting whites, harboring a runaway, and unlawful assembly.

[c]This category includes "whipping wife," creating a nuisance, carrying concealed weapons, and one fugitive from the "chain gang."

[d]This is a randomly selected sample.

TABLE 23

SENTENCES IN MEMPHIS RECORDER'S COURT
1856-1861

	Whites		Slaves		Free Blacks	
	No.	%	No.	%	No.	%
Not Guilty	148	15	103	12	50	20
Fined	852	85	217	26	167	66
Ordered to Leave	--	--	--	--	28	11
Work House[a]	354	42	15	2	44	22
Stripes	--	--	514	62	--	--
Unlisted	--	--	--	--	7	3
Total	1,000					

[a]These figures are not reflected in the totals because the individuals were also fined. They were sentenced to the work house only when they could not pay their fine.

TABLE 24

FREE BLACK FELONY PROSECUTIONS

	Individuals		Prosecutions	
	No.	%	No.	%
Rape[a]	3	2	6	4
Robbery[a]	3	2	3	2
Felonious Assault[b]	13	10	14	9
Murder	9	7	11	7
Counterfeiting[c]	2	2	3	2
Larceny[d]	62	48	73	49
Arson	1	1	1	1
Felony	3	2	3	2
Illegal Immigration	32	25	34	23
Insurrection	2	2	2	1
Total	130		150	

[a]Includes those charged with attempting to commit these crimes.

[b]Includes attempted murder, malicious shooting, and malicious stabbing.

[c]Includes forgery.

[d]Includes burglary, receiving stolen goods, obtaining goods by false pretense, as well as grand and petit larceny.

TABLE 25

COMPARISON OF WHITE AND FREE BLACK OFFENSES (BY PERCENTAGE)

	Knox, Davidson, Shelby		
	Whites	Free Blacks	Total Free Blacks
Crimes Against Persons	43.5	37	31
Rape	2	7	5
Robbery	2	4	3
Felonious Assault	28	14	13
Murder	11	12	12
Crimes Against Property	56.5	63	69
Counterfeiting	7	4	3
Larceny	48	60	66
Arson	1	--	1

This table includes neither unspecfied felonies nor felonies for which no whites were indicted, i.e., insurrection and illegal immigration into the state.

TABLE 26

OUTCOME OF TRIALS OF FREE BLACKS ACCUSED OF CRIMES OF VIOLENCE (BY RACE OF VICTIM)

	White		Black	
	No.	%	No.	%
Not a True Bill	1	6	--	--
Acquitted	4	22	--	--
Mistrial	3	17	1	7
Nolle Prosequi	4	22	3	20
Convicted	4	22	9	60
Other	2	11	2	13
Total	18		15	

TABLE 27

COMPARISON OF RESULTS OF TOTAL FELONY PROSECUTIONS OF WHITES AND FREE BLACKS (BY PERCENTAGE)

	Knox, Davidson, Shelby		
	Whites	Free Blacks	Total Free Blacks
Not a True Bill	5	5	3
Acquitted	25	17	19
Mistrial	4	7	5
Nolle Prosequi	31	23	27
Convicted	33	39	37
Other	2	10	9

TABLE 28

OUTCOME OF FREE BLACKS TRIALS

	Individuals		Prosecutions	
	No.	%	No.	%
Not a True Bill	5	4	5	3
Acquitted	28	22	28	19
Mistrial	--	--	7	5
Nolle Prosequi	37	28	41	27
Convicted	47	36	56	37
Other	13	10	13	9
Total	130		150	

TABLE 29

COMPARISON OF RESULTS IN COMMON FELONY PROSECUTIONS OF WHITES AND FREE BLACKS (BY PERCENTAGE)

	Knox, Davidson, Shelby		
	Whites	Free Blacks	Total Free Blacks
Not a True Bill	5	3	3
Acquitted	25	16	16
Mistrial	4	7	5
Nolle Prosequi	31	21	22
Convicted	33	45	47
Other	2	7	6

TABLE 30

COMPARISON OF PETIT JURY BEHAVIOR IN PROSECUTIONS OF WHITE AND FREE BLACKS (TOTAL FELONIES, BY PERCENTAGE)

	Knox, Davidson, Shelby		Total
	Whites	Free Blacks	Free Blacks
Acquitted	40	27	31
Mistrial	6	11	8
Convicted	54	62	62

TABLE 31

COMPARISON OF PETIT JURY BEHAVIOR IN PROSECUTIONS OF WHITES AND FREE BLACKS (COMMON FELONIES, BY PERCENTAGE)

	Knox, Davidson, Shelby		Total
	Whites	Free Blacks	Free Blacks
Acquitted	40	24	23
Mistrial	6	10	7
Convicted	54	66	69

TABLE 32

FREE BLACKS SENTENCES:
DAVIDSON CRIMINAL COURT

	Whites	Blacks
Mean Sentence	3.8 Years	4.5 Years
Median Sentence	3.0 Years	3.0 Years
Most Frequent Sentence	3 Years (27%)	3 Years (24%)
Second Most Frequent Sentence	5 years (18%)	1 year (19%)
Sentences of 5 Years or Less	85%	76%

BIBLIOGRAPHY

Unpublished Primary Sources

Tennessee Supreme Court

"Elijah, a slave, v. Tne State." Case Files, Middle Dis- Tennessee.

"Henry a Slave v. The State of Tennessee [1850]." Case Files, Middle District, Tennessee State Archives, Nashville, Tennessee.

"State v. Amos, a Slave." Case Files, Middle District, Tennessee State Archives, Nashville, Tennessee.

"State v. Bob and Jacob Slaves." Case Files, Middle District, Tennessee State Archives, Nashville, Tennessee.

"State v. Francis, a Free Woman of Color." Case Files, Eastern District, Tennessee State Archives, Nashville, Tennessee.

"State v. Grandison (slave)." Case Files, Middle District, Tennessee State Archives, Nashville, Tennessee.

"State v. Howell." Case Files, Middle District, Tennessee State Archives, Nashville, Tennessee.

"State v. Major alias Nig [1854]." Case Files, Middle District, Tennessee State Archives, Nashville, Tennessee.

"State v. Major alias Nig [1857]." Case Files, Middle District, Tennessee State Archives, Nashville, Tennessee.

"State v. Moses, a Slave." Case Files, Middle District, Tennessee State Archives, Nashville, Tennessee.

"State v. William Fields." Case Files, Middle District, Tennessee State Archives, Nashville, Tennessee.

"State v. William Holly." Case Files, Middle District, Tennessee State Archives, Nashville, Tennessee.

"William Holly v. State." Case Files, Middle District, Tennessee State Archives, Nashville, Tennessee.

Local Court Records

Bedford County. Chancery Court. Minutes, 1830-1861. Tennessee State Archives, Nashville, Tennessee.

__________. Circuit Court. Minutes, 1840-1861. Tennessee State Archives, Nashville, Tennessee.

Davidson County. Chancery Court. Minutes, 1846-1861. Davidson County Courthouse, Nashville, Tennessee.

__________. Circuit Court. Minutes, 1803-1842. Tennessee State Archives, Nashville, Tennessee.

__________. County Court. Minutes, 1783-1861. Tennessee State Archives, Nashville, Tennessee.

__________. Criminal Court. Minutes, 1842-1861. Davidson County Courthouse, Nashville, Tennessee.

Fayette County. County Court. Minutes, 1831-1861. Tennessee State Archives, Nashville, Tennessee.

Gibson County. Chancery Court. Minutes, 1840-1861. Tennessee State Archives, Nashville, Tennessee.

__________. Circuit Court. Minutes, 1824-1861. Tennessee State Archives, Nashville, Tennessee.

__________. County Court. Minutes, 1824-1861. Tennessee State Archives, Nashville, Tennessee.

Greene County. Chancery Court, Enrollment Docket, 1835-1845. Tennessee State Archives, Nashville, Tennessee.

__________. Chancery Court. Minutes, 1783-1861. Tennessee State Archives, Nashville, Tennessee.

__________. Circuit Court. Minutes, 1809-1861. Tennessee State Archives, Nashville, Tennessee.

__________. County Court. Minutes, 1773-1861. Tennessee State Archives, Nashville, Tennessee.

Hardeman County. Circuit Court. Minutes, 1833-1861. Tennessee State Archives, Nashville, Tennessee.

Hardin County. Chancery Court. Minutes, 1836-1861. Tennessee State Archives, Nashville, Tennessee.

__________. Circuit Court. Minutes, 1840-1861. Tennessee State Archives, Nashville, Tennessee.

Haywood County. Chancery Court. Minutes, 1842-1861. Tennessee State Archives, Nashville, Tennessee.

__________. Circuit Court. Minutes, 1837-1861. Tennessee State Archives, Nashville, Tennessee.

__________. County Court. Minutes, 1823-1861. Tennessee State Archives, Nashville, Tennessee.

Henry County. Chancery Court. Enrollment Docket, 1846-1855. Tennessee State Archives, Nashville, Tennessee.

__________. Chancery Court. Minutes, 1841-1861. Tennessee State Archives, Nashville, Tennessee.

__________. Circuit Court. Minutes, 1834-1861. Tennessee State Archives, Nashville, Tennessee.

__________. County Court. Minutes, 1824-1861. Tennessee State Archives, Nashville, Tennessee.

Johnson County. Circuit Court. Minutes, 1836-1861. Tennessee State Archives, Nashville, Tennessee.

__________. County Court. Minutes, 1836-1861. Tennessee State Archives, Nashville, Tennessee.

Knox County. Chancery Court. Minutes, 1832-1861. Tennessee State Archives, Nashville, Tennessee.

__________. Circuit Court. Minutes, 1810-1861. Tennessee State Archives, Nashville, Tennessee.

__________. County Court, Minutes, 1795-1861. Tennessee State Archives, Nashville, Tennessee.

Lauderdale County. Circuit Court. Minutes, 1836-1861. Tennessee State Archives, Nashville, Tennessee.

Lincoln County. Circuit Court. Minutes, 1849-1861. Tennessee State Archives, Nashville, Tennessee

__________. County Court. Minutes, 1849-1861. Tennessee State Archives, Nashville, Tennessee.

Maury County. Chancery Court. Minutes, 1829-1861. Tennessee State Archives, Nashville, Tennessee.

__________. Circuit Court. Minutes, 1810-1861. Tennessee State Archives, Nashville, Tennessee.

__________. County Court. Minutes, 1807-1861. Tennessee State Archives, Nashville, Tennessee.

Montgomery County. Chancery Court. Minutes, 1840-1860. Tennessee State Archives, Nashville, Tennessee.

__________. County Court. Minutes, 1802-1861. Tennessee State Archives, Nashville, Tennessee.

Robertson County. Circuit Court. Minutes, 1832-1861. Tennessee State Archives, Nashville, Tennessee.

__________. County Court. Minutes, 1796-1861. Tennessee State Archives, Nashville, Tennessee.

Shelby County. Circuit Court. Minutes, 1828-1861. Shelby County Microfilm and Public Records Office, Memphis, Tennessee.

__________. County Court. Minutes, 1820-1861. Shelby County Microfilm and Public Records Office, Memphis, Tennessee.

__________. City of Memphis. Criminal Court. Minutes, 1856-61. Shelby County Microfilm and Public Records Office, Memphis, Tennessee.

__________. City of Memphis. Recorder's Court. Dockets, 1856-1861. Memphis/Shelby County Archives, Memphis, Tennessee.

Tipton County. Circuit Court. Minutes, 1832-1861. Tennessee State Archives, Nashville, Tennessee.

Williamson County. Chancery Court. Minutes, 1825-1861. Tennessee State Archives, Nashville, Tennessee.

__________. Circuit Court. Minutes, 1810-1861. Tennessee State Archives, Nashville, Tennessee.

__________. County Court, Minutes, 1800-1861. Tennessee State Archives, Nashville, Tennessee.

Manuscripts

Nashville, Tennessee. Tennessee State Archives. Papers of Governor John Sevier.

__________. Tennessee State Archives. Papers of Governor William Carroll.

__________. Tennessee State Archives. Treasurer, "Journal, 1856-61", Record Group 23, Treasurer, 1796-1869.

__________. Tennessee State Library, Manuscript Division. Diary of John Nick Barker.

__________. Tennessee State Library, Manuscript Division. Scrapbook of Slavery Material, Jill Knight Garrett Collection.

__________. Tennessee State Library, Manuscript Division. William Trousdale Papers.

Published Primary Sources

Books

Caruthers, R. L., and Nicholson, A. O. P., comps. A Compilation of the Statutes of Tennessee, of a General and Permanent Nature, from the Commencement of the Government to the Present Time. Nashville, Steam Press of James Smith, 1836.

Catterall, Helen Tunniclifff, ed., Judicial Cases Concerning American Slavery and the Negro. Vol. 2: Cases from the Courts of North Carolina, South Carolina, and Tennessee. Washington, DC: Carnegie Institution of Washington, 1929.

Dupree, L.J., comp. A Digest of the Ordinances of the City Council of Memphis, From the Year 1826 to 1857: Together with All Acts of the Legislature of Tennessee which Relate Exclusively to the City of Memphis, with an Appendix. Memphis: Memphis Bulletin Company, 1857.

Haywood, John, rev. A Revisal of All the Public Acts of the State of North Carolina and of the State of Tennessee Now in Force in the State of Tennessee. Nashville: Thomas G. Bradford, Printer, 1809.

Meigs, Return J., and Cooper, William F., eds. *The Code of Tennessee, Enacted by the General Assembly of 1857-'8*. Nashville: E.G. Eastman and Company, State Publishers, 1858.

Schweninger, Loren, ed. *From Tennessee Slave to St. Louis Entrepreneur: The Autobiography of James Thomas* Columbia: University of Missouri Press, 1984.

Scott, Edward, comp. *Laws of the State of Tennessee, Including Those of North Carolina Now in Force in this State. From the Year 1715 to the Year 1820, Inclusive*. 2 vols. Knoxville: Heiskell and Brown, 1821.

Smith, John Hugh, and Lea, John M., comps. *The Revised Laws of the City of Nashville, With the Various Acts of Incorporation and Laws Applicable to the Town and City of Nashville, and a List of the Different Boards of Mayor and Aldermen, and other Officers of said City from the Year 1806 to 1850, Inclusive*. Nashville, Harvey M. Watterson, Printer, 1850.

Tennessee. General Assembly. "Comptrollers Report," *Appendix to the Senate and Hourse Journals, 1855-56.*

__________. General Assembly. "Comptrollers Report," *Appendix to the Senate and Hourse Journals, 1857-58.*

__________. General Assembly. "Comptrollers Report," *Appendix to the Senate and Hourse Journals, 1859-60.*

__________. General Assembly. *Journals of the Senate and House of the Second General Assembly of the State of Tennessee Held at Knoxville*. Kingsport, TN: Southern Publishers, Inc., 1933.

__________. General Assembly. *Journal of the House of Representatives at the First Session of the Fourth General Assembly of the State of Tennessee*. Knoxville: Printed by George Roulstone, Printer to the State, 1801.

__________. General Assembly. *Journal of the Senate at the First Session of the Fourth General Assembly of the State of Tennessee*. Knoxville: Printed by George Roulstone, Printer to the State, 1801.

———. General Assembly. *Journal of the Senate at the First Session of the Eighth General Assembly of the State of Tennessee, Begun and Held at Knoxville, on Monday, the Eighteenth Day of September, One Thousand Eight Hundred and Nine*. Knoxville: Printed by George Wilson, Printer to the State, 1809.

———. General Assembly. *Private Acts, Passed at the called Session of the Nineteenth General Assembly of the State of Tennessee*. Nashville: Allen A. Hall & F.S. Heiskell, State Printers, 1832.

———. General Assembly. *Private Acts Passed at the First Session of the Twentieth General Assembly of the State of Tennessee*. Nashville: Allen A. Hall & F.S. Heiskell, Printers to the State, 1833.

———. Supreme Court. *Reports*. Second Edition of Cooper's Edition. Vols. 1-41. Louisville, KY: Fetter Law Book Company, 1908.

U.S. Department of State. *Return of the Whole Number of Persons Within the Several Districts of the United States, According to "An Act providing for the Second Census or Enumeration of the Inhabitants of the United States*. Washington, D.C.: n.p., 1801.

———. Department of State. *Aggregate Amount of Each Description of Persons Within the United States of America, and the Territories thereof, Agreeable to Actual Enumeration made According to Law, in the year 1810*. Washington, D.C.: n.p., 1811.

———. Department of State. *Census for 1820*. Washington, D.C.: Printed by Gales and Seaton, 1821.

———. Department of State. *Fifth Census; or, Enumeration of the Inhabitants of the United States, 1830*. Washington, D.C.: Printed by Duff Green, 1832.

———. Department of State. *Sixth Census or Enumeration of the Inhabitants of the United States, as Corrected at the Department of State, in 1840*. Washington, D.C.: Printed by Blair and Rives, 1841.

__________. Department of Interior. Census Office. *The Seventh Census of the United States: 1850*. Washington, D.C.: Robert Armstrong, Public Printer, 1853.

__________. Department of Interior. Census Office. *Population of the United States in 1860; Compiled from Original Returns of the Eighth Census.* Washington, D.C.: Government Printing Office, 1864.

__________. Department of Interior. Census Office. *Agriculture of the United States in 1860; Compiled from the Original Returns of the Eighth Census.* Washington, D.C.: Government Printing Office, 1864.

Newspapers

Memphis Daily Appeal, 11 December, 14 December 1856.

Memphis Daily Eagle, 30 May 1849.

Nashville Daily Gazette, 13 February 1850-11 September 1861.

Nashville Republican Banner, 22 November 1854-27 March 1861.

Unpublished Secondary Sources

Bodenhamer, David Jackson. "Crime and Criminal Justice in Antebellum Indiana: Marion County as a Case Study." Ph.D. dissertation, Indiana University, 1977.

Corlew, Robert E. "Some Aspects of Slavery in Dickson County, Tennessee." M.A. thesis, Vanderbilt University, 1949.

England, James Merton. "The Free Negro in Davidson County." M.A. thesis, Vanderbilt University, 1936.

__________. "The Free Negro in Ante-Bellum Tennessee." Ph.D. dissertation, Vanderbilt University, 1941.

Flanigan, Daniel J. "The Criminal Law of Slavery and Freedom, 1800-1868." Ph.D. dissertation, Rice University, 1973.

Kinard, Margaret. "Frontier Development of Williamson County, Tennessee." M.A. thesis, Vanderbilt University, 1948.

Mooney, Chase Curran. "Slavery in Davidson County, Tennessee." M.A. thesis, Vanderbilt University, 1936.

__________. "Slavery in Tennessee." Ph.D. dissertation, Vanderbilt University, 1939.

Nash, Arnold Edmund Kier. "Negro Rights and Judicial Behavior in the Old South." Ph.D. dissertation, Harvard University, 1967.

Orr, Horace Eugene. "The Tennessee Churches and Slavery (With Special Reference to East Tennessee)." M.A. thesis, University of Tennessee, 1924.

Schafer, Judith K. "The Long Arm of the Law: Slave Criminals and the Supreme Court in Antebellum Louisiana, 1803-1862." Unpublished Paper, Read at the Southern Historical Association Convention, November 1984.

Schwarz, Phillip J. "Slave Criminality and the Slave Community: Patterns of Slave Assertiveness in Eighteenth-Century Virginia." 1979. (Typewritten.)

Van Dyke, Roger Raymond. "The Free Negro in Tennessee, 1790-1860," Ph.D. dissertation, Florida State University, 1972.

Wagner, Mary C. "The Settlement of Zion Community in Maury County, Tennessee, 1806-1860." M.A. thesis, Vanderbilt University, 1945.

Wiley, Bell Irvin. "Cotton and Slavery in the History of West Tennessee." M.A. thesis, University of Kentucky, 1929.

Published Secondary Sources

Books

Ayers, Edward L. *Vengeance and Justice: Crime and Punishment in the 19th-Century American South*. New York and Oxford: Oxford University Press, 1984.

Berger, Peter. Invitation to Sociology: A Humanistic Perspective. New York: Doubleday Company, Inc., 1963.

Berlin, Ira. Slaves Without Masters: The Free Negro in the Antebellum South. New York: Pantheon Books, 1974.

Brown, Richard Maxwell. Strain of Violence: Historical Studies of American Violence and Vigilantism. New York: Oxford University Press, 1975.

Calhoun, Daniel H. Professional Lives in America: Structure and Aspirations. Cambridge: Harvard University Press, 1965.

Campbell, Mary Emily Robertson. The Attitude of Tennesseans Toward the Union, 1847-1861. New York Vantage Press, 1961.

Cash, W.J. The Mind of the South. New York: Alfred A. Knopf, Inc., 1941.

Chambers, William Nisbet. Old Bullion Benton: Senator from the New West. New York: Little, Brown and Company, 1956.

Cobb, Thomas R.R. An Inquiry into the Law of Negro Slavery in the United States of America to which is Prefixed an Historical Sketch of Slavery. Savannah: W. Thorne Williams, 1858.

Curry, Leonard P. The Free Black in Urban America, 1800-1850: The Shadow of the Dream. Chicago and London: The University of Chicago Press, 1981.

Cutler, James E. Lynch-Law: An Investigation into the History of Lynching in the United States. Montclair, N.J.: Patterson Smith Publishing, 1969.

Davis, David Brion. The Problem of Slavery in Western Culture. Ithaca: Cornell University Press, 1966.

Fehrenbacher, Don E. The Dred Scott Case: Its Significance in American Law and Politics. New York: Oxford University Press, 1978.

Folmsbee, Stanley J.; Corlew, Robert E.; and Mitchell, Enoch L. Tennessee: A Short History. Knoxville: University of Tennessee Press, 1969.

Friedman, Lawrence M. A History of American Law. New York: Somon and Schuster, 1973.

Genovese, Eugene D. Roll, Jordan, Roll: The World the Slaves Made. New York: Pantheon Books, 1974.

Goodell, William. The American Slave Code. N.P.: The American & Foreign Anti-Slavery Society, 1853; reprint ed., New York: Negro Universities Press, 1968.

Hallum, John. The Diary of an Old Lawyer: Scenes Behind the Curtain. Nashville: Southwestern Publishing House, 1895.

Hartz, Louis. The Liberal Tradition in America: An Interpretation of American Political Thought Since the Revolution. New York: Harcourt, Brace & World, Inc., 1955.

Heiskell, S.G. Andrew Jackson and Early Tennessee History Illustrated. 2 vols. Nashville: Ambrose Printing Company, 1920.

Hindus, Michael S. Prison and Plantation: Crime, Justice, and Authority in Massachusetts and South Carolina, 1767-1878. Chapel Hill: University of North Carolina Press, 1980.

Hopkins, Vincent C. Dred Scott's Case. New York: Antheneum Press, 1971.

Jordan, Winthrop D. White Over Black: American Attitudes Toward the Negro, 1550-1812. Chapel Hill: University of North Carolina Press, 1968.

McBride, Robert M., and Robison, Dan M. Biographical Dictionary of the Tennessee General Assembly, 1796-1861. Nashville: Tennessee State Library and Archives and the Tennessee Historical Commission, 1975.

McLeod, Duncan J. Slavery, race and the American Revolution. London and New York: Cambridge University Press, 1974.

Miller, Elinor, and Genovese, Eugene D., eds. Plantation, Town and County: Essays on the Local History of American Slave Society. Urbana: University of Illinois Press, 1974.

Mooney, Chase C. Slavery in Tennessee. Bloomington: Indiana University Press, 1957.

Morgan, Edmund S. The Challenge of the American Revolution. New York: W.W. Norton & Company, 1976.

Nisbet, Robert A. The Social Bond: An Introduction to the Study of Society. New York: Alfred A. Knopf, 1970.

Packer, Herbert L. The Limits of the Criminal Sanction. Stanford: Stanford University Press, 1968.

Patterson, Caleb Perry. The Negro in Tennessee, 1790-1865. Austin: University of Texas, Bulletin No. 2205, 1922.

Patterson, Orlando. Slavery and Social Death: A Comparative Study. Cambridge and London: Harvard University Press, 1982.

Phillips, Ulrich B. American Negro Slavery: A Survey of the Supply, Employment, and Control of Negro Labor as Determined by the Plantation Regime. New York: D. Appleton and Company, 1918; reprint ed., Baton Rouge: Louisiana State University Press, 1966.

Rawick, George P., ed. The American Slave: A Composite Autobiography. Vol. 18: Unwritten History of Slavery. Westport, CT: Greenwood Publishing Company, 1974.

Sellers, Charles Grier, Jr. The Southerner as American. Chapel Hill: University of North Carolina Press, 1960.

Stampp, Kenneth M. The Peculiar Institution: Slavery in the Ante-Bellum South. New York: Vintage Books, 1956.

Tushnet, Mark V. The American Law of Slavery, 1810-1860: Considerations of Humanity and Interest. Princeton: Princeton University Press, 1981.

Wade, Richard C. Slavery in the Cities: The South 1820-1860. New York: Oxford University Press, 1964.

Wyatt-Brown, Bertram. Southern Honor: Ethics and Behavior in the Old South. New York and Oxford: Oxford University Press, 1982.

Articles

Clark, Cornelia Ann. "Justice on the Tennessee Frontier: The Williamson County Circuit Court 1810-1820." Vanderbilt Law Review 32 (January 1979): 413-45.

Clark, Ernest James, Jr. "Aspects of the North Carolina Slave Code, 1715-1860." North Carolina Historical Review 39 (April 1962): 148-64.

Coulter, E. Merton. "Four Slave Trials in Elbert County, Georgia." The Georgia Historical Quarterly 41 (September 1961): 237-46.

Dew, Charles B. "Black Iron Workers and the Slave Insurrection Panic of 1856." The Journal of Southern History 41 (August 1975): 321-38.

Eaton, Clement. "Mob Violence in the Old South." Mississippi Valley Historical Review 29 (December 1942): 351-70.

Edwards, John C. "Slave Justice in Four Middle Georgia Counties." The Georgia Historical Quarterly 57 (Summer 1973): 265-73.

Ely, James W., Jr. "Andrew Jackson as Tennessee State Court Judge, 1798-1804." Tennessee Historical Quarterly 40 (Summer 1981): 144-57.

England, James Merton. "The Free Negro in Ante-Bellum Tennessee." The Journal of Southern History 9 (February 1943): 37-58.

Fede, Andrew, "Legitimized Violent Slave Abuse in the American South, 1619-1865: A Case Study of Law and Social Change in Six Southern States." The American Journal of Legal History 29 (April 1985): 93-150.

__________. "Toward a Solution of the Slave Law Dilemma: A Critique of Tushnet's 'The American Law of Slavery.'" Law and History Review 2 (Fall 1984): 301-20.

Flanigan, Daniel J. "Criminal Procedure in Slave Trials in the Antebellum South." The Journal of Southern History 40 (November 1974): 537-64.

Hindus, Michael S. "Black Justice Under White Law: Criminal Prosecutions of Blacks in Antebellum South Carolina." The Journal of American History 63 (December 1976): 575-99.

Howington, Arthur F. "Not in the Condition of a Horse or an Ox: Ford v. Ford, the Law of Testamentary Manumission and the Tennessee Courts' Recognition of Slave Humanity." Tennessee Historical Quarterly 34 (Fall 1975): 249-63.

Kotlikoff, Laurence J., and Rupert, Anton J. "The Manumission of Slaves in New Orleans, 1827-1846." Southern Studies 19 (Summer 1980): 172-81.

Mooney, Chase C. "Some Institutional and Statistical Aspects of Slavery in Tennessee." Tennessee Historical Quarterly 1 (September 1942): 195-228.

Morris, Thomas D. "'As If the Injury was Effected by the Natural Elements of Air or Fire': Slave Wrongs and the Liability of Masters," Law and Society Review 16 (1981-82): 569-99.

__________."'Society is Not Marked by Punctuality in the Payment of Debts': The Chattel of Mortgages of Slaves," in David J. Bodenhamer and James W. Ely, Jr., eds., Ambivalent Legacy: A Legal History of the South (Jackson: University of Mississippi Press, 1984): 147-70.

Nash, A.E. Kier. "A More Equitable Past? Southern Supreme Courts and the Protection of the Antebellum Negro." North Carolina Law Review 48 (February 1970): 197-242.

__________. "Fairness and Formalism in the Trials of Blacks in the State Supreme Courts of the Old South." Virginia Law Review 56 (February 1970): 64-100.

__________. "Negro Rights, Unionism, and Greatness on the South Carolina Court of Appeals: The Extraordinary Chief Justice John Belton O'Neall." South Carolina Law Review 21 (Spring 1969): 141-90.

__________. "Reason of Slavery: Understanding the Judicial Role in the Peculiar Institution." Vanderbilt Law Review 32 (January 1979): 7-223.

__________. "The Texas Supreme Court and Trial Rights of Blacks, 1845-1860." The Journal of American History 58 (December 1971): 622-42.

Owsley, Frank L., and Owsley, Harriet C. "The Economic Structure of Rural Tennessee, 1850-1860." The Journal of Southern History 8 (May 1942): 161-82.

Patton, John W. "The Progress of Emancipation in Tennessee." The Journal of Negro History 17 (January 1932): 67-102.

Saunders, Robert M. "Crime and Punishmnent in Early National America: Richmond, Virginia, 1784-1820." The Virginia Magazine of History and Biography 86 (January 1978): 33-44.

Schwarz, Philip J. "Forging the Shackles: The Development of Virginia's Criminal Code for Slaves," in David J. Bodenhamer and James W. Ely, Jr., eds., Ambivalent Legacy: A Legal History of the South (Jackson: University of Mississippi Press, 1984): 125-46.

__________. "Gabriel's Challenge: Slaves and Crime in Late Eighteenth-Century Virginia." The Virginia Magazine of History and Biography 90 (July (1982): 283-309.

Schweninger, Loren. "The Free-Slave Phenomenon: James P. Thomas and the Black Community in Ante-bellum Nashville." Civil War History 22 (December 1976): 305-14.

__________. "A Slave Family in the Ante Bellum South." Journal of Negro History 60 (January 1975): 29-44.

__________. "Thriving Within the Lowest Caste: The Financial Activities of James P. Thomas in the Nineteenth-Century South." The Journal of Negro History 63 (Fall 1978): 353-64.

Sheldon, Marianne Buroff. "Black-White Relations in Richmond, Virginia, 1782-1820." The Journal of Southern History 45 (February 1979): 27-44.

Shingleton, Royce Gordon. "The Trial and Punishment of Slaves in Baldwin County, Georgia, 1812-1826." Southern Humanities Review 8 (Winter 1974): 67-73.

Stealey, John E. "The Responsibilities and Liabilities of the Bailee of Slave Labor in Virginia." American Journal of Legal History 12 (October 1968): 336-53.

Thompson, E. Bruce. "Reforms in the Penal System of Tennessee, 1820-1850." Tennessee Historical Quarterly 1 (December 1942): 291-308.

Trabue, Charles C. "The Voluntary Emancipation of Slaves in Tennessee as Reflected in the State's Legislation and Judicial Decisions." Tennessee Historical Magazine 4 (March 1918): 50-68.

Tushnet, Mark. "Approaches to the Study of the Law of Slavery." Civil War History 25 (December 1979): 329-38.

__________. "The American Law of Slavery, 1819-1860: A Study in the Persistance of Legal Autonomy." Law and Society 10 (Fall 1975): 119-84.

Watson, Alan D., "North Carolina Slave Court, 1715-1785," North Carolina Historical Review 60 (January 1983): 24-36.

Wish, Harvey. "The Slave Insurrection Panic of 1856." The Journal of Southern History 5 (May 1939): 206-22.

Wyatt-Brown, Bertram. "The Ideal Typology and Antebellum Southern History: A Testing of a New Approach." Societas 5 (Winter 1975): 1-29.

INDEX